Patrick F. Kavanagh

A popular history of the insurrection of 1798

Derived from every available written record and reliable tradition

Patrick F. Kavanagh

A popular history of the insurrection of 1798
Derived from every available written record and reliable tradition

ISBN/EAN: 9783742826848

Manufactured in Europe, USA, Canada, Australia, Japa

Cover: Foto ©ninafisch / pixelio.de

Manufactured and distributed by brebook publishing software (www.brebook.com)

Patrick F. Kavanagh

A popular history of the insurrection of 1798

A POPULAR HISTORY

OF

THE INSURRECTION OF 1798:

DERIVED FROM EVERY AVAILABLE WRITTEN RECORD AND
RELIABLE TRADITON.

BY

THE REV. PATRICK F. KAVANAGH.

The Tribune's tongue and Poet's pen
Must sow the seed in slavish men;
But 'tis the soldier's sword alone
Can reap the harvest when 'tis grown.

Second Edition, Revised and Enlarged.

DUBLIN:
M^cGLASHAN & GILL, 50, UPPER SACKVILLE-ST.
1874.

PREFACE.

THE story of the brief, but fierce and gallant, struggle made by the Patriots of '98 cannot but prove deeply interesting to their descendants. The heroic men who took part therein have, indeed, passed away to that happier country where the tears of the oppressed are dried—where might is no longer the enemy of right, where no tyrant threatens, and no slave weeps in fetters; but their memory still remains, a bright light to guide us through darkness to the holy Temple of Freedom. Nor is that memory less dear to us because the Flag they raised so boldly, and bore aloft so bravely, fell in the disastrous battle, and was trodden under the iron heel of the representative of brute force and unrighteous aggression. No; the Irish heart is of too generous a nature to bow down before the idol of power because success has crowned it, or to forsake a just cause because it has not proved triumphant. The Irish people know that the *charter of their country's liberty has been written by the hand of God*, and that of man can never efface the sublime record.

THE AUTHOR.

ADVERTISEMENT

TO THE SECOND EDITION.

IN the compilation of this second and much enlarged Edition of his History the author has had recourse to every available source of information, and has spared no pains to perfect his work. The pages of Hay, Gordon, Clooney, Teeling, and Plowden, have been diligently perused. Besides these standard authorities, others of less note have not been passed over: in fact, every document that helped to throw light on the subject in hand has been availed of. In selecting from these various sources of information the author has taken care to distinguish between what the narrators witnessed themselves and what they heard from others. But the writer of this volume claims to be something more than a mere compiler. Before he ever read a work on the subject of which he treats, he had acquired no small amount of information from those who were best calculated to impart it—*the actors in the struggle*. Born in the centre of the district where the contest was most fiercely waged, many of those who took part therein were his own near relatives, and from their lips he learned much of what he now narrates. He was, from the information thus obtained, enabled to discern whatever was erroneous in works previously written on the same subject. While he frankly acknowledges that his sympathies are wholly with the cause for which the insurgents suffered and laid down their lives, he has, nevertheless, striven to avoid the errors of the partizan—telling truth even when it seemed least favorable to those with whom he sympathises. If in his mention of the Orangemen of the period he verges sometimes towards asperity of expression, let his readers bear in mind that he views the *Orange Society* in the light of a *political faction*, inveterately hostile to the rights of the majority of his fellow-countrymen, and that their religious creed does not in the slightest degree influence him in the expression of his opinion: no one more gratefully acknowledges the sterling patriotism of those gallant leaders who, though they worshipped the same God, knelt before a different altar.

To those who would fain draw a veil over the past of this country, which, thank God, is still a nation, he would suggest that the struggles of a people for liberty form the most glorious page in their history, and constitute their most precious inheritance. We whose fathers have shed their blood in defence of civil and religious liberty should be dastards, indeed, did we suffer the memory of their struggles to be buried in oblivion. The author shall deem himself well rewarded for his labour in the compilation of this work if, while recounting the deeds of the *dead fathers*, he should awaken to a brighter glow the sacred flame of patriotism in the bosoms of the *living sons*.

In conclusion, it may not be amiss to express a hope that our onward journey towards long-lost liberty may be made by peaceful paths—that when the crown of an independent nation is placed upon the brow of Erin, no stain of blood may be seen upon its golden round.

Cork, *January* 10, 1874.

CONTENTS.

CHAPTER I.

England's jealousy of Ireland's prosperity under her native Parliament.—The course adopted by England to ruin her rival.—The Irish aristocracy of the period.—Brief account of the United Irish Society.—Its aims and origin.—Severity used by Government towards its chiefs.—Trial of Jackson, and flight of Theobald Wolfe Tone.—How Tone worked for Ireland in France and Holland.—The French and Dutch expeditions.—Severe measures adopted by Government.—Capture of the United leaders at Bond's.—Death of Lord Edward Fitzgerald.—Fate of other leaders, ... 1

CHAPTER II.

Outbreak of the insurrection.—Actions at Naas, Prosperous, and Kilcullen.—William Aylmer in Kildare.—Numerous conflicts between the people and the soldiery in the counties of Dublin, Carlow, Meath, and Wicklow.—Massacre of Catholic yeomen at Dunlavin. —Proclamations issued by the authorities.—How the Irish Parliament acted.—Colonel Maxwell's proposal.—Loyalty of the Catholic gentry and aristocracy.—Attack on Carlow.—Fate of Sir Edward Crosbie.—Engagement at Tara Hill.—Massacre at the Curragh; official account.—Insurrection in Cork county, ... 21

CHAPTER III.

Seizure of the Ulster chiefs retards the insurrection.—Junction of the Down and Antrim insurgents frustrated.—McCracken chosen commander of the Antrim force.—Insurgent advance upon Antrim.—Flight of the insurgents.—Gallant stand made by Hope.—Colonel Clavering.—McCracken descends from Donegore.—Saves his followers from capture.—Falls into the hands of his enemies, and is put to death, ... 41

CHAPTER IV.

Down men assemble at Saintfield.—Colonel Stapleton falls into an ambuscade.—Death of Mortimer.—Attack on Portaferry.—Rendezvous at Saintfield.—Munroe chosen commander-in-chief; his character.—Conflict at Ballinahinch.—Fatal mistake of the insurgents. —Their flight.—Official account of the affair.—Burning and pillage of Ballinahinch.—Romantic episode.—Death of Munroe, . . 47

viii   *Contents.*

CHAPTER V.
PAGE

No serious disturbance in Wexford apprehended by the Government.—Mr. McGee's description of Wexford.—People of Wexford not a Celtic race.—Population.—Hay and others on the social condition of the inhabitants.—Musgrave's and Maxwell's calumnies refuted. Relations existing between the middle and lower classes and the aristocracy.—The persecuting class encouraged by the Government.—Liberal Protestants dare not interfere.—How informers were made.—Burning of houses.—Instance given by the Rev. Mr. Gordon of death brought on by fear of torture.—Question of the number of United Irishmen in Wexford discussed.—Opinion of divers authors.—Arrival of the North Cork, who outdo the yeomen in cruelty.—Pitch-cap introduced.—County proclaimed.—Many people deliver up their arms.—Proceedings of Hunter Gowan and other persecutors.—Transportation.—Horrid rumours abroad during the week preceding the insurrection, ... 57

CHAPTER VI.

Wholesale massacres perpetrated by the Orangemen.—Father John Murphy the first to raise the standard of rebellion.—His first achievement.—His character.—Minor events in Wexford.—March of the militia and yeomanry to Oulart.—Burning of Darby Kavanagh's house.—Effects of the first insurgent success.—Insurgents proceed to Oulart Hill, ... 76

CHAPTER VII.

Slaughter of the peasantry at Kilmacthomas Hill.—Position taken by the insurgents on Oulart Hill.—The battle.—Total defeat of the loyalists.—Atrocities committed by the yeomanry during their flight.—Route taken by the victorious insurgents.—Joined at Ballinorrel by Father Michael Murphy.—Attack on Enniscorthy.—Its capture.—Flight of the loyalists.—Attempt made by the Orangemen to murder the prisoners in Enniscorthy jail frustrated.—Moderation of the insurgents.—Camp at Vinegar Hill reinforced.—Division in the insurgent councils.—Arrival of the Wexford deputation.—Its effect.—Insurgents arrive at the Three Rocks.—Surprise and defeat of the Meath militia on their way to Wexford.—Official account of the affair, ... 88

CHAPTER VIII.

Consternation in Wexford produced by the defeat at Oulart.—Attempt of the militia to put the prisoners to death.—Their design defeated.—Arrival of fugitives from Enniscorthy.—Wexford town a hotbed of Orangeism.—Preparation made by the loyalists for defence.—Reinforcements.—Terror of the Orangemen.—Precautions taken for the security of the town.—Loyalists send a deputation to the insurgents.—Arrival of Mr. Colclough in Wexford.—His message.—Sally headed by Colonel Watson.—Its result.—Loyalists resolve to evacuate the town.—Dishonest stratagem used by loyalists to retard the insurgent approach.—Strange scene of confusion exhibited in the flight of the military.—Entrance of the insurgents from Ferrybank.—Anger of insurgents on discovering the deceit practised on them by the soldiery.—Altered aspect of Wexford on the insurgent entry.—Two Orangemen put to death.—Excesses of the fugitive military.—Tranquillity in the town.—Departure of insurgents, . 103

CHAPTER IX.

Two divisions of the insurgent army march from Windmill Hill, taking separate routes.—Force under Father John reinforced.—Attack on Newtownbarry.—March of the royal troops from Gorey and Carnew against the insurgents on Carrickgrow.—Defeat and death of Col. Walpole.—Flight of General Loftus.—Mr. Plowden concerning the above-mentioned actions.—Esmond Kyan.—Joyful surprise of the people of Gorey.—Results of the above victories.—Appeal of Mr. Fox to the British House of Commons.—Loss already sustained by the British, ... 115

CHAPTER X.

Preparations made for the assault on New-Ross.—Harvey sends a flag of truce.—Death of the envoy.—Letter found upon his person.—Death of Lord Mountjoy.—Ross, its situation.—Dispositions made for its defence.—Various accounts of the battle.—How it began.—Marvellous bravery of the insurgents acknowledged even by their enemies.—Colonel Clooney's attack upon the military posted in the market-house and at Irishtown.—Subsequent return and final success of the loyalist troops.—True cause of the insurgent defeat.—Number of killed and wounded.—Accounts given by various writers.—Heroism displayed by a boy of 13.—A heroine.—Burning of Scullabogue.—Details of the massacre.—Examination of Mr. Frizell at the bar of the House of Commons.—Last proclamation of General Harvey.—His resignation.—The insurgents quit Carrickburn, and arrive at Slieve Kielter.—The forging of false despatches by loyalist officers proved, ... 120

CHAPTER XI.

Insurgents leave their camp on Gorey Hill to attack Carnew.—Flight of General Loftus.—Burning of Carnew.—Clemency shown by the peasantry.—Return of insurgents to Gorey Hill.—Condition of insurgent forces at this time.—Father John Murphy.—Bad news for the men on Gorey Hill.—The Wicklow men, ... 143

CHAPTER XII.

State of the county of Wexford.—Increased number of royal troops.—Orange atrocities.—Insurgents search for concealed Orangemen.—Imprisonment of Mr. Hunter.—Captain Keough military governor.—Measures adopted by him.—Barony Forth men arrive in the town.—Bagenal Beauchamp Harvey chosen commander-in-chief.—Unfitted for command.—Insurgent freedom from bigotry.—Ener-

b

getic preparations for resistance.—Bank-notes esteemed of no value.
—Provisions, their cheapness.—The Wexford "*fleet.*"—Capture of
Lord Kingsborough.—Reinforcements for the camp.—Orangemen
the objects of popular hatred.—Unreasonable fear displayed by the
Protestants.—Pretended converts.—Instance of liberality on the
part of the Catholics.—Hatred borne towards traitors.—Punishment inflicted upon informers.—Dixon's violence.—Requisitions.—
Tranquillity in the town.—Outrages become frequent.—Proclamation issued against Hawtrey White and his associates.—Catholics
refuse to permit the Protestant church to be used as a hospital.—
Popular anger excited by the discovery of a pitch-cap.—Kingsborough's danger.—Messengers from the camp demand ammunition
and reinforcements.—Good conduct of the Wexford gunsmen.—
Alarm of the loyalist prisoners.—Kingsborough's letter to the Lord
Lieutenant intercepted by Captain Dixon.—Tumult excited by the
latter.—How appeased.—Severe measures of retaliation adopted by
the insurgents at Vinegar Hill, ... 150

CHAPTER XIII.

Insurgents leave Gorey and march upon Arklow.—Their number and
equipment.—Battle of Arklow.—Death of Father Michael Murphy.
—Absence of Father John.—Contest between Esmond Kyan and
Col. Skerrit.—Return to Gorey.—Massacre of wounded insurgents
by the English soldiery.—Cannibalism of the "Ancient Britons."—
Losses on both sides.—Falsehood of General Needham's despatch
proved by various authors.—State of the country.—Merciful spirit
displayed by the insurgents.—Their respect for the fair sex contrasted with the brutality of the loyalist officers and men, . . 164

CHAPTER XIV.

Movements of the insurgents and royalists.—Position of the contending forces.—Vaunts of the royalist general.—Retreat of the royal
troops.—Insurgent challenge refused.—Insurgents proceed to Vinegar Hill.—Attack on Borris House.—Battle of Longmig or Fooke's
Mill, ... 174

CHAPTER XV.

Alarm of the Government at the long-continued resistance of the Wexford men.—Combined movements of the English generals.—The entrance of Wexford harbour blocked up by men-of-war.—How the
insurgents at Vinegar Hill prepared to encounter the enemy.—
Commencement of the battle.—General Needham charged with
cowardice.—Scarcity of ammunition among the insurgents.—Number engaged on both sides.—Sir Jonah Barrington's description of
the conflict.—Women take part in the fight.—Operations of the
insurgents under Father Kearns and Mr. Barker.—Fall of Father
Clinch.—Retreat of the insurgents towards Wexford.—Wounded insurgents slaughtered by the soldiery.—Fate of Barker.—Slaughter
of the defenceless people who followed the insurgent retreat.—
Small number of the fighting-men slain at Vinegar Hill.—The Insurgents from Vinegar Hill and those from New-Ross meet at
Wexford.—General Edward Roche covers the insurgent retreat, . 183

CHAPTER XVI.

On the rumours of a French invasion the Government redouble their efforts to quell the insurrection.—Great increase of the English forces.—Insurgents resolve to maintain the struggle to the last extremity.—Concentrate their forces at Vinegar Hill.—Anxiety felt by the townspeople.—Reinforcements despatched from town to the chief rendezvous.—Captain Dixon plots the destruction of the Orange prisoners.—Steps taken by Mr. Hay to foil the captain. —Mr. Hay, on his return from the Three Rocks, finds the town occupied by a fresh force of insurgents under General Roche.—The latter fails in persuading his men to accompany him to the "Hill." —Frenzied state of the multitude.—Resolve to put the Orangemen to death.—Efforts made by Mr. Hay to save them.—Dixon prevails by the aid of two Orange informers.—Execution of prisoners on the bridge.—Father Carrin hastens to the rescue.—His successful appeal to the people.—Esmond Kyan's intercession.—Noise of the engagement heard in Wexford.—Lord Kingsborough sends for Mr. Hay.—Inhabitants assemble to concert measures for their safety.— Captain Keough delivers up his sword.—Dixon and his friends oppose the capitulation.—Despatch sent to General Lake, and his answer thereto.—Route taken by the defeated insurgents.—They demand the same terms as the townspeople obtained.—Kingsborough's promises.—Timothy Whelan attempts to put an end to the negociation for the surrender of the town.—Town surrendered to General Moore.—His humanity.—Wounded insurgents in the hospital put to death by yeomen.—Disappointment of General Lake.— His character, ... 193

CHAPTER XVII.

How the insurgents acted after the disastrous retreat from Vinegar Hill.—March out of town in two divisions.—The route taken by the division under Father John Murphy and Gen. Edward Roche.— Held a council of war at the Three Rocks.—Father Phillip Roche goes on his fatal embassy.—His character.—Miles Byrne not a leader.—March towards Longraig.—Insurgents penetrate into Carlow and Kilkenny.—Put the yeomanry who oppose them to flight. —Conflict at Kiledmond.—Force the passage of the River Barrow.— Wexford militia made prisoners—Cruel deed committed by the militia.—The Hessians.—Their brutal character, . . . 203

CHAPTER XVIII.

Insurgents arrive at the village of Dunain, where they are joined by the colliers.—Attack on Castlecomer.—Attempt to take possession of Lady Anne Butler's mansion.—Burning of Castlecomer.—Flight of Sir Chas. Asgill.—Strange apathy of the people of Kilkenny and Queen's County.—Insurgents retrace their steps towards Wexford. —Treachery of the colliers.—Insurgents force their way through Scollagh Gap.—Father John captured.—Insurgents again separate into two bodies, taking different routes, ... 213

CHAPTER XIX.

The insurgents halt at Monaseed, where they hear of fresh Orange atrocities.—They fall in with the force they are in quest of.—How the division of insurgents under Garret Byrne, on their way to Wicklow, are met by a horrid spectacle at Gorey.—They take vengeance on the murderers of women and children.—The engagement at Hacketstown.—Just retribution that befel the Ancient British cavalry.—Defeat of the Orangemen at Ballyrakeen Hill.—Attack on Capt. Chamney's house.—Resolve to destroy all strongly-built mansions, ... 217

CHAPTER XX.

Insurgents proceed to the Wicklow Gold Mines, where they burn the English camp.—Receive a reinforcement from Killaughrim Wood.—"The babes in the wood."—They attack General Sir James Duff, and force him to retreat.—Mr. Plowden's narrative of the battle of Cranford or Ballygullen.—Insurgents divide their force.—Wexford men return to Carrickgrew.—Wicklow men retreat to Glenmalure.—Wexford insurgents quit Carrickgrew and proceed to Kildare to join Aylmer.—March towards Athlone.—Attack a fortified house occupied by Lieutenant Tyrrell.—The Wexford men separate from the Kildare insurgents and penetrate into Meath.—Encountered by the Limerick militia and forced to retreat.—Capture and execution of Father Kearns and Anthony Perry.—The Wexford insurgents cross the Boyne and enter Louth.—Attacked by a large force of cavalry near Ardee.—Approach within seven miles of the metropolis, where they are routed by a squadron of the Dumfries dragoons.—The Rev. Mr. Gordon's account of the last stand made by the Wexford insurgents, ... 229

CHAPTER XXI.

Great numbers thrown into prison on the entry of the military into Wexford.—Cruel treatment of prisoners.—Heroism of the boy Lett.—General Needham's troops and the Hempesch dragoons.—Executions in Wexford.—Kelly of Killane.—Gen. Hunter's clemency.—Lord Lieutenant's proclamation.—Orange ferocity.—Esmond Kyan's death.—Hunter Gowan.—"Mr. Massacre."—False alarms raised by the Orangemen.—Major Fitzgerald's courage and prudence.—The island discovered by Hawtrey White cannot be found when sought for.—Landing of the French expedition under General Hardi.—Surrender of the insurgent general Edward Roche.—Execution of Walter Devereux and James Redmond, ... 238

A POPULAR HISTORY

OF THE

INSURRECTION OF 1798.

CHAPTER I.

England's jealousy of Ireland's prosperity under her Native Parliament.—The course adopted by England to ruin her rival.—The Irish Aristocracy of the period.—Brief account of the United Irish Society, its origin and aims.—Severities used by Government towards its members.—Trial of Jackson, and flight of Theobald Wolfe Tone.—How Tone worked for Ireland in France and Holland.—The French and Dutch Expeditions.—Severe measures adopted by Government.—Capture of the United Chiefs at Bond's.—Seizure and death of Lord Edward Fitzgerald.—Fate of other leaders.

THE Irish Parliament, for a long period the fettered slave of the English Legislature, and used only as an instrument of oppression, sprang from its feebleness into life and vigour at the imperious summons of the Volunteers.

Under the fostering care of her native Parliament thus enfranchised, Ireland in a brief time became marvellously prosperous. But England's jealousy took alarm when she beheld the slave she had unwillingly liberated assuming the aspect of a rival, and the nation by whose plunder she had been enriched, and whose blood she had so prodigally wasted, now controlling her own revenues, and, freed in a great measure from foreign oppression, bidding fair to become in time as great as she was independent.

The courage of England had failed her at the sight of the drawn swords and loaded cannon of the Volunteers; but these determined patriots being disarmed and rendered powerless by aristocratic treachery,* she again took heart, and resolved to reduce to her former state of abject slavery her hated rival. To effect the degradation of Ireland, by wresting from her a native Parliament, was rightly judged too perilous an undertaking so long as her sons were united. Myriads of armed Irishmen would have laughed to scorn the threats of England, and at the command of their own Parliament would have defied her power in the field. But English ministers did not dream of employing force against a united Irish nation. No! there was another method by which their object might be more surely achieved.

The glorious fabric of Irish independence might have withstood the rudest shock of armed violence, but the brand of religious discord, thrown with a skilful hand, could hardly fail to consume its proud walls with irresistible conflagration. This brand was thrown by the hand of the English Prime Minister. The popular Viceroy, Lord Fitzwilliam, was recalled, and Lord Camden sent in his place, charged with the detestable mission of fomenting religious discord. The hopes of the long-persecuted Catholics had risen with the rise of the Volunteers, for though this force was mainly composed of Protestants, they were of the middle-class,

* "An attempt, a month later, to reassemble the Convention was dexterously defeated by their President, Lord Charleville."—*M'Gee's History of Ireland*, p. 251. "Lord Charlemont did not oppose but he duped them."—*Sir Jonah Barrington's Rise and Fall of the Irish Nation*, p. 376.

who are often inclined to concede to others that liberty of conscience they seek to secure for themselves.

Now that the Volunteers were disbanded, the class from which they sprung had lost influence in the government of the country, and the aristocracy once more enjoyed unlimited power. Never was any country cursed with so powerful, and, at the same time, so bitterly hostile an aristocracy as Ireland.*

Foreign in race and creed, having no sympathy with the people, but regarding them as helots born to slavery, whose cry for liberty was to be smothered in their blood, they beheld with reluctant eyes the grand triumph of the Volunteers, and now that the latter had disappeared from the scene, and that the English

---

* In proof of this assertion, we may remind our readers, that King William III. would have granted religious freedom in Ireland but for the persistent opposition offered by the Irish Parliament, then, and long afterwards, composed exclusively of members of the aristocracy—that in the reign of Queen Anne, and in subsequent reigns, they passed the terrible penal laws which deprived the Catholics of all civil rights—that in many instances they urged the confiscation of the estates of the ancient Irish families, such as that of the MacCarthy More of Cork, in opposition to the known inclination of the English sovereigns. In truth, it was not till the democratic element appeared in the Irish Parliament that any measure favouring the freedom of the masses was conceded. The Protestants of the middle class have ever proved themselves the sincerest friends of their persecuted fellow-countrymen of another creed, while the aristocracy, with the lower rabble, their clients and dependents, their most relentless enemies. This course of hostility to the rights of their fellow-countrymen they continued till, at length, the time came when they consummated their guilty career by aiding in the destruction of the legislative independence of their native country. Concerning their conduct at that crisis, Sir Jonah Barrington observes : " They perpetrated the most extraordinary act of legislative suicide which ever stained the records of a nation." The Irish nation can never forget that they owe the Union and all its lamentable consequences to the Irish aristocracy.

Government was bent on reducing Ireland to her former misery by the destruction of her native Parliament, they resolved to afford her their most strenuous aid. Grattan nobly struggled at the head of his glorious minority to obtain toleration for his Catholic fellow-countrymen, but, as might have been foreseen, with an audience predeterminedly hostile, he failed, and the halls of Ireland's desecrated Senate no longer echoed to the voice of the great orator. Bigotry achieved an inglorious triumph, and the chains were but more firmly riveted on the prostrate form of the Catholic. A gloom settled over the land, for the rising sun of hope was darkened by the clouds of religious bigotry. But its light was not utterly extinguished, and nothing less would content the English Minister. Ireland still possessed a native though venal Parliament, and even of this last vestige of independence she was destined to be deprived.

It was now plain to all reflecting men that a great effort must necessarily be made to foil the efforts of the English Government by preserving to Ireland the invaluable right of self-government; and that the union of all creeds and classes was the only means by which this could be accomplished. To effect this union the leaders of the United Irishmen used their utmost endeavours.

It is outside our present purpose to enter into a detailed and lengthened narrative of the United Irish Society, but inasmuch as with that famous body the idea of armed resistance to British tyranny was in those days revived in Ireland, and as, moreover, many of its leading members took an active part in the subsequent insurrection, we deem it well to furnish our readers with a brief account of their proceedings. When the Society in question came into existence, the population of Ireland was divided into various jarring factions. In the North the Presbyterian " Peep o' Day Boys " contended with the Catholic " Defenders." The agrarian societies of the South, known as " Right Boys" and " Ribbonmen," waged a midnight warfare against the tyrant lords of the soil and the rapacious tithe-proctors. The spirit of animosity and hatred was equally rife among the higher classes. The gentlemen, lay and clerical, who formed the Catholic Association, found their bitterest opponents in the Whig Club, composed of the leading men of the Protestant aristocracy, whose persistent accusations of disloyalty they thought themselves obliged to refute by no less constant protestations of their ardent loyalty to the British Crown. To reconcile these jarring and hostile factions, to unite them in a unanimous effort to obtain the rights desired by all, was the noble aim of the United Irishmen. In the June of 1791, the Society was instituted in Belfast, at a meeting of a number of merchants and professional men, inhabitants of that city and its neighbourhood.

To Samuel Neilson, a Belfast merchant, must be given the credit of starting the Society; to Theobald Wolfe Tone, a distinguished member of the bar, the honor of being its chief organiser and most able pensman. The programme adopted by this important meeting was prepared by Wolfe Tone, and contained three propositions: that "English influence" was the great danger of Irish liberty; that a reform of Parliament was needed as a counterpoise to that influence; that such a reform should include Irishmen of all religious denominations.

In the November of the same year, a second club was instituted in Dublin. To give publicity to their proceedings and to propagate their opinions, the *Northern Star* newspaper was started in Belfast, and subsequently, in 1797, another called the *Press*, in Dublin. During the first three years of its existence, the Society made no very rapid progress, and seemed to attract but little notice from the Government; yet it did not altogether elude its vigilant observation. In 1792, two members of the Dublin Club, the Hon. Simon Butler and Oliver Bond, were summoned before the bar of the House of Lords for having acted as chairman and secretary at one of their meetings, and condemned each to a fine of £500 and six months' imprisonment. In 1794, Archibald Hamilton Rowan was convicted of having published and circulated a proclamation exhorting the Volunteers to resume their arms, and the Protestants of Ireland to meet in general convention and to make common cause with the Catholics; for this offence, Rowan, a gentleman of the highest character, was, though defended by Curran, condemned to a long imprisonment in Newgate. Notwithstanding the many difficulties the United Irishmen had to contend with—the determined opposition of the Orange Protestants, the indifference, if not hostility, of the higher classes of the Catholic population, and the constant efforts of the Government and its agents to keep alive the fires of bigotry they so laudably endeavoured to extinguish—they made a steady if slow progress. Amongst other objects which they laboured to attain was the repeal of the penal laws; and there is little doubt that the passing of the Catholic Relief Bill, in 1793, was, in great measure, if not wholly, owing to the strenuous exertions of the United Irish Society. The Government feared lest despair of obtaining relief from the yoke of those cruel laws, under which they had so long groaned, might impel the Catholics to join *en masse* the ranks of a society which had already grown sufficiently formidable. Having, in great measure, conciliated the latter by the granting of this long-hoped-for boon, the Government began to direct its undivided attention to the United Irishmen; and with a view towards the more effectual suppression of their society, enacted two bills, one called the Gunpowder and the other the Convention Act—the first of those acts declaring it illegal to import arms or any kind of ammunition into the kingdom, and forbidding the keeping of the same without licence; the second prohibiting the election or appointment of conventions or other unlawful assemblies, under the pretence of preparing or presenting public petitions or other addresses to his Majesty or his Parliament. The Government soon began to turn the arms it had just forged against the obnoxious society. The most celebrated of the clubs was that of Dublin, where its most eloquent orators and most honoured chiefs used to assemble. Here Butler, Bond, Tone, Tandy, Keough, and M'Cormick were wont to meet and address great multitudes of people. On the night of the 4th of May, 1794, the agents of Government burst into the assembly, arrested the officers, seized the papers, and dispersed the meeting. From that date the Society began to assume a new form. Hitherto it had carried on its proceedings openly, and, ostensibly at least, aimed at nothing beyond parliamentary reform, a reform which would concede equal rights to all Irishmen, and place Ireland on a footing of equality with England.

But now, driven perforce to become a secret society, it became at the same time a military one: forbidden to seek for freedom by constitutional means, it was compelled to recur to the final arbiter of all disputes—the sword. The change that took place is thus described by a modern historian:* "For reform of Parliament was substituted in the test or oath, representation ' of all the people of Ireland;' and for petitions and publications, the enrolment of men by baronies and counties, and the appointment of officers, from the least to the

---

* T. D. M'Gee.

highest in rank, as in a regular army. The unit was a lodge of twelve members, with a chairman and a secretary, who were also their corporal and sergeant; five of these lodges formed a company, and the officers of five such companies a baronial committee, from which again, in like manner, the county committees were formed. Each of the provinces had its Directory, while in Dublin the supreme authority was established in an 'Executive Directory' of five members. The orders of the Executive were communicated to not more than one of the Provincial Directors, and by him to one of each County Committee, and so in a descending scale, till the rank and file were reached; an elaborate contrivance, but one which proved wholly insufficient to protect the secrets of the organization from the ubiquitous espionage of the Government."

But subsequent events proved too well that no society can long remain secret from a Government that has gold to bribe the spy and informer. In such societies there is no touchstone by which the traitor can be detected and excluded—no one is more willing than he to take an oath for whose sanctity he has no respect. Skilled to enact to the life the part he assumes, no eye can penetrate his disguise and see the treachery that lurks in his heart, till the mine he has dug beneath the feet of his dupes explodes, and the complicated fabric of their organization is shattered into fragments, and they themselves lie crushed and bleeding amongst its ruins. It is sad to pursue the career of the society and the fortunes of the many noble characters connected with it to its final and melancholy collapse.

In 1795, the arrest of an Anglican clergyman named Jackson, sent by the French Republic, as its agent, to Ireland, led to the flight of Theobald Wolfe Tone, who had compromised himself by communicating with him. However, the loss (great as it was) sustained in the services of the daring and energetic Wolfe Tone was more than counterbalanced to the society by its gain in being joined by Lord Edward Fitzgerald, whose great name, associated with the most noted periods of Irish history, gave a vast additional prestige to the cause of the patriots. But the character of Lord Edward had no need of any adventitious circumstance of great wealth or high lineage to win for it the respect and admiration of his fellow-men. Nature seemed to have moulded him for a chief fitted to lead a generous and enthusiastic people like the Irish. Brave but gentle, generous yet not prodigal, of dignified manners yet divested of haughtiness, he was formed to be the idol of his fellow-countrymen.

Reviewing the characters of the United Irish chiefs, we must admire the extraordinary energy of Theobald Wolfe Tone, the heroic fortitude and perseverance of Neilson, the chivalrous honour of Rowan, the courage and honesty of all; but in the noble Fitzgerald we behold a union of all the qualities that form a unique and perfect character. In the same year the society was joined by other gentlemen of the highest social standing. Of these we may mention, Arthur O'Connor, who was a nephew of Lord Longueville, and a lineal descendant of the last Ard-righ of Ireland; Thomas Addis Emmet, and Dr. M'Nevin. All three were subsequently elected members of the Executive Directory.

In 1796 two important measures were passed in Parliament, namely: The Indemnity Bill, by which the magistrates were secured from being called to account for any excess in the administration of their powers; and the Insurrection Act, by which it was ordained that any seven magistrates might proclaim any district they judged to be tainted with disloyalty. This Act authorised them to search for arms in private houses, and to punish all persons absent from their homes at unreasonable hours. In the same year the Habeas Corpus was suspended, whereby power was given to arrest suspected persons, and detain them in prison for an unlimited period without assigning any cause. Soon after, the yeomanry were embodied to reinforce the regular troops, who were now poured into the country in great numbers. The great and daily increasing severities exercised by Government had the effect of driving numbers who had hitherto kept aloof to enrol themselves in the society. Towards the end of the year '97, half a million* of men had taken the test; of this number about 300,000 were armed either with pikes or firelocks. Of this immense but undisciplined force Lord Edward Fitzgerald was chosen commander-in-chief. On the other side, the Government could number an army of 160,000 men, 80,000 of whom were regular troops—the remainder being composed of militia and yeomanry.

In the beginning of the year '95, Lord Fitzwilliam was sent over to Ireland as Lord Lieutenant. This measure afforded great satisfaction to the Catholics, and raised their hopes of complete emancipation to a high pitch. Their expectations, however, were not destined to be realized, for, within three months from the date of his appointment this popular governor was recalled, and Lord Camden sent in his place. A feeling of deep despondency now pervaded the nation. It was felt that the Government had determined on the passing of the Union, as a preliminary step, to drive the people into insurrection. In the same year the Orange Society was formed, whose test was: "In the awful presence of God, I, A. B., do solemnly swear that I will, to the utmost of my power, support the King and the present Government; and do further swear that

---

* Sir Jonah Barrington, in his "Rise and Fall of the Irish Nation," estimates the number of *armed* men at 125,000—p. 434. A far greater number were sworn in.

I will use my utmost exertion to exterminate all the Catholics of the Kingdom of Ireland." To prevent the union the United Irishmen desired to effect of all Irishmen, the Government endeavoured, through its agents, to kindle afresh the fires of religious bigotry. To this end all manner of horrid rumours were disseminated of massacres to be perpetrated by the Catholics upon the Protestants, and *vice versa*. So well did they succeed in their iniquitous schemes that, in this year alone, seven thousand of the Catholic population in the county of Armagh were either killed or driven from their homes by the Orangemen.* Theobald Wolfe Tone who, as we have seen, was forced to fly the country, sought refuge in America. Having tarried there but a short space, he betook himself to France—in those days, as it had been for centuries before, the second home of exiled Irishmen.

There he exerted himself to the utmost in persuading the rulers of the Republic to stretch forth a helping hand to his beloved country. He succeeded so well in his efforts that on the 16th of December, 1797, a large fleet, having on board 15,000 picked troops, under the command of General Hoche, sailed from Brest for Ireland. But on sea, as on land, an unpropitious fortune dogged the footsteps of the gallant patriot. A dense fog enveloped the fleet during the voyage, a moiety of the ships losing their way therein, while the remainder, driven off the coast by a furious storm, were forced to return to France. The ill success of his first attempt did not crush the iron energy of Tone. He repaired to Holland—then styled the Batavian Republic—where, aided by the influence of Hoche, he succeeded in procuring the equipment of a fresh expedition. A fleet of sixteen ships, with 15,000 men on board, under

* See Mr. Plowden's " Review of the State of Ireland."

the command of Admiral de Winter and General Dandaels, was prepared for the Irish expedition. On the 8th of July they were ready to put to sea, but adverse winds setting in, detained them in harbour for five weeks, and at the end of that time the weather proving still unfavourable, the Dutch Directory resolved to land the troops and postpone the expedition, to the infinite vexation of the baffled exile. Toward the end of the next month, Tone's devoted friend, Hoche, died. With a saddened heart, Tone, still bent on carrying out his darling project, sought the French Directory, who lent a favourable ear to his eloquent pleading, and issued orders for the formation of "The Army of England," of which Bonaparte was named commander-in-chief. The great general seemed to take no slight interest in the proposed expedition—had frequent interviews with Tone—putting many questions to him relative to the British Isles, at times giving vent to bitter execrations of the English and the Jacobites. A vast army was now set on foot; Tone's hopes rose to a high pitch as the time for embarkation drew nigh. But these high hopes were destined to end in the bitterest disappointment, when, on the 20th of May, 1798, Bonaparte violated his promise to Tone, and directed his course, not towards the hills of "Holy Ireland," but the Pyramids of Egypt. At a later period, when the fire of insurrection, that timely aid might have kindled into irresistible conflagration, was quenched in the blood of thousands of patriots, Wolfe Tone, having accompanied the insignificant expedition under General Hardi, was taken prisoner in the naval conflict that ensued—recognised by an English officer—tried by court-martial, and sentenced to be hanged.* The proud spirit of Tone

* The following is an extract from the speech made by Tone on the occasion of his trial:—"Into the service of the French

shrank from this degradation—he requested his captors to grant him at least a soldier's death. This was cruelly denied. He then attempted to commit suicide—failed in the attempt, but died of the self-inflicted wound a week after, on the 19th of November.

We may hope that in the interim, this noble and dauntless spirit repented him of the rash and guilty deed that no possible circumstance could palliate or justify.

In the meantime, affairs in Ireland assumed, day by day, a more gloomy and hopeless aspect. Every dire instrument of oppression and cruelty was employed to madden the people and goad them into premature insurrection.*

Republic I originally entered with a view of serving my country. From that motive I have encountered the toils and terrors of the field of battle. I have braved the dangers of the sea, covered with the triumphant fleets of the power I opposed. I have sacrificed my prospects in life; I have courted poverty; I have left my wife unprotected, and my children fatherless. After doing this for what I thought a good cause, it is but little that I die for it. In such a cause as this success is everything. I have attempted that in which Washington succeeded and Kosciusko failed. What awaits me I am aware of, but I scorn to supplicate or complain. Whatever I have written, spoken, or acted in relation to this country, and its connexion with Great Britain, which I conceived to be the bane of its prosperity, I here avow, and am now ready to meet the consequence. Having sustained a high rank in the French service, I only wish, if the court possess such a discretionary power, that they will award me the death of a soldier."

* Sir Jonah Barrington, p. 457:—"Those transactions were dreadful, even to the recollection; they were the ruin of the nation and its character, but are only mentioned to give some idea of that worst of all scourges, Civil War, and of the most cruel of all tribunals, Courts Martial, a situation into which Mr. Pitt craftily permitted the Irish nation to fall in order to promote his purpose of a Union." And, in another page of the same work he affirms that, "The insurrection of 1798 was excited by the artifices of Mr. Pitt to promote a Union."

In the May of '97, an order was issued by the British Commander-in-chief that placed the whole country under the fearful yoke of Martial Law. It ran as follows:—"In obedience to the order of the Lord Lieutenant in council, the Commander-in-chief commands that the military do act without waiting for directions from the civil magistrates in dispersing any tumultuous or unlawful assemblies of persons threatening the peace of the realm and the safety of the lives and properties of His Majesty's loyal subjects wheresoever collected." To form an adequate idea of the terrible sufferings of the Irish people during this period, we have but to consider that every law which protected the rights of the subject was suspended; that their bitterest enemies who had sworn to exterminate them, were constituted at once their judges and executioners. A large volume might be filled with well-authenticated accounts of the cruelties inflicted upon innocent individuals. How many thousand victims suffered, whose sufferings were unrecorded, Heaven alone knows!

In vain had the United Irishmen endeavoured to conceal their operations from Government, in whose service a whole host of spies assiduously laboured to possess themselves of their secret. Men in all ranks of life were enrolled in the "Battalion of Testimony," from such as held the position of gentlemen, like Captain Armstrong, to gutter-bred miscreants of the type of Jemmy O'Brien. But, though differing in social rank, they were all alike in the vileness of their character. Placed by their paymasters upon the track of their victims, they hunted them down with the cunning of the fox and the ferocity of the bloodhound. A conspicuous victim of these wretches was William Orr, of Ferranshane. He was found guilty of having administered the United Irishman's oath to a soldier named Wheatley on the evidence of the same person, by a packed jury, and was inhumanly executed on the 14th of October, '97, although the Crown witness, struck with remorse, acknowledged that he had perjured himself, and many of the jury deposed on oath that they were drunk when the verdict was found. For commenting upon the conduct of the Lord Lieutenant in refusing to respite this innocent man, Mr. Fennessy, the proprietor of the *Press*, was tried for libel, found guilty, and sentenced to two years' imprisonment. The commander-in-chief, Lord Carhampton, does not seem to have been entrusted with the plans of the Prime Minister, and his energetic proceedings seemed likely to prevent the breaking out of the insurrection and the consequent bloody repression when the prostrate and enfeebled country, bleeding from a hundred wounds, was despoiled of her native government.

Being constantly thwarted in his military plans, he resigned his command, and was replaced by General Abercrombie. But this honest soldier, within two months from the time of his appointment, threw up his commission in disgust, declaring that "The army in Ireland was formidable to every one but the enemy." To Abercrombie succeeded General Lake, and to Mr. Pelham, the Chief Secretary (who also resigned), Lord Castlereagh, both, no doubt, well fitted to play their parts in the horrid tragedy now about to be enacted.

With a view to concert measures for the successful conduct of the insurrection which was shortly to take place, the Leinster delegates, to the number of thirteen, assembled together on the 12th of March, '98, at Bridge-street, in Dublin. But information of the intended assemblage had been previously imparted to Government by Mr. Thomas Reynolds, who had some time before been sworn a member of the society and elected delegate for Kildare county. They were surprised in their deliberations by Major Swan and twelve sergeants in coloured clothes, their papers seized and themselves taken into custody. Messrs. Emmet, Bond, Henry and Hugh Jackson, M'Nevin and Sweetman, were lodged in prison, and warrants issued for the apprehension of Lord Edward Fitzgerald and of Messrs. Sampson and M'Cormick. To fill the vacancy thus created in the executive of the society, the brothers John and Henry Sheares were elected to take charge of the Leinster clubs, and handbills were circulated amongst the people cautioning them against " being either goaded into untimely violence, or sunk into pusillanimous despondency." "If Ireland," concludes the handbill, "be forced to throw away the scabbard, let it be at her own time, not theirs." From the 30th of March, the date of the proclamation of Martial Law, the severities exercised upon the people pass all description. The most horrible tortures were made use of to extort a confession of guilt from suspected persons, houses were plundered and burnt, and men and women shot and hanged without even the formality of a trial. These atrocities were not confined to any single district, but were perpetrated throughout the entire country. To the truth of this statement not only such writers as Hays and Gordon bear witness, but others whose testimony admits no shadow of doubt, or suspicion of partiality to the people, as Sir John Moore, Sir Ralph Abercrombie, and Lord Moira. On the 21st of May the brothers John and Henry Sheares were arrested on the information of Captain Armstrong, who had wormed himself into their confidence, and dined with them the very day previous to their capture.

But the work of the Government was incomplete while Lord Edward remained at large. He had escaped arrest by being absent from Bond's when the other leaders were seized. A reward of £1000 was now offered for such information as would lead to his capture.

By constantly changing his quarters he was able, for the space of three months, to evade capture. But the moment, fatal alike to himself and to his country, at last came. On the night of the 18th he arrived at the house of Mr. Murphy, a feather merchant, of 153, Thomas-street. He appeared to his host to be ill, and complained of cold and sore throat, the result of the hardships and exposures he had undergone. On the following morning a woman brought to Murphy a parcel containing Lord Edward's uniform, which the former secreted in his warehouse. About mid-day Murphy, alarmed at seeing a party of soldiers passing up the street, communicated the intelligence to his guest, who requested to be conducted to some safer part of the house. Murphy led him to the top of the house, to one of the valleys formed by the roofs of the warehouse, where he remained for some time. All this while his faithful friend, Neilson, regardless of his own safety, continued walking up and down the street keeping guard, and occasionally interrogating Murphy as to Lord Edward's safety. Dinner-time arrived, and the alarm created by the appearance of the soldiery having somewhat subsided, Murphy, Neilson, and Lord Edward sat down to partake of the repast. When the cloth was removed, Neilson abruptly rose from the table and hurriedly quitted the house, and soon after, Mr. Murphy being summoned to attend to some business matter, went down stairs, leaving his guest alone. Returning after a few minutes' absence, he perceived that Lord Edward had left the dining-room and retired to his bed-room, where he found him lying, with his coat off, upon the bed. Ten minutes had hardly elapsed from Neilson's departure, and Murphy and Lord Edward were engaged in conversation, when a trampling was heard up the stairs, and Major Swan entered the room. The instant he perceived Swan, Lord Edward sprang from his reclining attitude, and advanced towards the unwelcome visitor. The latter immediately discharged a small pocket-pistol at him, but without effect. While Lord Edward was advancing towards Swan, a soldier burst into the apartment, who, at Swan's command, seized upon Murphy. Lord Edward now struck at Swan with a dagger which he had with him in the bed, but before he had time to repeat the blow another enemy presented himself upon the scene. This was Ryan, a captain of yeomanry, who, armed with a sword-cane, immediately attacked the Fitzgerald. As Swan's pistol had been ineffectually fired at Lord Edward, so the blade of Ryan's sword bent upon his breast, but so violent was the thrust that it threw him backward upon the bed. Ryan then threw himself upon him, and endeavoured to hold him down, but in the struggle that ensued received some desperate stabs from the dagger of the prostrate nobleman. Lord Edward at length arose from the grasp of his wounded enemy, who with Major Swan still clung to him, and advanced towards the door, dragging them both with him in his progress, clutching in his right hand the dagger with which he had wounded Ryan. Before he reached the entrance of the chamber he was confronted by Major Sirr, with half a dozen soldiers at his back. Sirr drew a pistol, and with a truer aim than Swan, shot Lord Edward in the right arm, upon which the dagger fell from his grasp. Although wounded and unarmed, the gallant Geraldine continued to struggle fiercely with his captors, endeavouring to shake off the grasp of Swan and the wounded Ryan, and making desperate efforts to gain the door. Sirr, fearing lest this terrible enemy might escape, summoned the soldiers to his assistance, who, after a severe struggle, succeeded in overpowering him, but so great was the strength he displayed in his efforts to rise from the ground, that they had to cross their firelocks over his prostrate body. It was during this struggle that a wretched drummer basely wounded the noble chief with his sword in the back of the neck.

An attempt was made by an unarmed crowd of citizens to effect the rescue of the prisoner, but proved unsuccessful, being defeated by the military, who, in anticipation of such an event, had hurried to the spot from the nearest posts. The illustrious captive was immediately conveyed to Newgate, where he might have recovered from his wounds, none of which were mortal, but the agony arising from hopes so wofully disappointed, aggravated by the inhumanity of his gaolers in refusing to admit to his bedside his beloved relatives, brought on his death, which took place on the 4th of June, his remains being interred in St. Werburgh's Church.

Thus perished, in a dark English dungeon, the hope of his country and the terror of his enemies, the lion-hearted Geraldine—the best and bravest of his princely race.

"So closed" (writes Mr. M'Gee, in his *History of Ireland*) "the memorable year 1798 on the baffled and dispersed United Irishmen. Of the chiefs imprisoned in March and May, Lord Edward had died of his wounds and vexation; Oliver Bond of apoplexy; the brothers Sheares, Father Quigly, and William Michael Byrne on the gibbet. In July, on Samuel Neilson's motion, the remaining prisoners in Newgate, Bridewell, and Kilmainham, agreed, in order to stop the effusion of blood, to expatriate themselves to any country not at war with England, and to reveal the general secrets of their system, without inculpating individuals. Those terms were accepted, as the Castle party needed their evidence to enable them to promote the cherished scheme of Legislative Union. But that evidence, delivered before the Committee of Parliament, by Emmet, M'Nevin, and O'Connor, did not altogether serve the purpose of Government. The patriotic prisoners made it at once a protest against and an exposition of the despotic policy under which their country had been goaded into rebellion. For their firmness they were punished by three years' confinement in Fort George, in the Scottish Highlands, where, however, a gallant old soldier, Colonel Stuart, endeavoured to soften the hard realities of a prison by all the kind attentions his instructions permitted him to show these unfortunate gentlemen. At the peace of Amiens (1802), they were at last allowed the melancholy privilege of expatriation. Russel and Dowdal were permitted to return to Ireland, where they shared the fate of Robert Emmet, in 1803; O'Connor, Corbet, Allen, Ware, and others cast their lot in France, where they all rose to distinction; Emmet, M'Nevin, Sampson, and the family of Tone were reunited in New York, where the many changes and distractions of a great metropolitan community have not even yet obliterated the memories of their virtues, their talents, and their accomplishments. It is impossible to dismiss this celebrated group of men, whose principles and conduct so generally influenced their country's destiny, without bearing explicit testimony to their heroic qualities as a class. If ever a body of public men deserved the character of a brotherhood of heroes, so far as disinterestedness, courage, self-denial, truthfulness, and glowing love of country constitute heroism, these men deserved that character. The wisdom of their conduct and the intrinsic merits of their plans are other questions. As between their political system and that of Burke, Grattan, and O'Connell, there always will be, probably, among their country-men, very decided difference of opinion. That is but natural: but as to the personal and political virtues of the United Irishmen, there can be no difference—the world has never seen a more sincere or more self-sacrificing generation."

CHAPTER II.

<small>Outbreak of the Insurrection.—Actions at Naas, Prosperous, and Kilcullen.—William Aylmer in Kildare.—Various conflicts between the soldiery and the people in the Counties of Dublin, Carlow, Meath, and Wicklow.—Massacre of Catholic yeomen at Dunlavin.—Proclamation issued by the authorities on the outbreak of the Insurrection.—How the Irish Parliament acted on the same occasion.—Colonel Maxwell's horrid proposal.—Loyal address of the Catholic gentry and aristocracy.—Attack on the town of Carlow by the insurgents.—How it ended.—Fate of Sir Edward Crosbie.—Engagement between the insurgents and Lord Fingal's Yeomanry at Tara Hill.—Massacre at Gibbet Rath, on the Curragh.—Official accounts of the affair.—Insurrection in Cork.</small>

It had been resolved by the Directory to commence the insurrection by making themselves masters of the capital, and then to proceed to overpower by simultaneous attacks the armed forces of the Government stationed throughout the provinces. The attempt to obtain possession of the capital proved a total failure, in consequence of the great precautions taken for its security. Dublin seemed changed from a peaceful city to an armed garrison; every partisan of the Government was armed to the teeth—the very judges appearing on the bench in military uniform. The guards stationed at every public building of importance were trebled, and all the avenues of the city were watched with the most vigilant care. The day of the 23rd of May was an anxious and disturbed one for the inhabitants of Dublin; however, it passed over in tranquillity, and within the city but one feeble attempt was made to kindle the fire of insurrection. Between the hours of nine and ten o'clock at night a body of men approached to attack

Newgate Prison, with intent to possess themselves
thereof. Their leader,* Samuel Neilson, posting his
men at some distance from the building, advanced
alone towards it for the purpose of reconnoitring.
While thus engaged he was recognised by one of the
officials, seized, and, after a few moments of desperate
but ineffectual resistance, found himself an inmate of the
dungeon. On seeing his capture his followers dispersed,
and thus terminated their bootless enterprise.

Some hours after, news reached the city that the
mail-coaches had been attacked and destroyed on their
way thither; that the Belfast mail was burned at
Santry; the Athlone, at Lucan; and that from Cork,
at Naas. From this night of the 23rd till the 31st of
May, no mail arrived from the provinces in Dublin.

The insurrection may be said to have commenced
with the attack on Naas, a small town distant about
fourteen miles from Dublin. In this place were stationed
a force composed of 400 of the Armagh Militia,
together with 100 of the cavalry regiment of Ancient
Britons, under the command of Lord Gosford.
On the evening of the 23rd, Lord Gosford had received
an anonymous letter warning him of the attack, and,
in consequence, had his troops under arms and fully
prepared to encounter their expected assailants. At the
hour of one on the following morning the insurgents, to
the number of about 1000 men, under a leader named
Reynolds, began the attack. They were received with
a well-directed fire by the troops stationed in security
behind the barrack walls. This fire they sustained
for some time with great resolution, the few of their
number who were possessed of firearms feebly return-

---

* Neilson struggled desperately with his captors, receiving
upwards of twenty wounds before being secured.—*Biography of
Lord Edward Fitzgerald*—Thomas Moore, Esq.

ing the incessant and fatal volleys from the garrison. The insurgents, at length, disheartened by the great loss they had sustained, began slowly to retreat. When the military saw their baffled assailants retiring, they issued from their shelter, and charging down upon them succeeded in putting them to utter rout. In this action the loss of the insurgents amounted to about one hundred men, while of the soldiery, two officers and fifty privates were slain.

A letter written by the parish priest of Naas to Dr. Troy, contains some interesting particulars concerning this affair. We give the following extracts:—

"*Naas, June* 25th, 1801.

"My Lord—I have remarked, in the account which Sir Richard Musgrave has given in his book on the late rebellion, that he has, in the article regarding Naas, made very great mis-statements. He says there was a Captain Davis wounded, &c.; not one word regarding that fact is true. There was no Captain Davis in the garrison at that time. Captain Davis came in a short time after, and is yet alive. All the officers then in the garrison of Naas know this to be the fact. Sir Richard also states that two hundred rebels were killed in the attack on Naas. The officers alluded to can give testimony, as they were witnesses, that more than nine or ten rebels did not fall on the occasion; but, in the course of three or four hours after, fifty-seven of a crowd in the street were killed. Many of these were shot when escaping from their huts, which were set on fire; others were taken out of their houses, from off their gardens, and brought to 'the Ship,' as the expression was, and hanged in the street." . . "The same day a young man of the name of Walsh was brought into Naas, who was said by a female to be the person who shot Captain Swayne, in the action at Prosperous. It is now well known that he was not within sixteen miles of Prosperous when the action took place there; nevertheless, he was taken, without any form of trial, to 'the Ship,' and there hanged, dragged naked through the street to the lower end of the town, and there set fire to; and when half burned, his body opened, his heart taken out and put on the point of a wattle. . . . . . When the body had been almost consumed, a large piece of it was brought into the next house, where the mistress of it, Mrs. Nowland, was obliged to furnish a knife, fork, and plate, and an old woman of the name of Daniel was obliged to bring them salt. These two women heard them say that 'Paddy ate sweet,' and confirmed with a 'd—n their eyes.' These women are living, and worthy of credit, being judged honest and respectable in their line and situation of life.—Signed,

"R. Donne, P. P.

"*Rev. Dr. Troy, Dublin.*"

At about the same hour a party of the North Cork Militia, under the command of Captain Swayne, stationed at the village of Prosperous, were surprised by the insurgents. The barrack was set on fire, and its inmates, while endeavouring to escape from the burning fabric, fell by the pikes of the peasantry. Had these men been true soldiers, their fate might have deserved our sympathy, but when we consider how cruel and merciless they were, we can feel but little pity for them. John Esmond, a Catholic gentleman and a lieutenant of the Sallins Yeomanry, was soon after hanged for his alleged complicity in this attack. He was, moreover, charged with the blackest treachery towards Captain Swayne, with whom he was said to be on the most intimate terms. It is due, however, to the unfortunate gentleman to say, that the charge of treachery, at least, is quite unfounded, for he and Swayne, instead of being on terms of amity, were known to have had entertained a cordial dislike towards each other. At a later hour on the same day, a body of three hundred pikemen were encountered near the bridge of Old Kilcullen by an equal number of the King's troops. The latter consisted of the 5th Light Dragoons and Romney Fencibles, under the command of Captain Eskrine. The English cavalry charged thrice with great fury on the insurgent ranks, but were as often repulsed, and, being in turn charged by the insurgents, were completely routed, leaving two officers and thirty privates dead on the field.

Thus far successful, the insurgents pursued their march in triumph towards Kilcullen, the quarters of General Dundas; but fortune, that had so lately favoured, now deserted them, for on arriving at the village, they were attacked by a detachment of infantry, and routed with considerable loss.

Concerning the two actions that took place near Kilcullen, the Rev. Mr. Gordon, rector of Killegny, in the diocese of Ferns (Wexford), in his excellent and impartial *History of Ireland*, remarks: "The action at Kilcullen, at seven o'clock, was remarkable only for an early proof of the total unfitness of cavalry for combat with embattled pikemen. Three hundred of the latter were three times furiously charged, without the least impression, by a body of cavalry, consisting of Light Dragoons and Romney Fencibles, who lost two captains and thirty privates by the pikes of the enemy. Yet these victorious pikemen were, a few minutes after, totally routed by twenty-two Fencible Infantry, led against them by General Dundas."

The insurgents, whom we have seen so successful in their attack on Prosperous, marched thence towards the village of Slane, where a detachment of the royal troops were stationed. In this action, however, they did not come off triumphant, for the military, though dispersed at the beginning of the attack, sallied forth from their different billets, and making a courageous stand, succeeded in repulsing the attack and in inflicting severe loss on their assailants.

William Aylmer took the place of Lord Edward as leader of the United Irishmen of Kildare. In the conduct of hostilities in that county the young chief had more than ordinary difficulties to contend with. Kildare, a flat and open country without hill or fastness, could afford neither shelter nor rallying place to his raw and undisciplined troops, while those very characteristics rendered it peculiarly favourable to the evolutions of a regular army. "Lord Edward's county" had, moreover, the disadvantage of being represented in the Directory by the traitor Thomas Reynolds, and consequently its organization was better known to Government than that of any other district. Within a day's march of the Metropolis, and but a short distance from several garrison towns, General Wilford, the royalist commander, at the head of nearly 4000 men, with a powerful train of artillery, might well consider the ill-armed and undisciplined force opposed to him an easy conquest.

But his brave and skilful opponent kept him long at bay, and held out till the insurrection was totally quelled in other quarters, when, more fortunate than other chiefs, he escaped with life and liberty. Mr. Teeling, in his "Personal Narrative," describes the struggle maintained in Kildare in the following terms:—"Aylmer was pursuing, at this time, a species of fugitive warfare. Totally defective in artillery, and commanding in an open champaign country, he was unable to maintain, for any considerable time, a stationary war; but the velocity with which he moved, and the prompt decision that marked his action, rendered him a more formidable foe, and his warfare more harassing and destructive to his enemies. At night, on the extended plains of Kildare, in the morning twenty miles in advance, cutting off the supplies of the enemy, storming their posts, or driving back the advance of their army in full march to lay waste some devoted village or town; always on the alert, indefatigable in his pursuits and exhaustless in enterprise, his military character seemed a perfect copy of the 'Great Dundee.' Even after the termination of the Wexford campaign, the defeat of the united forces in Ulster, and the general cessation of hostilities, we find Aylmer at the head of his invincible band, 'winning, by his courage and conduct, the admiration of hostile ranks,' and never laying down the arms which he had borne with manly pride until the last of his companions were guaranteed in life and safety by a solemn treaty with the British General Dundas."

Besides those we have narrated, numerous conflicts took place during the first and second days of the insurrection between the insurgents and their trained foes within the limits of Dublin, Kildare, Carlow, Meath, and Wicklow. At Rathfarnham Lord Ely's yeomanry corps were attacked by a force of insurgents under Messrs. Ledwich and Keough, numbering some 400 men. The yeomanry were on the point of defeat when the arrival of Lord Roden's dragoons to their aid turned the scale of success against their assailants. Sir Jonah Barrington thus mentions the affair:—" The Lord Lieutenant ascertained that such an attempt [a night attack on the city] was to be made on the 23rd of May, by a large body of insurgents then collecting on the north of Swords and Santry, and on the south under the Rathfarnham mountains, less than five miles from the city . . . The insurgents on the south intended to take the castle by surprise, while the Santry men assailed the barracks; but their plan was disconcerted

by Lord Roden at the head of his dragoons (called the
fox-hunters, from their noble horses). His lordship
marched rapidly upon them, surprised the few who had
collected; and being supported by a small number of
light infantry, completely succeeded in his attack. A
few were sabred, and some few made prisoners; but
the body dispersed with little resistance. Roden received a ball on his helmet, but was only bruised, and
some dragoons were wounded; the other (county of
Dublin) men retreated to join the Kildare men, the
southerns marched to unite themselves with those of
Wicklow."

Of the two leaders, Ledwich was taken prisoner, and
hanged the next morning; Keough was desperately
wounded, but recovered, and was pardoned by Lord
Camden. Sir Jonah adds:—"He did not, however,
change his principles, and was ultimately sent out of
the country."

At Dunboyne, a small body of the Reay Fencibles
(Scotch), while passing through the village, were
attacked and slain by the peasantry. At Barretstown,
a similar defeat was inflicted upon a detachment of the
Suffolk Fencibles.

In their attack upon Monasterevan the insurgents
were repulsed with loss, their opponents being in this
instance the Catholic loyalists of the town, led by Captain Cassidy; they were, however, successful in their
attacks upon the little towns of Rathangan and Blessington, the latter place remaining in their possession for
some days. At Tallaght, Lusk, Hacketstown, and
Callan, unimportant, and, on the part of the insurgents,
unsuccessful actions took place.

Similar attacks were made by the insurgents upon
the military barracks at Dunlavin and at Baltinglas (in
Wicklow), proving, as such attempts generally did, unsuccessful. At Dunlavin, the local yeomanry being

suspected by other corps of complicity in the insurgent attack, were surrounded and disarmed. Twenty-eight of these unfortunate men (nineteen Wexford and nine Kildare men, all Catholics), were (after a mock trial, during which no evidence of their guilt was adduced), summarily executed. The fact of their being "Papists" was deemed by their fellow-yeomen a quite sufficient proof of their disloyalty. This shocking massacre of their co-religionists drove many of the Catholic yeomen into the insurgent ranks, where their previous military training enabled them to do good service.

On receiving intelligence of the outbreak of the insurrection, the chief authorities in Dublin, the Lord Lieutenant, the Lord Mayor, and the Commander-in-Chief of her Majesty's forces issued each a proclamation.

The Viceroy announced that orders had been despatched to punish by Martial Law all persons in any way participating in the rebellion. The civic Chief Magistrate issued *his* mandate to the citizens to register, without delay, whatever firearms they possessed, and to affix to the doors of their houses a list containing the names of their inmates. General Lake declared his intention to exercise fully the great powers entrusted to him, and ordered that all persons not in military uniform should remain in their respective houses from nine in the evening till five in the morning.

On the same day (the 24th of May) the Parliament met, and by a unanimous vote approved of all these vigorous measures, and expressed, at the same time, in forcible terms, their enthusiastic adherence to the present Government of the country. The resolution then moved and passed unanimously, was as follows:—
"That an humble address be presented to his Excellency the Lord Lieutenant to express our cordial acknowledgment for the message sent this day by his Excellency to the House. We entirely approve the decisive mea-

sures his Excellency has taken, by the advice of the Privy Council, however we may lament its necessity. We renew our engagement of support; we reflect on the general firmness and vigour which are manifested; we feel the fullest assurance that the rebellion will be speedily crushed."

Colonel Maxwell, who rose to second the motion, took occasion to make the atrocious suggestion to the House, that, "As it was expedient to crush the rebellion as quickly as possible, it would be well to put all the United Irish leaders, then in prison, to death—as such a measure would much discourage their brethren at present in arms." This horrible proposal of the savage soldier did not, however, meet with the approbation of the House, even Castlereagh himself rose up to express his disapproval. The celebrated minister, though cold-hearted and indifferent to human suffering, had no desire to shed human blood when no political end could be gained thereby. With the view of imparting greater solemnity to their address, the members, with the speaker at their head, walked in procession through the streets to the Viceregal residence to present it with due formality to the King's representative. This done, they adjourned for a week.

The Catholic aristocracy and gentry of Ireland resolved not to be behind-hand with the Protestant Parliament in professions of devoted loyalty to a government, which it appears had earned their enthusiastic gratitude, by treating them for centuries as Pariahs—by depriving them of all civil rights, and forbidding them, under the severest penalties, the exercise of their religion. They, too, presented an address. This precious document, the emanation of meanness and selfishness, is as follows:

"The Address of the Roman Catholics of Ireland, presented to his Excellency the Lord Lieutenant, on Wednesday, May the 30th, 1798.

"MAY IT PLEASE YOUR EXCELLENCY,—We, the undersigned, his Majesty's most loyal subjects, the Roman Catholics of Ireland, think it necessary at this moment publicly to declare our firm attachment to his Majesty's royal person, and to the constitution under which we have the happiness to live; we feel, in common with the rest of his Majesty's subjects, the danger to which both are exposed from an implacable and enterprising enemy, menacing invasion from abroad, and from the machinations of evil and disaffected men, conspiring treason within his Majesty's kingdom; under these impressions, we deem it necessary to remove, by an open and explicit declaration, every idea of countenance afforded on our part to a conduct bearing even the appearance of indifference and indiscretion, much more to a conduct holding forth symptoms of disaffection and hostility to the established order of government in this kingdom, in the preservation of which, though we differ from it on some points of spiritual concern, we feel too deeply interested to look with an indifferent eye on its overthrow. Allow us, then, to assure your Excellency, that we contemplate with horror the evils of every description which the conduct of the French Republic has produced on every nation hitherto weak enough to be deluded with its promises of liberty, and offers of fraternity; we anticipate similar misfortunes as awaiting this his Majesty's Kingdom, in the deprecated event of successful invasion; with confidence we state our determination not to be outdone by any description of our fellow-subjects, in zealous endeavours for averting that calamity; and that, although anxious to enjoy, free of every restriction, the full benefit of our constitution, we reject with indignation any idea of removing the restrictions, under which we still labour, by means of foreign invasion, or by any other step inconsistent with the known laws of the land; we prefer, without hesitation, our present state to any alteration thus obtained; and, with gratitude to the best of kings, and to our enlightened Legislature, we acknowledge such a share of political liberty and advantage already in our possession, as leaves us nothing to expect from foreign aid, nor any motive to look elsewhere, than to the tried benignity of our Sovereign, and the unbiassed determination of the Legislature, as the source of future advantage. We cannot avoid expressing to your Excellency our regret at seeing, amid the general delusion, many, particularly of the lower orders, of our religious persuasion, engaged in unlawful associations and practices. Yet we trust that your Excellency's discernment will lead you to make every just allowance for the facility with which men, open to delusion from their situation in life, are led astray from their political duty: it shall be our endeavour to call such men to a sense of that duty, by pointing out to them how inconsistent their conduct is with their real interest, and how contrary to the maxims of the religion which they profess; nor shall we less endeavour, by our conduct, to convince all descriptions of our fellow-subjects, how much we are impressed with the necessity of laying aside all considerations of religious distinctions, and joining in one common effort for the preservation of our constitution, of social order, and of the Christian religion, against a nation whose avowed principles aim at the destruction of them all. We request your Excellency will make these our sentiments known to his Majesty, and we rely with confidence on your Excellency's acknowledged candour and generosity, that you will represent us in that light, to which we venture to hope our conduct and principles have given us a just claim.

"FINGAL.   SOUTHWELL.
"GORMANSTOWN.   KENMARE."

With seventy-two baronets, gentlemen of distinction, and professors of divinity, together with the Rev. Peter Hood, D.D., President of the Royal College of Maynooth, for himself and students of said College, and above 2,000, whose names are too numerous to be inserted.

Another address of similar tenor was presented at the same time to the Lord Lieutenant, by the same four noblemen, bearing, besides the signature of Dr. Troy, Archbishop of Dublin, the Honourable Mr. Barnewall, Denis Thomas O'Brien, Hugh Hamil and George Goold, Esqrs., and of a great number of the higher class of the Roman Catholics of Dublin.

To these servile and sycophantic effusions, the representative of the "best of kings"[*] returned the following answer: "I have the highest satisfaction in receiving your address. The loyalty of the principles you profess will, I doubt not, be fully evinced by your public and effectual exertions. The present unhappy conjuncture calls equally upon men of all religious persuasions to mark their attachment to their sovereign and our constitution, by counteracting the spirit of anarchy and rebellion which had disgraced the country. The influence of your example and authority may be of essential service; and you may be assured of my determination to do justice to your efforts, in repressing every species of turbulence and insubordination."

Between one and two o'clock, on the morning of the 25th, a body of peasantry, to the number of about four thousand men, assembled on the lawn of Sir Edward Crosbie's mansion, situate about a mile and a half from the town of Carlow, with the intention of attacking the

---

[*] Of George III., Lord Macaulay writes in his essay on William Pitt: "As a sovereign he was resentful, unforgiving, stubborn, cruel;" and again, "Dull, obstinate, unforgiving, and, at the same time, half mad." Thus does England's great historian describe "the best of men."

large force of the King's troops that occupied the place.

The force of Royal troops stationed at Carlow, was under the command of Colonel Mahon, of the 9th Dragoons, and amounted to some fifteen hundred men, composed of detachments of the Armagh and North Cork Militia regiments, with several corps of yeomanry. As had happened in other places, the English commander was apprised beforehand of the intended attack, and had full time to make all the preparations that he deemed requisite. At daybreak, the insurgents quitted their place of assembly, with their whole force divided into four bodies, equal in numbers. They proceeded, with a rude imitation of military order, towards the town which was the object of their combined attack. One of the four divisions, desirous to be the first to engage the enemy, outstripped the others, and entered the town before them. As they entered the silent and apparently unguarded town, some of the wilder and more reckless spirits could not refrain from giving vent to their exultation by loud shouts of triumph. Their hopes of surprising their enemies were, however, ill-founded; for the latter were but too well prepared for their attack. They were suffered to penetrate unmolested into the centre of the place, whose inhabitants seemed still buried in sleep, when the report of a sentinel's musket gave warning of their approach to his watchful comrades. Then from the barracks and adjacent houses a terrible fire was poured into the centre of that band of surprised and dismayed peasantry. The effect of such a surprise upon the bravest and best disciplined troops is often disastrous—it was fatal to the unfortunate insurgents. For some moments they kept together, while volley after volley came crashing into their midst, from a foe they could not see. At last, utterly panic-stricken and disheartened, they fled on all sides, each striving to save himself. Some succeeded in escaping outside the fatal town, while others, and these were far the greater number, sought for safety in the surrounding houses. This movement, however, had been anticipated by their foes, who instantly set fire to a number of these buildings. It is computed that one hundred and fifty houses, in which the terrified peasantry had sought refuge, were set on fire by the soldiery; and these houses being largely formed of inflammable material, which was now dried by the great summer* heat, burned with a rapid and fearful conflagration. In a brief space the unhappy fugitives were enveloped in fire. Those who managed to escape from the raging flames were shot or bayonetted in the streets by their vengeful and cruel enemies, while the greater number never emerged, but were burned alive in the place of retreat. Within an incredibly short time five hundred of the unfortunate peasantry had ceased to exist. The yet blazing houses were full of the charred remains of human bodies, while the streets were strewn with the bleeding corpses of such as escaped from the fury of the burning element only to meet with as merciless a foe. Not less than five hundred of the insurgents lost their lives on the occasion, while two hundred persons, not engaged in the affair, were accused of complicity therein, tried by court-martial, and executed. Amongst the latter was the "gentlemanly knight," Sir Edward Crosbie.† No more lamented victim underwent death by the sentence of this most merciless and unjust tribunal. The accusation put forward by his enemies was complicity in the plans of the insurgents; but the real cause of his condemnation and death was his avowed detestation of,

* The summer of 1798 was unusually warm.
† See Appendix.—Further particulars concerning Sir Edward Crosbie, and an account of the cruelties exercised by the Carlow Orangemen.

and opposition to, the fell system of Orangeism. His trial was a mere mockery of justice; for soldiers were stationed, with fixed bayonets, at the doors of the courthouse, to prevent the entrance of any one who should come to give evidence in his favour. After his execution, his senseless remains were brutally abused, and his gory head placed, in barbarous triumph, upon a spear. Thus did the English Government of the day teach Protestant gentlemen what a crime it was in their eyes to sympathise with their oppressed countrymen of another creed.

26th.—On this day, a body of three thousand insurgents, assembled on the Hill of Tara, were attacked by a large body of yeomanry. These yeomen, who formed one of the most efficient corps in the kingdom, were mostly composed of Catholics, and were under the leadership of the gallant but unpatriotic nobleman, the Catholic Lord Fingal. They came into the field excellently well equipped, and, moreover, provided with a piece of artillery of large calibre. Their insurgent foes were wretchedly armed, few of them bearing fire-arms; not a moiety of them were furnished even with pikes, while the rest carried no offensive or defensive arm, save the rustic scythe or pitchfork. Notwithstanding all their disadvantages, they bore, for the long space of four hours, the spirited attacks of their assailants, often during that time repulsing the cavalry who charged them. At length, however, they were forced to abandon their position, with greatly diminished numbers, leaving four hundred of their number dead upon the field.

On the royalist side, in addition to Lord Fingal's cavalry, three companies of the Reay Fencibles, under Captain M'Clean, the Kells and Navan yeomanry, under Captain Preston, took part in this hard fought action. Mr. Teeling thus speaks of the same action, whose loss he attributes to the want of competent leaders on the insurgent side:—" This circumstance (the lack of officers) was never more conspicuous than in the disastrous affairs of Meath. Admirably posted, on the princely Hill of Tara, and with a force sufficient to combat twice the number of their assailants, they had not an officer who knew the advantage of the ground, or to whose sole authority they acknowledged obedience. Each separate leader of division looked only to those who were under his immediate control; and, though many were qualified for inferior command, none assumed that superiority so essential to the direction of the field, in the arrangement of forces who had no combined system of action. Had they marched under men who possessed the talents of Fitzgerald, of Redmond, of Clony, of Roche, or a hundred others, whose names are conspicuous in the Wexford campaign, Tara would not have been the field of an easy bought victory, where courage was abundant, and arrangement only deficient."

The Kildare, Dublin, and Carlow insurgents, meeting with such ill success in their encounters with the forces of the Government, became disheartened and inclined to discontinue what had appeared, from the outset, a hopeless struggle. Success might have encouraged them to prolong the unequal struggle; but that wanting, nothing remained to them but submission. A body of about two thousand insurgents, under the leadership of one Perkins, who had assembled on the hill of Knockalwin, near the Curragh of Kildare, hearing of the defeats sustained by their countrymen in other quarters, resolved no longer to struggle against what they supposed their irresistible ill-fortune.

Acting on this resolve, they despatched a messenger to General Dundas, to treat for terms of surrender. This officer, not being devoid of humanity, readily granted the terms they sought—leave to surrender their arms and retire unmolested to their homes. In consequence of this wise clemency of the English general, great numbers of the peasantry met at Gibbet Rath, on the Curragh, with the hope of obtaining the like terms. General Dundas willingly conceded the same terms to these as he had before granted to their fellow-insurgents, and immediately despatched General Gosford to receive the arms they had promised to surrender. But the affair was not to end so peacefully. It happened that Major-General Sir James Duff was at the time on his march from Dublin to Limerick, and being informed of the assemblage of peasantry on the Curragh, and of their having surrendered to General Dundas, he without delay directed his march to the Curragh, with the apparent intention of carrying out the wish of his superior officers. But Duff evidently knew the road to promotion in the English army, and was well aware that any severity he might exercise upon the *mere Irish* would meet with the approval of his masters. Doubtless, too, he deemed that it would be a mistake to neglect such a splendid opportunity of cutting off a number of the rebellious natives. He required but a pretext to give a colour of justice to his cruel purpose. Unhappily that pretext was afforded by the thoughtless folly of one of the insurgents, who, in silly bravado, discharged his musket in the air before he surrendered it. Upon this General Duff ordered his soldiers to fire on the betrayed, and then almost disarmed, multitude, who immediately fled in terror. Then was beheld a scene of indiscriminate slaughter. The infantry poured volley after volley upon the flying insurgents with fearful effect, while Lord Jocelyn at the head of his mounted yeomen pursued and cut them down without mercy. The unfortunate peasantry, terrified by this unexpected onslaught, fell an easy prey to their bloodthirsty pursuers—the wide open plains of the Curragh affording them no shelter from their foes—and it is reckoned that fully 400 of them fell on the occasion.

Insurrection of 1798.

The massacre on the Curragh is thus described by Lord Camden in his despatch to the Duke of Portland:—

"*Dublin Castle*, *May 29th.*

"My Lord,—I have only time to inform your grace that I learn from General Dundas that the rebels on the Curragh of Kildare have laid down their arms, and delivered up a number of their leaders. By a despatch which I have this instant received, I have the further pleasure of acquainting your grace that Sir James Duff, who, with infinite alacrity and address, has opened the communication with Limerick (that with Cork being already open), had arrived at Kildare whilst the rebels had possession of it, completely routed them and taken the place.

"I have the honour to be, &c.

"Camden."

Sir James Duff thus describes the same transaction:—

Extract of a letter from Major-General Sir James Duff to Lieutenant-General Lake, dated Monasterevan.

"I marched from Limerick on Sunday morning with sixty dragoons, Dublin Militia, three field-pieces, and two curricle guns to open the communication with Dublin, which I judged of the utmost importance to Government. By means of cars for the infantry I reached this place in forty-eight hours. I am now, at seven o'clock this morning (Tuesday) marching to surround the town of Kildare, the head-quarters of the rebels, with seven pieces of artillery, 150 dragoons and 350 infantry, determined to make a dreadful example of the rebels. I have left the whole country behind me perfectly quiet and well protected by means of the troops and yeomanry corps. I hope to be able to forward this to you by the mail coach, which I will escort to Naas.

"I am sufficiently strong. You may depend on my prudence and success. My guns are well manned, and all the troops in high spirits. The cruelties the rebels have committed on some of the officers and men have exasperated them to a great degree. Of my future operations I will endeavour to inform you.

"P.S.—Kildare, two o'clock, P.M.—We found the rebels retiring from the town on our arrival, armed; we followed them with the dragoons. I sent on some of the yeomen to tell them, on laying down their arms, they should not be hurt. Unfortunately, some of them fired on the troops;* from that moment they were attacked on all sides—nothing could stop the rage of the troops. I believe from two to three hundred of the rebels were killed. We have three men killed and several wounded. I am too much fatigued to enlarge."

In Munster but one attempt was made to shake off the English yoke.

On the 19th of June an attack was made by some 300 of the Cork peasantry on a body of king's troops, consisting of 200 Westmeathean yeomanry and 100 of the Caithness legion, while on their march from Clonakilty to Bandon. The peasantry sprang from their ambuscade and charged the Westmeatheans with their pikes, giving them no time to form. It might have fared ill with the latter had not the Caithness legion hurried up to their assistance, and pouring a sharp fire on the insurgents, put them to flight. The peasantry lost in this action about fifty men, but the loss of the military could not be ascertained, for, *as was customary*, their dead and wounded were borne away, and a report issued by the commander more creditable to his powers of invention than to his truthfulness.

* The Rev. Mr. Gordon, referring to this, says: "On the most futile pretence they attacked the unresisting multitude."

CHAPTER III.

The seizure of the Ulster chiefs retards the insurrection in that province.— How the intended junction of the insurgents of Down and Antrim was frustrated.—Henry Joy M'Cracken chosen to command the men of Antrim.—His first measures.—Advance of the united army upon Antrim.— The attack.—Panic and flight of the insurgents.—Gallant stand made by Hope.—Colonel Clavering and M'Cracken.—M'Cracken quits Donegore.—Saves his followers from capture.—Falls into the power of his enemies, and is put to death.

THE unexpected seizure of their chiefs, on the very eve of their preconcerted rising, was a severe blow to the Northern United Irishmen. It seemed indeed to have completely paralysed their energies for a time. Far better organised than their Southern confederates, they were from that very circumstance less capable of action when deprived of their chiefs.

Ulster might not inaptly be compared at this crisis to a piece of ordnance loaded and primed, whose gunner had been shot down when about to discharge it at the foe.

Their hesitation at this critical period, when every hour was precious, may perhaps in some measure be attributed to that cautiousness which forms the distinguishing trait in the character of the Scottish race, from which many of them derived their origin. They lacked that fiery temperament, which renders the true Celt, when his spirit is thoroughly aroused, so reckless of danger, so willing to encounter the greatest odds. But the men of Ulster though slow in action were sincere in purpose, at length resolved to make an effort to shake off the intolerable yoke under which they had so long groaned, and to maintain with their strong arms those principles they had ever secretly cherished in their hearts. The insurgents of Antrim and Down having chosen leaders to fill the places of Russell and Neilson, who were in prison with the other chiefs, agreed to assemble on the 5th of June at an appointed place in their respective counties. But fortune seemed adverse to them from the very outset. The Rev. Steele Dickson, the newly-selected leader of the Down men, was arrested with two of his staff, while on his way to the appointed rendezvous, and his followers, on hearing of his capture, dispersed to await the election of another chief. Their Antrim brethren, who had assembled on the same day, were not a little disconcerted by the arrival of a messenger from Down to announce what had befallen their comrades in that county, and to urge the postponement of their enterprise till a new leader had been chosen, and both parties might act in conjunction. This was not the only discouraging circumstance that occurred at this critical period, for it was soon after announced that their own leader had resigned his command, and declined to take further part in the affair.

This succession of mishaps naturally threw the insurgents into a state of great confusion, and produced serious difference of opinion, if not positive dissension amongst them. Some of the officers declared for instant action, while others urged the prudence of delay. While this confusion prevailed amongst them a horseman came on the spur into the camp bearing the startling news that a large body of cavalry was advancing towards them, and had already reached within a mile of their rendezvous. This put an end to their indecision. Deeming it now more perilous to disperse than to stand their ground, they resolved to choose without delay some one from their number to lead them against the enemy. Their election was soon made, and fell upon Henry Joy M'Cracken, than whom they judged no one could be found more fitted for the arduous post of leader. On being chosen to the chief command, M'Cracken's first care was to take such measures as would secure his men against the danger of being surprised by the enemy.

To this end he posted sentinels around his camp, and formed a sufficient guard to be relieved at regular hours. He then proceeded to draw up a manifesto addressed to the united troops of Ulster in the following terms:—

"Army of Ulster, to-morrow we march on Antrim; drive the garrison of Randalstown before you, and haste to form a junction with the commander-in-chief.— Signed, HENRY JOY M'CRACKEN, 1st year of Liberty, 6th day of June, 1798." At an early hour on the 7th, the Northern insurgents marched from Cregarogan fort (an ancient and ruined fortress near which they had assembled) directing their course towards the town of Antrim. The gunsmen, drawn up four deep, formed the van; behind these came the pikemen, a far more numerous body, while a small band brought up the rear, with a few field-pieces, the only artillery they possessed. Chanting in chorus the warlike and soul-stirring "Marseillaise," M'Cracken's little force, amounting to no more than three thousand men, pressed forward rapidly towards Antrim, before whose walls they arrived about mid-day. On their way thither they were joined by some five hundred men from Temple-Patrick and Killead. Meanwhile, the royalist garrison, consisting of the 22nd regiment of light dragoons, under Colonel Lumley, together with several corps of yeomanry and a strong reinforcement recently arrived from the camp at Blaris Moore, had employed the interim in making preparations to resist the insurgent attack. Their foot had taken up a position in front of the castle gate, the main entrance to the town, while the cavalry took post at the opposite extremity of the place behind the high strong wall that enclosed the cathedral. Their cannon was planted in the middle of the main street, which extended between the two positions above-mentioned. Against the royal troops, thus advantageously posted, the insurgents advanced in two divisions, one of which was ordered to force an entry through the castle gate, and the other to carry the position occupied by the cavalry. About 2 o'clock in the afternoon the assault began. The first division of the insurgent army advancing against the position occupied by the cavalry, was received by that body with a heavy fire, which they returned with such good effect that their opponents were forced to abandon their post and take refuge in the adjoining grave-yard—the low strong walls and numerous tombs of which furnished an excellent cover for marksmen. Meantime the second division of the insurgent army attacked the town from the opposite direction, and bringing a small cannon they had with them to bear on the infantry posted at the castle gate, drove them thence to a more advantageous position under the walls. The first division of the insurgent army having succeeded in driving their enemy before them, had gained the centre of the town, but there they found themselves exposed to a destructive fire of cannon and musketry directed against them by men who lay in security behind stone walls and earthen barriers. To drive the foe from their cover, and to occupy it themselves, was their next effort, and to effect this the pikemen were brought into action. Having received orders to charge, they rushed forward with great impetuosity, and though driven back several times, the grape-shot making dreadful havoc in their ranks, they at length succeeded in gaining the desired position, whence the combat could be maintained on more equal terms. The body of insurgents who had driven the soldiery from the castle gate, maintained their position for some time, but at length a well-directed shot from the hostile artillery dismounted their only piece of cannon. Colonel Lumley regarding this as a favourable opportunity, charged down with his regiment of cavalry upon the pikemen who guarded it. The latter encountered the onset of the dragoons with great gallantry, and after a fierce struggle, in which Lumley was wounded, drove them back in confusion: However, this repulse did not deter the brave loyalist officer from leading his men once more to the attack. But this time he was assailed by a new foe, for the body of pikemen who had shortly before gained the shelter of the grave-yard, now rushed forward to aid their brethren at the gate, and the dragoons, attacked at once both in front and rear, began to fall in great numbers; however, cheered on by their gallant chief, they continued for some time to offer a determined resistance.

At this juncture, M'Cracken, summoning together all his force not engaged with the dragoons, led them against the infantry, and succeeded after a fierce contest in seizing upon their cannon, and driving them outside the town to join the cavalry, who, by this time completely routed, had taken refuge in flight. The insurgents had scarce time to congratulate themselves upon their hard-won victory, when an incident occurred which turned the scale of success against them. While the cavalry who, as we have seen, were defeated at the castle gate, were in rapid retreat from the scene of their disaster, they were met by a body of insurgents from the north of the county on their way to aid their countrymen in the town; these men, beholding the large body of cavalry advancing towards them, mistook their flight for a charge, and seized with a sudden panic fled in the utmost disorder. The sight of a flying and terrified enemy restored courage to the disheartened dragoons; they discontinued their flight, and being soon after reinforced by fresh troops from Belfast and Blaris Moore, retraced their steps to the town, and became in their turn assailants. The unexpected return of their vanquished enemies, so strongly reinforced, filled the insurgents with such dismay, that despite the utmost efforts of their brave leader, they began to fly from the town in confusion; being pursued in their flight towards Randalstown and Slane's Castle, they were cut down in great numbers.

One small band alone had the courage to maintain their ground for some time under a leader named Hope, but being repeatedly charged by the enemy's cavalry, they at length were compelled to retreat to the neighbouring hill of Donegore, where they found M'Cracken, with a few of his faithful adherents. That brave chief could now muster but a small band of about 100 men out of the thousands he had led to the assault of Antrim. But brave men never despair, and with this handful of men, the undaunted chief resolved to hold out to the last, and terminate with honor, if not with success, the enterprise of which he was the head. Within a short distance of Donegore lay a British force four times more numerous than his own, under the command of a Colonel Clavering; that officer, relying more on the power of negociation than the force of arms, and unwilling to encounter brave men whom adverse fortune had rendered desperate, offered entire amnesty to all save four of the leaders, for each of whom he offered a reward of £400. We need hardly say that these terms were rejected with contempt by the insurgents, who revenged themselves for the insult offered them by supposing them capable of betraying their devoted chiefs, by proclaiming Colonel Clavering an enemy to the union of Irishmen, and offering a reward of £400 for his capture alive or dead.

Foiled in this base attempt to bribe the followers of M'Cracken to betray him, and lacking courage to attack him in his present position, the British officer threatened to fire the surrounding country, in case he persisted in remaining upon the hills.

Unwilling to be the occasion of ruin to so many unoffending people, M'Cracken descended from the heights with his little band, whom he dismissed to seek their safety as best they could. He himself, with seven companions, effected a retreat in the darkness of the night to the lesser Collon. Being pursued to this retreat by his enemies to the number of fifty men, he contrived by rapidly changing his ground, and appearing on different heights at short intervals, to deter his pursuers from a nearer approach, till those who accompanied him were enabled to effect their escape in safety.

However, this brave man soon after fell into the hands of his enemies, and perished on the scaffold, dying with a noble fortitude in keeping with his life.

Thus the insurrection in Antrim, with the death of its leader, and the dispersion of his trusty adherents, came disastrously to an end.

CHAPTER IV.

The men of Down assemble at Saintfield.—Colonel Stapleton falls into an ambuscade.—Death of Mortimer, Rector of Comber—Attack on Portaferry.—Rendezvous at Saintfield.—Munroe chosen commander-in-chief.—His character.—The steps he took on being appointed.—Advance of the English from Belfast and Downpatrick.—Conflict at Ballinahinch.—Fatal mistake of the insurgents.—The flight.—Official accounts.—Burning and pillage of Ballinahinch.—Romantic episode.—Death of Munroe.

THE men of Down, notwithstanding the disheartening failure of their brethren of Antrim, resolved to try the fortune of war. On the 9th of June they assembled in arms in the neighbourhood of Saintfield. However, before their whole force had mustered, news came that the British soldiery, stationed at Newtownards, was on the march to attack them. This force consisted of a regiment called the York Fencibles under Colonel Stapleton, with two corps of yeomanry and two pieces of artillery. In preparation for the expected attack, the insurgents stationed themselves in ambuscade behind the hedges which bordered the road along which their enemies were advancing. The latter soon came in sight, and already half their force had entered the ambuscade when the rashness of one of the insurgents prevented the complete success of the stratagem. This man, perceiving in the ranks of the yeomanry a Protestant minister named Mortimer, the rector of Comber, discharged his piece at the martial clergyman, who fell from his saddle severely wounded. On this, the royal troops, becoming aware of the presence of their hitherto concealed enemies, came to a sudden halt, too late, however, to save those of their number who had advanced within the line of the hedges. The English troops, thus taken by surprise, behaved with great bravery; the light company which marched in front under the command of Captain Unit, breaking through the hedges, and attacking the insurgents stationed behind them; but only to meet with a speedy death at the hands of the pikemen. Thus far successful, the insurgents proceeded to attack the remainder of the English force. But these having taken advantage of the preceding contest to prepare for the assault, met the impetuous onset of their foe with great firmness, and finally succeeded in effecting a retreat in good order to Comber, while the insurgents retraced their steps to Saintfield, where they remained during the night.

On the ensuing day, the united Irishmen of the barony of Ards proceeded to the attack of Portaferry, at the time garrisoned by a large body of yeomanry, commanded by Captain Matthews, a veteran officer of the line. The officer in question placing but small reliance upon the valour of his yeoman garrison resolved to leave them no alternative but to fight. Having timely information of the approach of the insurgents he posted his men in the market-place of the town, and forthwith sent orders to the commander of a revenue cruiser, then moored in the river, to bring his guns to bear on the street, so that all without exception who showed therein might be exposed to their fire. The yeomen were thus compelled to await the onset of the insurgents, who soon appeared advancing against the market house. Their approach was greeted with a volley from the gunsmen stationed there, by which several of their number fell. However, they pushed resolutely forward, receiving as they advanced another volley from their sheltered foes. At this juncture the guns of the cruiser sent a shower of grape-shot amongst them, while the yeomen, inspirited by the presence of this powerful auxiliary, delivered volley after volley with greater coolness and accuracy. Dismayed by this double fire from foes on land and water, the insurgents hastily retreated from the town, bearing with them their dead and wounded.

Saintfield now became the rendezvous of the Down insurgents, and on the 11th, about 7000 men were assembled there. They acknowledged as their chief Mr. Henry Munroe, a tried patriot, who deserved and possessed their entire confidence. Munroe, though in many respects well calculated to undertake the successful guidance of his countrymen in the untried and perilous path they were about to tread, was, unhappily, imbued with romantic ideas of military honour, better suited to a knight of the age of chivalry than to a leader in a desperate struggle against the unscrupulous chiefs who led the power of England. How fatally this trait in his character militated against the success of the enterprise he conducted will appear in the sequel.

We now proceed to detail the steps he took in his new capacity of commander of the Down insurgents.

On the evening of the 11th, having evacuated Saintfield, he took post on the heights in the vicinity of that town, whence he despatched a force under the command of one of his officers named Townsend, to take possession of Ballinahinch. This command was executed without much difficulty, the royal garrison offering no very determined resistance.

On the ensuing day Munroe himself set out with the main body of his troops for the same town, taking the precaution to leave a sufficient force on the Crevy Rocks to protect the rear of his army. In the meantime a British force had started from Belfast under the joint command of Generals Nugent and Barber, at the same time that a large body of troops was on its way from Downpatrick to form a junction with them. These divisions formed a force of about 2000 men, consisting of the Argyleshire Highlanders, the Monaghan regiment of militia, and several corps of yeomanry—amongst which the most noted was the Hillsborough. Munroe, apprised of the approach of this large force, proceeded to dispose his troops for the coming encounter. The town of Ballinahinch, where the insurgents had assembled, stands nearly in the centre of a circle of hills of considerable height.

The road by which the royal army approached the town skirted the base of these hills. The first eminence they passed in their advance is that called the Windmill-hill. This hill is cultivated nearly to its summit, its sloping sides divided into fields, separated by the usual breast of high ditches which rise one above the other in irregular lines as they near the top. Behind the lowest of these convenient breastworks the insurgent commander posted in ambuscade a considerable force of gunsmen under an officer named M'Cance to await the advance of the King's troops. To the south of the town, and almost parallel with the last mentioned hill, rises the bolder eminence of Ednevady; upon this he himself with the main body of his forces took up a position. In the town, which is situate between these heights, he also placed a considerable force. Thus, with one division on Ednevady height, and another on Windmill-hill, with a third in Ballinahinch, the insurgent chief awaited the approach of the British commander. He was not long kept in suspense, for the reflection of distant fires, kindled by the advancing soldiery, plainly signalled their approach. At the same time the insurgents, from their elevated position, could discern the advance of another hostile division coming from the direction of Downpatrick, and evidently intending to form a junction with the first seen body, who were the royal troops under General Nugent from Belfast. To prevent, if possible this junction, Munroe despatched a body of men to occupy an eminence that rose in the line of their advance. However, before the insurgents could gain the desired position, the English troops diverged from the road, rapidly crossed the fields that stretched between them and their comrades, and effected the intended junction. At length, General Nugent came within artillery range of the insurgent main-body posted on Ednevady, and at the same time in close vicinity to the detachment which lay in ambuscade on the slope of Windmill-hill. No sooner had he opened fire with his artillery on the main body than a deadly fusilade was poured into his midst from the neighbouring ambuscade.

This fire, so unexpected and destructive, retarded his further advance, and compelled him to direct his efforts to dislodge this daring foe. Accordingly, bringing up his artillery he began to use it with vigour in demolishing the earthen barrier that sheltered the insurgents. Despite this heavy fire, now poured upon them, the latter gallantly maintained their ground for upwards of an hour, inflicting the while no small loss upon the royal army. At length they were forced to retreat, and betake themselves to the summit of the hill, where they maintained the combat with unshaken firmness for a considerable space, repulsing several attempts made to dislodge them—the English soldiers evincing great reluctance to climb the hill in the face of the deadly fire poured upon them from its summit. While a detachment of General Nugent's force were engaged with their enemies posted on Windmill-hill, the main body, drawn up in square between that eminence and Ballinahinch, directed the fire of their artillery against the insurgents on Ednevady and those who yet held possession of the town. Unable to return with effect the heavy fire of the hostile artillery, Munroe deemed it prudent to withdraw his forces from both the assailed positions, and to concentrate them with the main body under his immediate command on the heights of Ednevady. This resolution taken, he despatched orders to Townsend and M'Cance to quit their posts and join him. The order was promptly obeyed by Matthews, but M'Cance, unwilling to relinquish his hopes of victory, refused to obey the first and second summons sent by his commander, and requested instead that a reinforcement might be despatched by whose aid he would be able to hold his ground. However, on receiving a third summons, he reluctantly obeyed, and abandoned the position he had defended so long and with such undaunted resolution. Soon after his departure, the hill was occupied by a British force. His whole force being now concentrated, Munroe offered battle to the enemy, but the latter declined the contest and contented themselves with shelling the hill. At length, when darkness had fallen, the British troops entered Ballinahinch where they spent the night in every species of riotous excess, revenging the losses they had sustained during the day upon the wretched inhabitants.

Outside the town the wearied insurgents rested on their arms, while their brave chief passed from band to band exhorting them to maintain discipline, and cheering them with the assurance of a signal success on the morrow. During the night a messenger from the town arrived at Munroe's camp, and representing the disorder that prevailed among the royal troops, urged the insurgents to make an instant attack upon them with a certainty of achieving a complete success. On receiving this intelligence a council of war was hastily summoned, in which the general voice proclaimed itself in favour of an immediate attack, but Munroe's chivalrous scruples prevailing over his better sense, he obstinately withstood the earnest entreaties of his officers, and avowed his determination to defer the attack till the day had fully dawned. So dispirited were the insurgents by this unwise decision of their chief that an entire division amounting to 700 men quitted the camp during the night.

At an early hour on the following morning (13th), Munroe prepared for action. The contest began with a discharge of the few small cannon possessed by the insurgents, to which the heavy guns of the enemy instantly replied with vigour proportioned to their greater number and larger size. To obtain possession of the town was now the object of the insurgent leader, to retain it that of the royalist general. Munroe having divided his force into two bodies, despatched one of them to force an entrance on the left, while he himself led a more numerous body to assault it on the right. Part of General Nugent's force, formed in solid square, withstood for a time the onset of the first division of the insurgents, but were, after a spirited struggle, during which their leader fell, driven headlong into the town, hotly pursued by their fierce and elated foe. While this furious contest was taking place on one side of the town, Munroe had penetrated it on the other, driving the enemy before him, who took shelter behind the cannon planted in the market-square. From their position in the rear of the cannon the royalists kept up a destructive fire of musketry upon their assailants, while the artillery belched forth volley after volley of grape-shot with terrible effect.

At this critical juncture Munroe's ammunition failed him, and nothing remained for the insurgents but to essay a charge with the pike. So irresistible was the charge now made by the pikemen that the artillerymen were forced to abandon their guns, and the British general, finding that further resistance was impossible, ordered a retreat to be sounded, and led his routed forces out of the town, taking a northernly direction.

A singular and lamentable error on the part of the insurgents now occurred to change the fortunes of the day, and convert what would have proved a glorious victory into a lamentable defeat. Blinded by the thick smoke that shrouded the battle-field they heard the English bugles sounding a retreat, and judging it to be the signal of the arrival of fresh troops on the side of the enemy, they were seized with a panic—halted in their advance, broke their ranks, and in an instant were flying in the wildest confusion from the town by the way they had entered. Thus, by a strange coincidence, it happened that the insurgents and the royalists were evacuating the town at the same moment, one flying from a real and the other from an imaginary foe. The flight being soon perceived by the retreating royalists, a halt took place—discipline and courage returned with the welcome sight of their flying enemy. The 22nd Light Dragoons received orders to charge them as they fled, while the infantry, recovering from the panic, joined the cavalry in the pursuit. The aspect of affairs was now entirely changed, the lately triumphant insurgents, flying in a disordered crowd, while the English cavalry rode amongst them, hewing them down with their long keen sabres, at the same time that the infantry poured volley after volley into their fugitive masses. It was in vain that the gallant Munroe strove to rally the terrified fugitives. Of the large force he had led to the attack of Ballinahinch, he could only muster about one hundred and fifty men whom he led back to Ednevady Hill. As no quarter was given by the British, the number of the insurgents who fell on this occasion must have been very large.

The official bulletin of this action is as follows:—

"*Dublin Castle, eleven o'Clock,* A. M.,
"*June* 14, 1798.

"Intelligence is just arrived from Major-General Nugent stating, that on the 11th instant he had marched against a large body of rebels who were posted at Saintfield. They retired on his approach to a strong position on the Saintfield side of Ballinahinch, and there made a show of resistance, and endeavoured to turn his left flank; Lieutenant-Colonel Stewart arriving from Down with a pretty considerable force of infantry, cavalry, and yeomanry, they soon desisted, and retired to a very strong position behind Ballinahinch.

"General Nugent attacked them next morning at three o'clock, having occupied two hills on the left and right of the town to prevent the rebels from having any other choice than the mountains in their rear for their retreat. He sent Lieutenant-Colonel Stewart to post himself with part of the Argyle Fencibles and some yeomanry, as well as a detachment of the 22nd Light Dragoons, in a situation from whence he could enfilade the rebel line, whilst Colonel Leslie with a party of the Monaghan militia, some cavalry and yeoman infantry, should make an attack upon their front. Having two howitzers and six six-pounders with the two detachments, the Major-General was enabled to annoy them very much from different parts of his position. The rebels attacked impetuously Colonel Leslie's detachment, and even jumped into the road from the Earl of Moira's demesne to endeavour to take one of his guns, but were repulsed with slaughter. Lieutenant-Colonel Stewart's detachment was attacked by them with the same activity, but he repulsed them also, and the fire from his howitzer and six-pounder soon obliged them to fly in all directions. Their force was, on the evening of the 12th, near 5000, but as many persons were pressed into their service, and almost entirely unarmed, the general does not suppose that on the morning of the engagement their numbers were so many.

"About four hundred rebels were killed in the attack and retreat, and the remainder were dispersed all over the country. Parts of the towns of Saintfield and Ballinahinch were burned.....Three or four green colours were taken, and six one-pounders, not mounted, but which the rebels fired very often, and a considerable quantity of ammunition."

We need scarcely say that no credit can be given to such accounts as the above, manufactured, as they were, to please the official eye, without the slightest regard to truth. In this action, at Ballinahinch, an episode of a romantic but melancholy nature took place. A beautiful young lady, named Elizabeth Grey, followed her brother and lover to the field, where she fought bravely at their side during the entire conflict, and perished together with them in the flight that ensued.

Having completed the discomfiture of the insurgents,

Insurrection of 1798.

the British troops returned to Ballinahinch, which they pillaged and set on fire.

Munroe was soon after captured by his enemies, tried by court-martial, and put to death in front of his own house, in the above mentioned town, of which he was a native. His head was cut off, fixed on a pike, and exhibited, a ghastly trophy, over the market-place. Thus, at the early age of 31 years, perished upon a scaffold, the brave Munroe. But, though his enemies awarded a felon's death, his country will cherish his memory, as one of her most devoted patriots.

With this disastrous action, the insurrection in the North of Ireland may be said to have ended; but the unfortunate inhabitants long after continued to feel the vengeance of their triumphant and merciless enemies. The gibbets in Ulster were hung with victims, and the dungeons thronged with prisoners.

CHAPTER V.

Authorities did not apprehend any serious disturbance in Wexford.—M'Gee's description of Wexford.—The people of Wexford not a Celtic race.—Population.—Hay and others on the social condition of the people.—Musgrave and Maxwell's calumnies refuted.—Relations existing between the people and the gentry.—The persecuting class encouraged by Government.—Liberal Protestants dare not interfere.—How informers were made.—Burning of houses.—Instance given by Mr. Gordon of death brought on by fear of torture.—Question of the number of United Irishmen in Wexford discussed.—Opinions of divers authors given.—Arrival of the North Cork, who outdo the yeomen in cruelty.—Pitch-cap introduced.—County proclaimed.—Many people deliver up their arms.—Proceedings of Hunter Gowan and other persecutors.—Transportation.—Horrid rumours abroad during the week preceding the Insurrection.

WHILE the Insurrection manifested itself in a series of feeble and desultory attempts in the northern counties of Leinster, which the Government found little difficulty in repressing, their attention was imperatively called to its outbreak in another district, in the most southern county in the same province, where it burst forth with a violence as great as it was unexpected. Wexford was the stage upon which the last and most thrilling scene of the tragedy was to be enacted. So little apprehension was entertained by the authorities of any serious disturbance in that county, that, in addition to the recently embodied yeomanry corps, only about five hundred of the regular army had been stationed* there. Soon, however, the whole available military power of England, under her ablest generals, was to be gathered together within its narrow limits—a force greater than in after years sufficed to overthrow the conqueror of Europe, upon the plains of Waterloo.

Before entering into the details of this remarkable struggle, and the events that immediately preceded it, we deem it not amiss to furnish our readers with a brief description of the county and its inhabitants.

Mr. T. D. M'Gee, in his excellent History of Ireland, thus expresses himself on the subject: "Wexford, geographically, is a peculiar county, and its people are a peculiar people. The county fills up the south-eastern corner of the island, with the sea south-east, the River Barrow to the west, and the woods and mountains of Carlow and Wicklow to the north. It is about fifty miles long by twenty-four broad; the surface undulating and rising into numerous groups of detached hills, two or more of which are generally visible from each conspicuous summit. Almost in the midst flows the River Slaney, springing from a lofty Wicklow peak, which sends down, on its northern slope, the better known River Liffey. On the estuary of the Slaney, some seventy miles south of Dublin, stands the county

---

* This fact tends to confirm the statement of Hay and others, that the United Irish Society had gained but few adherents in Wexford.

town, the traveller journeying to which, by the usual route then taken, passed in succession through Arklow, Gorey, Ferns, Enniscorthy, and other places of less consequence, though familiar enough in the fiery records of 1798. North-westward, the only road in those days from Carlow and Kilkenny, crossed the Blackstairs at Scollagh Gap, entering the county at Newtownbarry, the ancient Bunclody; westward, some twenty miles, on the River Barrow, stands New Ross, often mentioned in this history, the road from which to the county town passes through Scullabogue and Taghmon (Ta'mon), the former at the foot of Carrick-byrne rock, the latter at the base of what is rather hyperbolically called "The Mountain of Forth." South and west of the town, towards the estuary of Waterford, lie the baronies of Forth and Bargy, a great part of the population of which, even within our own time, spoke the language Chaucer and Spencer wrote, and retained many of the characteristics of their Saxon, Flemish, and Cambrian ancestors. Through this singular district lay the road towards Duncannon fort, on Waterford harbour, with branches running off to Bannow, Ballyhack, and Dunbrody."

The Wexford people can hardly be called a Celtic race. The surnames of Lacy, Prendergast, Fitzgerald, Devereux, Whitty, Walsh, Synnot, Furlong, Harvey, Boxwell, and Brown, indicate their descent from Norman, Welsh, and Flemish ancestors;* while such names as Cornock, Godkin, and Lambert, remind us of the latest addition to the foreign element in the time of the redoubted Cromwell. The Celtic element, if we judge by the far greater frequency of such names as the above,

* The following is a list of the surnames of a grand jury sworn in during the current year, 1873, in the town of Wexford: Browne, Devereux, Furlong, Power, Robinson, Sinnot, Cooney, Mechan, Roche, Crosbie, Stafford.

forms but a small proportion of the population. The Irish language has long since wholly disappeared, and even such unmistakably Irish names as are yet found, have dropped the ancient prefixes of O' and Mac.

It is strange, indeed, that such a population should have offered to the English the fiercest and most determined resistance they ever encountered in Ireland, while the people of purely Celtic counties "made no sign," but remained sunk in disgraceful apathy, while the fortunes of their native country hung trembling in the balance. The population of Wexford, in 1798, was, according to Mr. Bushe's estimate, 132,912 inhabitants. That of the town of Wexford itself was upwards of 9,000 souls. Others have estimated the entire population at 150,000, which I judge to be nearer the truth. Treating of the social condition of the county, Mr. Hay makes the ensuing observation: "The County of Wexford had long been remarkable for the peaceful demeanour of its inhabitants, and their good behaviour and industry have been held out as an exemplar for other parts of Ireland. So little and so seldom infested with disturbance or riots of any kind, that an execution for a capital crime rarely took place there; and, in the calendar of its criminals, it has as few on record as any part either of Great Britain or Ireland. This county bore such reputation, that landed property was considered of higher value in it than in many other parts of the country, purchasers not hesitating to advance some years' rental more for lands in the county of Wexford than for the like in most other parts of Ireland." But as Mr. Hay was himself a Wexford man, and might not unreasonably be suspected of partiality for his native county, I shall take the liberty of quoting a few extracts from the work* of an English gen-

---

* Letters on the condition of the People of Ireland, by Thomas

tleman, published at a later period, in which he treats of the same subject. After lauding, at some length, the superior civilization of the Wexford people, he asks, "To what can this great difference in the appearance of the country, in the state of cultivation, in the progress of civilization, in comfort, in cleanliness, in order and good conduct be owing—for this county is in Ireland, and subject to the same laws as every other part of Ireland?" This, as an Englishman, he naturally attributes to their English descent, derived from Strongbow's little army, all natives of Pembrokeshire, which, though situate in Wales, he asserts to have had a Saxon population. In continuation he remarks: "In the baronies of Forth and Bargy, at this day, it is difficult to see any marked difference between the appearance of the country or the people and England or its population. There are the same cleanliness, order, and neatness. Great industry prevails amongst a *peaceable and well-disposed people.* . . . comfort and contentment, the rewards of industry, are everywhere seen." We have thought it fitting to furnish our readers with the foregoing extracts from an authority that even those who would afford but slight credence to statements less evidently impartial must respect, as a conclusive answer to the calumnies heaped upon a peaceable and well-disposed people, by certain authors, whose works have obtained a wide circulation. We ourselves, in our younger days, have been intimately acquainted with many of these men described by Musgrave and Maxwell, and other writers of their bigoted and narrow-minded class, as *ferocious and ignorant peasants*—and we must say, that we have never met with finer specimens of a manly and intelli-

Campbell Foster, Esq., of the Middle Temple, Barrister-at-law ("*The Times*" Commissioner). London: Chapman and Hall, 1846.

gent race. Amidst the numerous Catholic peasantry of Wexford, there abode a great number of small landed proprietors. The majority of these were good landlords, and often kind neighbours, willing to live on terms of amity with their humbler fellow-countrymen, although they differed with them in religious tenets. It is true that even these, well-disposed as they were, regarded the Catholics as a far inferior class, and were little inclined to admit them to any degree of social equality. This class included men of the highest standing in the county, and of the most extensive landed possessions. But unhappily for the peace of the country, there existed at the time another class, which rather stood on the boundary of the aristocratic circle than fairly within its area, whose principles and practice were essentially different.

For the most part meanly born, or if well born of ruined fortune, and of spendthrift habits, they had emerged from obscurity into baneful prominence by taking advantage of the encouragement given by the Government to all who were willing to become their instruments in hunting down the adherents of the ancient creed. The men thus encouraged by Government, were violent in their denunciations of Papists—untiringly energetic in the discovery of the disloyal schemes which, it seems, these unfortunate Papists were always hatching. Every post carried long epistles from the worthies in question to the authorities of the Castle, containing accounts of the discoveries they had made of conspiracies, formed by the same Papists, of course, having for their end the overthrow of the British Government in His Majesty's kingdom of Ireland. In every private circle to which they were admitted, and in every public meeting at which they assisted, they poured forth revilings, accusations, and threats against the objects of their hatred. Of this class Mr. Hay speaks in the following terms:—

"Slaves to their superiors, but tyrants to their inferiors, these needy adventurers became the tools of prevailing power; justices of peace were selected from this class, and these, by this degree of elevation (certainly to them the station is an exalted one), think themselves raised to a level of equality with the most respectable gentlemen of the country. But their ignorance is so preposterous, and their behaviour so assuming, that men of education, talents, and fortune, are induced to withhold themselves from a situation they would otherwise grace, as it might oblige them to confer with fellows with whom they would not by any means hold communion or keep company. Thus are the very men who ought to be the magistrates of the country, and who would cheerfully accept the office, deterred from holding commissions of the peace; while the justice and police of the community is left to ignorant, presuming, and intemperate upstarts, devoid of all qualification and endowment, except that alone, if it may be termed such, of unconditional submission and obedience to the controlling nod of their boasted patrons. If they faithfully adhere to this, they may go all lengths to raise their consequence, and enhance their estimation with the multitude. These creatures have therefore the effrontery to push themselves forward on every occasion, and after a series of habitual acts of turpitude, whenever an opportunity offers itself, they become the scourges and fire-brands of the country."

Thus it was that the Government, instead of treating these men as disturbers of the public peace, sowers of discord, hatred, and suspicion amongst a people who had hitherto lived in some degree of peace and harmony, evinced its approbation of their conduct by bestowing upon them honors which it denied to worthier men, and arming them with authority to carry into execution all their nefarious schemes. Besides being vested with the magisterial power, they generally were appointed to the command of a corps of yeomanry; and at the head of these myrmidons, they roamed through the country to the terror of the unfortunate inhabitants, whose lives and properties were now wholly at their mercy, since the Act of Indemnity had freed them from all danger of being called to account for their excesses. In their train followed a number of vile satellites who were at all times prepared to swear to the guilt of any one whom their employers chose to consider disloyal. Orangemen, themselves, they claimed for the members of the society to which they belonged, a species of monopoly in loyalty, so that outside their unhallowed circle there was no safety for any man. Liberal Protestant gentlemen were in their eyes as much objects of suspicion and hatred as the Papists themselves.

And it is but fair to say that Protestant gentlemen were found virtuous enough to earn the detestation of such vile men, whose hatred was their highest eulogy.

But the liberal magistrates, being aware that the course pursued by the persecutors was approved of and sanctioned by the Government, deemed it both useless and dangerous to interfere. Had they entertained any doubt upon the subject it would have been wholly dissipated by an incident which took place during this period—the arrest and imprisonment of Messrs. Colclough and Harvey, whose sense of justice, stronger than their prudence, led them openly to denounce what they deemed the most cruel and wicked oppression. Some persons may be inclined to condemn the silence of others at such a time as cowardly and guilty; but not all men have courage to advocate the cause of the

Insurrection of 1798.

oppressed, when tyranny, armed with irresponsible power, is seated upon the tribunal. The actual force of these instruments of a cruel policy might be in itself contemptible, but the sanction of the law and the whole strength of the government rendered them truly formidable. At a later period it was thought prudent to restrain, and even to punish them, but for the time they were useful, and none might presume to interfere with or thwart their proceedings till their task was completed, and the people, maddened with oppression, rose as one man to shake off a yoke that galled them beyond all endurance. To discover and to hunt down the members of the United Irish Society was the object to which they chiefly directed their efforts. To discover them they needed informers, and in case these were not at hand, they undertook to make them. In this species of manufacture they were skilful workmen. The pitch cap, the scourge, and the rope of the executioner were the instruments they employed. Mr. Alexander, a respectable Protestant inhabitant of Ross, gives us an account of the tortures inflicted upon two men named Driscol and Fitzpatrick, in order to compel them to enact this infamous part. The first-named of these men was half strangled three times, and flogged four times, to force him to swear informations, but continued, notwithstanding, steadfast in his refusal to do what was required of him. The other man, Fitzpatrick, a poor village schoolmaster, old and infirm, was engaged in teaching his little school, when a magistrate entered and tendered to him the oath of allegiance. The poor man having taken the oath with great willingness, was informed by his visitor that in further proof of his loyalty he must swear to the whereabouts of all the pikes and the owners of them in his neighbourhood of which he had any knowledge. In vain he protested that he knew nothing about pikes or insurgents, and consequently could not, without perjury, swear to what he had no knowledge of. His protestations were of no avail. He was forthwith conveyed to Ross, and there flogged with great severity, of which flogging Mr. Alexander was a witness, and "it was not (he adds) with dry eyes, that I saw the punishment inflicted on this humble pioneer of literature."

These barbarities became of such frequent occurrence that the terror-stricken people abandoned their houses and sought refuge in the open fields. Concerning the burning of houses and the forcing of people by torture to become informers, Mr. Hay makes the following remarks:—

"The proclamation of the county of Wexford having given greater scope to the ingenuity of magistrates to devise means of quelling all symptoms of rebellion, as well as of using every exertion to procure discoveries, they soon fell to burning of houses wherein pikes or other offensive weapons were discovered, no matter how brought there; but they did not stop here, for the dwellings of suspected persons, and those from which any of the inhabitants were found absent at night, were also consumed. This circumstance of absence from the houses very generally prevailed through the country, although there were the strictest orders forbidding it. This was occasioned at first, as was before observed, from the apprehension of the Orangemen, but afterwards proceeded from the actual experiences of torture by the people from the yeomen and magistrates. Some, too, abandoned their homes from fear of being whipped, if on being apprehended confessions satisfactory to the magistrates could either be given or extorted, and this infliction many persons seemed to fear more than death itself. Many unfortunate men, who were taken in their houses, were strung up as it were to be hanged, but were let down now and then to try if strangulation would oblige them to become informers. After these and the like experiences, several persons languished for some time, and at length perished in consequence of them. Smiths and carpenters, whose assistance was considered indispensable in the fabrication of pikes, were pointed out on evidence of their trades as the first and fittest objects of torture. But the sagacity of some magistrates became at length so acute, from habit and exercise, that they discerned a United Irishman even at the first glance, and their zeal never suffered any person whom they deigned to honor with such distinction to pass off without convincing proof of their attention. Many innocent persons were thus taken up (continues the same author) while peaceably engaged in their own private concerns, walking along the road, or passing through the market in the several towns, without any previous accusation, but in consequence of military whim, or the caprice of magisterial loyalty; and those who had been at market, and passing by unnoticed, had the news of a public exhibition to bring home, for the unfortunate victims thus seized upon were instantly subjected to the torture of public whipping. People of timid dispositions therefore avoided going to market, fearing that they might be forced to display the same spectacle. Provisions of course became dear, for the want of the usual supply in the market towns; and the military, to redress this evil, went out into the country and brought in what they wanted, at what price they pleased, the owners thinking themselves well treated if they got but half the value of their goods; and in case of a second visit, happy if they escaped unhurt, which, however, was not always the case, and thus were the minds of the people brought to admit such powerful impressions of terror that death itself was sometimes the consequence."

So great was the terror inspired by torture so fre-

quently employed, that men expired from the very
apprehension of being subjected to it. Of this Mr.
Gordon gives an instance:—" Whether an insurrrec-
tion in the then existing state of the kingdom would
have taken place in the county of Wexford, or in case
of its eruption, how far less formidable and sanguinary
it would have been if no acts of severity had been
committed by the soldiery, the yeomen, or their sup-
plementary associates, without the direct authority of
their superiors, or command of the magistrate, is a
question which I am not able positively to answer.
In the neighbourhood of Gorey, if I am not mistaken,
the terror of the whippings was in particular so great,
that the people would have been extremely glad to
renounce for ever all notions of opposition to government if they could have been assured of permission to
remain in a state of quietness. As an instance of this
terror I shall relate the following fact:—

"On the morning of the 23rd of May, a labouring
man named Denis M'Daniel came to my house with
looks of the utmost consternation and dismay, and
confessed to me that he had taken the United Irishman's oath, and had paid for a pike, with which he had
not yet been furnished, nineteen pence halfpenny, to
one Kilty, a smith, who had administered the oath to
him and many others. Whilst I sent my eldest son,
who was a lieutenant of yeomanry, to arrest Kilty, I
exhorted M'Daniel to surrender himself to a magistrate,
and make his confession; but this he positively refused,
saying that he should in that case be lashed to make
him produce a pike, which he had not, and to confess what he knew not. I then advised him, as the
only alternative, to remain quietly at home, promising
that if he should be arrested on the information of
others, I would represent the case to the magistrates.
He took my advice, but the fear of arrest and lashing

had so taken possession of his thoughts that he could neither eat nor sleep, and on the morning of the 25th he fell on his face, and expired in a little grove near my house."*

Authors differ considerably in their statements concerning the extent and influence of the United Irish Society in Wexford. Mr. Hay, who on most points is an excellent authority, seems convinced " that the system of the United Irishmen had not diffused itself through the county of Wexford to the extent so confidently affirmed by Sir Richard Musgrave, whose veracity in almost every other instance appears equally questionable. The truth is that no authentic proof existed at the time to support these arrogant assertions, and subsequent information confirms how little the county of Wexford was concerned in that conspiracy, as no return appears of its being organized in the discoveries of the secret committees of the Houses of Lords and Commons. It would be contrary to truth, however, to say that there were no United Irishmen in the county of Wexford; but by every statement worthy of credit that has ever appeared, their numbers were comparatively fewer in this than in any other county in Ireland." Treating of the same subject the Rev. Mr. Gordon remarks:—" The county of Wexford had not been otherwise than very imperfectly organized."†

Sir Richard Musgrave, with a view to justify the cruelties exercised by his brother Orangemen, the persecuting magistrates of Wexford, affirms the country to have been completely organized. But no statement put forward by such a man can be regarded as deserving of any credit, being notorious for his virulent and reckless mendacity, heedless of what assertion he made

---

* History of Irish Rebellion, p. 87.
† History of Ireland, p. 395.

to vilify a people for whom he cherished a most envenomed hatred. In the "Memoirs of Miles Byrne," the "Macamores" (the ancient name of the present baronies of Shilmalier) are mentioned as well organized.

Mr. T. D. M'Gee holds a contrary opinion. In his "History of Ireland" we find the following:—

"The most formidable insurrection—indeed the only really formidable one—broke out in the county of Wexford a county in which it was stated there were not 200 United Irishmen, and which Lord Edward Fitzgerald had altogether omitted from his official list of counties organized in the month of February."

From these conflicting statements it is not easy to deduce any very definite conclusion; but having weighed them all we may hazard an opinion that the organization existed in the county for a considerable time before the outbreak of the insurrection, but made little progress, owing both to the opposition offered to it by the priests as a secret society, and to the peculiar character of the Wexford people, who have been always averse to secret societies of every description; but that driven to despair by the extreme measures adopted by the Government, they resolved upon resistance, and then began to take the oath in great numbers.

The reign of terror which we have feebly endeavoured to describe did not attain its full height till the arrival of Lord Kingsborough at the head of the merciless corps called the "North Cork." Their arrival took place in the beginning of April, about three weeks before the proclamation of the county. This infamous horde, who came to riot in the blood of an unoffending people, and finally to perish themselves by the vengeance of the same people roused to madness by oppression, were enlisted from the dregs of the Orange population of Cork. However, the infamy attached to their memory casts no dark shadow on the fair name of that patriotic county, for though they lived amongst the people, they were by no means of them, and would have willingly exercised the same cruelty upon them as they did on the inhabitants of Wexford.

These cruel mercenaries were adepts in the villanous arts by which the most peaceable are roused into vengeful retaliation; and the unfortunate people amongst whom they came found that even the native yeomen might be exceeded in cruelty. The latter, indeed, soon became emulous imitators of the new comers, and evinced that they lacked not the will to rival them in deeds of ruthless cruelty. What pen can adequately describe the horrors which were now daily exhibited! Never, surely, in any civilized country were such scenes beheld as were now enacted under the eyes, and with the sanction, of the English Government.

Had the history of these events been written only by those who might be considered partial to the sufferers there might be room to impugn its truthfulness, but men who, in principles and politics widely differed, have confirmed it by their united testimony.

But we prefer to hurry over those scenes of horror, merely tarrying amongst them sufficiently long to see by what means a peaceable people were driven into armed resistance to constituted power—a resistance which, though it proved unavailing, yet gave a lesson to tyrants not soon forgotten. The chief actors in those scenes of blood were the infamous North Cork before mentioned, and to the diabolical ingenuity of their leader must be attributed the invention of the pitch-cap. This most dreaded instrument of torture was a spacious cap, made of strong thick paper, shaped so as to cover the entire head, fitting close to it. This cap being previously smeared inside with boiling pitch, was placed on the head of the individual condemned to the torture, and pressed down upon it, so that the heated pitch should come into contact with the scalp, on which the hair had been cut short, that the victim might experience all the intensity of the torment. So great was the agony experienced by the unhappy wretches subjected to this cruelty, that often, bursting from the grasp of their torturers, in the madness of the intolerable pain, they dashed their brains out against some neighbouring wall, and thus put an end at once to their life and misery.

But for such as were not driven by excessive pain to self-destruction, an additional torment remained, for when the pitch had cooled, and the cap became firmly attached to the head of the sufferer, it was seized, and torn violently off the head, bringing away with it all the hair, and oftentimes the entire scalp, leaving the wretched victim writhing in agonies to which death would have been mercy.

This species of torture, which might be truly deemed a refinement upon the scalping of the North American Indians, must not be thought to have been seldom exercised, for it was one of the most common, and was used as a means of extorting evidence to sustain unfounded accusations. It was inflicted without trial at the mere caprice of every petty officer of yeomanry or militia. As these bands of torturers and executioners traversed the country the unfortunate peasantry whose homes they approached fled in terror to hide themselves in the fields, and from their places of concealment beheld the progress of the flames that consumed the humble roof that should no more afford them shelter. While these horrors were in progress the magistrates of the county assembled at Wexford, and commanded the inhabitants under pain of death to deliver up all arms in their possession within fourteen days.

The result of their deliberations appeared in the

following notice which was distributed through the country:—

"NOTICE.—We, the high sheriff and magistrates of the county of Wexford, assembled at sessions, held at the county courthouse in Wexford, this 23rd day of May, 1798, have received the most clear and unequivocal evidence, private as well as public, that the system and plans of those deluded persons who style themselves, and are commonly known by the name of United Irishmen, have been generally adopted by the inhabitants of the several parishes in this county, who have provided themselves with pikes and other arms for the purpose of carrying their plans into execution. And whereas we have received information that the inhabitants of some parts of this county have, within these few days past, returned to their allegiance, surrendering their arms, and confessing the errors of their past misconduct. Now we, the high sheriff and magistrates assembled, as aforesaid, do give this public notice that if, within the space of fourteen days from the date hereof the inhabitants of the other parts of this county do not come in to some of the magistrates of this county and surrender their arms, or other offensive weapons, concealed or otherwise, and give such proof of their return to their allegiance as shall appear sufficient, an application will be made to Government to send the army at free quarters into such parishes as shall fail to comply, to enforce due obedience to this notice.

"Signed by—Edward Percival, Sheriff, Courtown, John Henry Lyster, James Boyd, George Le Hunte, Thomas Handcock, John James, John Pounden, Hawtrey White, James White, Ebenezer Jacob, William Hore, Edward D'Arcy, John Heatly, John Grogan, Archibald Jacob, Edward Turner, Isaac Cornock, Cornelius Grogan, Francis Turner, William Toole, Richard Newton King, Charles Vero."

Terrified by the extreme cruelty wherewith those were treated with whom arms had been discovered, many of those who as yet possessed them hastened to give them up, hoping that being unarmed they might be left in peace.* The Catholic clergy, too, advised their flocks to adopt this course, relying with groundless confidence on the promises of their faithless and merciless rulers. This error of judgment, however, they afterwards nobly redeemed, by fighting valiantly against their relentless foes. As might have been foreseen, this submission on the part of the people proved utterly unavailing to obtain any respite from persecution, and their sufferings, instead of being mitigated, increased day by day. Nothing was now heard in the country but the frightful screams of the tortured victims of the scourge or of the pitch-cap. But as man must ever cloak his guilt under some specious pretext, this was done, forsooth, to force the victim to confess crimes of which he was suspected of being guilty.

Despair took possession of the public mind, as the men, under whose eyes, and by whose orders, such cruelties were practised, were the magistrates of the county, from whose sentence there was no appeal. Amongst those bloodthirsty and inhuman wretches, to whose tender mercies the unfortunate peasantry were delivered up by the English Government, some may claim more especial attention. Hunter, Gowen, Archibald, Hamilton, Jacob, and Owens, a Protestant minister, earned for themselves an infamous notoriety for the

* Many who had not pikes procured them now in order to obtain on delivering them up a written protection from the magistrates.—HAY.

savage energy wherewith they used the power that the law had placed in their hands. Gowen entered the town of Gorey at the head of his troops, holding his sword aloft with a human finger stuck on its point, and afterwards adjourning to an inn to refresh himself after his labours, and to recount to his friends the infamous exploits of the day, stirred his punch with the bloody trophy. Of a character equally infamous was Jacob of Enniscorthy, who scoured the country accompanied by a wretch as villainous as himself, who filled the double office of torturer and executioner. Besides those who underwent the various tortures in the power of such miscreants to inflict—and we have seen that their ingenuity was almost equal to their power, which was unbounded—numbers were sentenced to transportation, after a trial which was indeed a mockery of justice.

Mr. Hay states that for months previous to the insurrection, groups of from twelve to fifteen cartloads of persons condemned to transportation in other counties, passed daily through the county of Wexford, on their way to Duncannon Fort. The Wexford magistrates soon began to put the precedent thus afforded in practice to a fearful extent. Many of the condemned appealed to the court of quarter sessions, held as described on the 23rd, but, as might have been expected, all the sentences passed by individual magistrates were confirmed by the twenty three thereat assembled. Amongst the expatriated victims was a priest named Dixon, who was found guilty upon the evidence of an informer, although three respectable witnesses gave testimony—by swearing an alibi—sufficient to acquit him in any court of justice. During the week preceding the insurrection all manner of horrid rumours were rife in Wexford. As fourteen days were granted by the proclamation issued on the 23rd, for the submission of the people and the delivering up of their arms, it was hoped by many that a cessation of the persecution hitherto maintained might take place. But this hope was grievously disappointed. The various implements of torture were plied as vigorously as before; the brand of the legal incendiary still gave to flames the once peaceful homes of the people, and the demons of cruelty and revenge alone rejoiced amidst the scene of universal horror and desolation.

CHAPTER VI.

Wholesale massacre perpetrated by the loyalists.—Father John Murphy the first to raise the standard of rebellion.—His character.—His first achievement.—Minor events in Wexford.—March of the militia and yeomanry to Oulart.—Burning of Darby Kavanagh's house.—Effects of the first success of the insurgents.—The Boolevogue insurgents proceed to Oulart Hill.

DURING the week preceding the insurrection two events occurred in Wicklow calculated to deepen, if possible, the feelings of horror which the state of affairs in their own county had already excited in the breasts of the Wexfordians. Hitherto individuals had suffered death or torture, but now it seemed wholesale massacres were determined upon. One of the events we allude to occurred at Dunlavin, and is recorded in a foregoing chapter; the other, no less shocking in its details, took place at Carnew, and is thus related in the "Irish Magazine," published in 1811, while the affair was still recent. "The armed loyalist yeomen of Coolatin and Carnew traversed the country, threatening the inhabitants that unless they came into Carnew for protection they should be all put to death. The people suspecting the real design remained at home. However, thirty-six unfortunates went, and on their arrival they were seized and thrust into prison, and, in the interim, another summons was despatched to the country people to come into Carnew. This second invitation they treated as the first. The loyalists then proceeded to sacrifice the wretched people who had placed themselves in their power. They tied the thirty-six in couples, back to back, conveyed them to the ball-alley, placed them against the wall, in pairs, and shot every one."

The reign of terror may be said to have reached its height when those unhappy yeomen were thus cruelly murdered by their comrades on the mere suspicion of being less bloodthirsty than they. Men stood aghast on hearing of such a deed of wholesale slaughter. It now seemed plain that no man, however innocent, could deem himself safe—to be a "Papist," or even a liberal Protestant, was a crime that sufficed to bring down destruction on his head. Brave men might think of resistance, but unarmed and unorganised as they were, what could it avail but to render their ruin more complete? In this dreadful crisis, however, a man was found fearless enough in the midst of an oppressed and dismayed people to raise the standard of revolt, and bid a brave defiance to the tyrants of his country.

This man had been known hitherto only as a kind, zealous, and a true Irish priest, who, though he had won the highest honors of scholarship in a foreign university, yet had ever lived amongst his humble flock as one of themselves. A gentleman by profession and education, and by acquired accomplishments and natural gifts fitted to move in the highest circles, he preferred to be the poor man's friend than the rich man's flatterer. He, like others of his sacred calling, had believed in the faith of the faithless, and had counselled his flock to deliver up their arms at the mandate of their rulers.

He now saw with bitter disappointment that the submission had been of no avail; that mercy was shown to none; not even to the old and helpless, nor to those whose sex should have been a sufficient defence.

From the surrounding parishes reports came of fearful outrages daily committed, and at length the storm burst forth in full violence within the district whose inhabitants called him pastor. On the 26th of May twenty houses were set on fire in the parish of Boolevogue. The church soon after shared the same fate, and soon the humble temple wherein a virtuous and peaceful people had often gathered together to worship God in the religion of their fathers, was reduced to a mass of smoking ruins, and the zealous priest, who had prayed and preached therein, found himself without home or altar, a homeless and hunted fugitive.

The often repeated, and, I believe, commonly received statement that the burning of Father John's house and chapel was what impelled him to take part in the insurrection, is quite unfounded. Like the majority of the Catholic clergy of the time, he had no house that he could call his own, but lodged in that of a parishioner, and the chapel of Boolevogue was not burned till the morning of Sunday the 27th of May, when the insurrection had already begun by the fight at the Harrow.*

---

* The author received the above account of the burning of the chapel, and the outbreak of the insurrection, from a respectable farmer of the parish, whose father was an intimate friend of Father John Murphy's, and accompanied him through the entire struggle. The same account is given by other old people of the neighbourhood of Boolevogue, where the people are perfectly familiar with the events of the memorable year of '98, having heard them from their fathers and grandfathers. It has never, we believe, been published before. For further particulars concerning Father John, see Appendix.

Father John had indeed opposed the organization of the United Irishmen, not, as may be supposed, from any lack of patriotism, but because he deemed it unlawful, as unable to effect what it aimed at, while he trusted that in time the English Government might adopt a policy more just and merciful towards his unfortunate country.

In this expectation he was, as we have seen, disappointed, for matters assumed, day by day, a gloomier aspect, till the good priest and true patriot perceived at length that oppression had risen to a height that justified, because it necessitated, resistance. The step he designed to take was perhaps hastened by the following event:—

Saturday, the 26th of May, was the day appointed for the peasantry of Boolevogue and its neighbourhood to deliver up their arms to a magistrate named Cornick, who was to meet them at Ferns. On arriving at that place, according to appointment, they did not, as they expected, meet Cornick, but were fiercely assailed by a large number of the "black mob," as the Orange yeomen of the period were called by the peasantry. Their enemies, who out-numbered them by two to one, were all provided with swords and muskets, which they used with fatal effect. Overpowered by numbers, but still fighting bravely, the peasantry retreated towards home, turning now and then as their enemies pressed them too closely. On arriving at Milltown, they were met by Father John, who had ridden up on hearing of the affray. On seeing the arrival of the priest, the Orangemen, ceasing the pursuit, came to a halt, and presently afterwards returned to Ferns. It was this desperate and unprovoked attack, together with the burning of the houses in his parish, that decided the hitherto wavering mind of Father Murphy.

Father John luckily happened to be absent when the houses above-mentioned were given to the flames, but he beheld the conflagration from a distance, and sought refuge in a neighbouring thicket. To this place of refuge, also, came many of his people involved in the same calamity. Here, surrounded by a crowd of weeping and tearful women and children, and of men, who trembled not for themselves, but for their helpless wives, mothers, and sisters, and their more helpless little ones, the great-souled Soggarth thought more of their sorrow than of his own, and now deeply deplored his infatuation in counselling the people to deliver up their arms, and thereby leaving themselves at the mercy of foes whose hatred could be content only with their utter destruction. He now resolved to retrieve, if possible, this error of judgment.

Hitherto he had been their leader in peace, now they should follow him in the struggle for freedom. The contest was, indeed, unequal ; but as his eye rested upon the stalwart forms of those sturdy men, who stood before him in dejected attitudes, his spirit aroused itself from the torpor almost of despair into which it had sunk, and formed a brave resolve to change them into soldiers of freedom. His resolution taken, Father John motioned to the people to gather more closely around him, and began, in a direct and homely style, to speak of the deep sympathy he felt for them in their present affliction, which he might truly say grieved him more than his own mischance. He confessed his mistake in the matter of the arms, and finally declared that the time was come for resistance, and that he himself would lead to the field those of his parishioners who were willing to follow him, for he deemed it better to die like men, with arms in their hands, than wait to be butchered like dogs in the ditches.

Self-sufficient ignorance may presume to censure the counsel given by this good priest to his people, but there are times when resistance to tyranny becomes, if not a duty, at least a thing just and lawful, and who but the falsest, vilest, or most ignorant, can deny that it was thus in the case of men who took up arms to defend life itself, and what true men value more than their own, the lives of those who are dear to them. There are histories of this period written by men in the service of the English Government, in which the acts and motives of the insurgent peasantry and of their leaders are foully misrepresented. The authors of such pretended histories basely calumniate the brave men who made so grand a struggle against their far too numerous and too powerful foes. They are not ashamed to call them "deluded wretches," and to stigmatise their high-souled leader as a "ferocious bigot who delighted in blood."

Alas, Ireland has been sadly prolific of such vipers as those so-called historians—men who, living on property wrested by iniquitous laws from the people, and fattening on Irish soil, habitually utter the vilest calumnies against the truest and loyalest of her sons.

The men they calumniate might have been uneducated, but was it their own fault or that of the ruler who banned the schoolmaster and set a price on his head? They had their faults, no doubt, but in all the qualities that make men estimable they were far superior to their calumniators. They were honest men who lived by honest labour—not on the wages of dishonour—they were not descendants of Cromwell's bloodstained hypocrites, robbers, and regicides, with, perchance, a title of honour that but made their native meanness more conspicuous by the contrast—but were the sons of honest men with humble but stainless names—names which this history intends to prove they sullied by no craven or unworthy act.

When Father John had concluded his brief speech, an exulting cheer burst forth from all the men of his audience, and they forthwith declared their willingness to follow him through every danger. Well might those bold peasants accept with joy their proffered leader, for he had been cast by nature in the mould of those who lead men to victory.

Father John was rather under than over the ordinary stature of his countrymen, but broad-chested and strong-limbed, of remarkable activity as well as strength. His complexion was florid, his features rather handsome, but their beauty lay more in the expression than in the shape. His white forehead rose over bright blue eyes, which, though they usually beamed with a cheerful smile, could at times flash forth a glance that indicated the fiery and intrepid soul which in a just cause defies danger, and boldly confronts death itself. To personal advantages he united a most determined spirit, and a power, invaluable in a leader, of inspiring confidence into his followers.

Had he received the advantages of a military education he might have successfully aspired to the highest honours offered by the career of arms, but he has obtained for himself a higher and a prouder name than any of the epaulotted tools of tyrants; for the soldier who falls in the cause of an oppressed people builds for himself a monument of fame that outlives that of granite or marble.

Father John, thus chosen by acclamation the first captain of the insurgents, determined to commence his new career by a daring deed that would strike terror into the hearts of tyrants. He proposed that an attack should be made on the Camolin yeomen cavalry as they returned that night from one of their daily forays on the defenceless people, to Camolin Park, the residence of their Colonel, Lord Mountnorris. The people were to disperse, provide themselves with whatever arms they could procure, and return, when night had fallen, to the appointed place.

In pursuance of this plan Father John and his brave men met as soon as darkness had set in at the appointed place, and having thrown a barricade across the road by which the cavalry were to return on their homeward way, they concealed themselves behind the ditches on either side of the way. They had not been long in their place of concealment when they heard the welcome sound of horses' hoofs breaking in upon the silence of the night, and in a brief while their ruthless persecutors came full in view, discussing in loud tones their achievements during the day, and gloating over the horrible details of acts of demon-like wickedness, little dreaming that their last foray had been ridden and that the avengers were so close at hand.

Riding thus leisurely along they arrived at length within sight of the barricade—halted at a short distance from it while one approached closely to ascertain its nature. Then a wild yell rising from behind the ditches told them of the presence of those they had good reason to fear as their deadliest foes. But they had little time for reflection, and but little for action. They had time only to fire one hasty and ill-aimed volley from their pistols when the foe was in their midst.

The contest was brief—the pitchfork with its long sharpened prongs wielded by vigorous arms, and the deadlier scythe were more than a match for the sabre. After a fight that lasted but for a few minutes, every saddle was empty of its yeoman rider, and of those who had ridden forth in the morning on their cruel errand of bloodshed and plunder, the greater number now lay upon the highway bleeding and disfigured corpses.* The horses and accoutrements of the fallen yeomen became now the spoil of the joyful victors, who, elated with this first and decisive success, determined to march to Camolin Park and take possession of the arms therein stored, which had been given up by the surrounding peasantry. In this enterprise they were also completely successful, capturing, in addition to what they expected, a number of new carbines, provided by Lord Mountnorris for the arming of the new corps he had organised. Well was it for the noble colonel that he had not ridden out with his corps on this fatal day!

Although this successful effort on the part of the insurgents had taken place during the night, the tidings of it had before midnight been heard with joy in many a distant cottage and farm-house, and before morning dawned the victorious band were augmented by many a brave recruit, prepared to brave all dangers fighting for the good old cause. Leaving Father John and his men to rejoice in their first victory, and to plan others, we will take a view of the state of the country, and briefly recount minor events that occurred during the night of the 23rd, and on the ensuing day.

The tidings of the successful surprise and defeat of the Camolin cavalry spread with great rapidity throughout the entire county. Turner, a magistrate, who escaped with difficulty from the pursuit of his long-hunted foes, at last turned to bay, brought the startling news to Wexford early on Sunday morning.

The North Cork then stationed in the barracks, to the number of 100 men, and the Shilmalier Yeomen Cavalry immediately got under arms, and were soon on their march towards Oulart Hill, whereon it was said that their peasant foe intended to take up their position.

* Lieutenant Bookey was piked, and a man named Donovan, who rode on before the others to the barricade, was shot. Some accounts state that only these two were slain.

The yeomanry and militia who quitted Wexford on this expedition marched by different routes—the former taking the road that runs through the village of Castlebridge, and the latter choosing that by the seaside. They met by agreement at Ballyfarnock, and proceeding together as far as Ballinamonabeg they halted with the intention of quenching their thirst and laying in a stock of "Dutch courage" at a public house* there belonging to a man named Kavanagh. Not finding the owner at home, they proceeded to indulge in copious libations, and when they had drunk what they considered enough, under the circumstances, these loyal defenders of the country and sustainers of the tottering constitution, by way of payment, set fire to the house they had plundered. Thus, not content with robbing the unfortunate proprietor, they satisfied their brutal instinct of destruction by burning his house.

This is but an illustration of the infamous treatment the unfortunate people were forced to endure at the hands of those whom frequent acts of injustice and cruelty seemed to have transformed into demons. The leader of these wretches, bear in mind, gentle reader, was a magistrate armed with the power of life and death. The news of the defeat of the Camolin cavalry reached

---

* The *Wexford delegates of United Irishmen* happened to be assembled in the house at the time, but having received warning of the approach of the yeomen, they effected their escape a few moments before the latter arrived at the place. The owner of the house was at Oulart when his house was burned, where he had an opportunity of evincing his gratitude for the patronage of such *honest* customers.

The victim of Orange atrocity in this instance was the author's grandfather, who was wont, when speaking of the destruction of his house, to mention also the fact of the delegates being present. The day before he had surrendered a pike to Colonel Lehunte, but with praiseworthy providence had reserved another for Oulart, of which I have no doubt he made good use.

Gorey long before dawn, and the militia quartered there, apprehending that the victors might direct their march thither, were seized with terror, and forthwith fled from the town. They, however, returned soon after on hearing that they had gone in the direction of Oulart, and as cowards are ever cruel, they showed their satisfaction at this intelligence by torturing the prisoners they had taken.*

A young man named Jeremiah Donovan, disguised as a groom, bearing fictitious letters, directed to Lord Mountnorris, brought the news of the defeat of the yeomen at the Harrow to Castlebridge, whence it spread rapidly over the entire country. Next day he returned in time to take part in the fight on Oulart where he fell—the only man killed on the insurgent side.†

If the tidings of the successful result of the first encounter between the insurgents and their enemies served to raise the hope of the peasantry, it filled the various corps of yeomanry with a determination to take the direst vengeance—not that these cravens desired to meet in fair fight the half-armed peasantry, for they had it in their power to take a safer if less soldier-like revenge.

The aged parents, the helpless wives and children of their feared and hated foes were in their power, and on these poor victims they would wreak their vengeance. Filled with this fell purpose they sallied forth from their various stations, and commenced putting to death all persons they encountered on their way, and those were chiefly the feeble and unarmed, for the young and strong shunned the highway. They set fire to the

* See Gordon and Hay's " Histories of the Insurrection."
† For this fact and many others the author is indebted to Mr. Nicholas Donovan of Boolevogue, a nephew of the Jeremiah Donovan referred to above. The old chapel stood on the farm of the Donovans, as the new one does at present.

houses of those they designated as "rebels, Papists, disaffected croppies," and in many instances the unfortunate inmates were consumed in the flames amidst the exulting yells of their destroyers. An historian of the period, himself a witness, affirms that on a march of some seven miles one corps alone set fire to one hundred houses!

Such achievements as this—the burning of the old, the helpless, and the innocent in their houses—the Orange historians of the time mention in terms of mild deprecation, while they pour out the vials of their most wrathful denunciation upon the heads of the hunted peasantry, because they dared to retaliate upon such ruthless enemies. Meantime Father John's force, considerably augmented, amounting to about 3,000 men, badly armed, indeed, but filled with a determination to conquer or die, set out about mid-day on Sunday, the 27th, for the Hill of Oulart, where they arrived about noon. This course their leader chose, to give the people of the neighbouring parishes an opportunity of joining his standard.

CHAPTER VII.

Slaughter of the peasantry at Kilmacthomas Hill.—Position taken by the insurgents at Oulart Hill.—The Battle.—Total defeat of the loyalists.—Atrocities committed by the yeomen during their flight.—Route taken by the victorious insurgents.—Joined at Ballicorrel by Father Michael Murphy.—Attack on Enniscorthy.—Capture of the town.—Flight of the loyalists.—Attempt made by the Orangemen to murder the prisoners in Enniscorthy jail frustrated.—Moderation of the victorious insurgents.—Insurgents' camp at Vinegar Hill reinforced.—Division in their councils.—The arrival of the Wexford deputation.—Its effect.—Insurgents arrive at the Three Rocks.—Surprise and defeat of the Meath Militia on their way to Wexford.—Official account of the affair.

DURING the night of the 26th, a number of peasantry assembled on the hill of Kilmacthomas, an eminence about nine miles to the west of Gorey. This multitude was largely composed of women and children, and had assembled, as it seemed, more in the hope of escaping the fury of the yeomanry and militia than with a determination to fight. While on his way to celebrate mass (it being Sunday morning), Father Michael Murphy was encountered by some of these people who besought him to accompany them to the hill. He had from the outset been strongly opposed to armed resistance, considering it hopeless, and therefore, unlawful; but, at the same time he declared, that if it were attempted, "He would go with the people." In the fulfilment of this promise he proceeded to Kilmacthomas. Against the unorganised crowd assembled on the eminence in question, two hundred yeomen marched out from Carnew, and advancing boldly, probably encouraged by the presence of the women and children, came within musket range, and poured volley after volley into the unresisting crowd, who soon fled in wild terror, while their foes pursued and succeeded in slaughtering about three hundred of their number. The Rev. Mr. Gordon states that after this massacre the yeomen in a march of seven miles burned a hundred cabins, and two Roman Catholic chapels. We turn with pleasure from this slaughter of helpless women and children to follow the fortunes of the brave peasants encamped on Oulart hill.

About three thousand people accompanied Father John to the hill of Oulart, but of that large number there were not more than three-hundred fighting men. The rest of the multitude consisted of women, children, old infirm men, and unarmed striplings. Across the brow of the hill where it looks towards the *old* village of Oulart,* about a mile distant, there extends a breast-high ditch, forming a dividing line between two of the numerous small fields into which the cultivated surface of its rounded summit is divided. Behind this convenient breastwork Father Murphy stationed all the best armed men of his force. Of this small force the majority had pikes, but others were furnished with no more efficient arms than scythes and pitchforks. At some distance in the rear of this body he placed the women and children, with the old men and boys, whose too advanced or unripe age unfitted them for the approaching contest. Amongst these, however, there were many who afterwards did good service. The insurgent force thus disposed remained upon the hill-top, awaiting in anxious expectation the approach of their enemies from the direction of Wexford. It was the Sabbath day, and the summer sun had attained his meridian height, and was already verging towards the west, when the anxious watchers on Oulart Hill beheld a long line of red-coated men advancing towards them along the road that leads from Wexford, and crossing the summit of a swell of ground called the hill of Bōlūbwee (thus pronounced). They halted on coming within a short distance of the base of Oulart. These men were the North Cork Infantry, who had marched out of Wexford at an early hour that morning.

* The modern village of the same name is situate several miles distant from the hill.

From their elevated position the insurgents could plainly discern all the movements of the hostile body. The Shelmalier Cavalry, under Colonel Lehunte, who accompanied the militia, were first seen to get in motion, extending their force so as to enclose the hill, evidently with the design of depriving their enemies of all chance of escape or retreat in case of their defeat by the militia.

The latter deploying into line began to advance at a quick pace up the ascent from the southern side. The peasantry awaited their approach in silence, permitting them to come within musket shot of their earthen bulwark. Major Lombard, the second in command, rode somewhat in advance of his men, and not seeing, as he drew near the ditch, anything to denote the presence of the enemy, he concluded that they had fled; under this impression he spurred his steed forward, waving his sword aloft, and calling loudly to his men to follow, exclaiming that "the course was clear."

The words of ill-timed exultation had scarce passed his lips when a bullet from the musket of one of the watchful insurgents pierced his breast—he instantly fell from his horse, and lay dead upon the field. On beholding their officer fall, the militia raised a shout of rage, and pressed forward at a quickened pace to avenge his death. While the military were thus advancing, one of the insurgents suggested to his comrades that it would be well to raise their hats, placed on the points of their pikes, over the top of the ditch, as thereby they might draw a volley from the advancing militia. This suggestion was instantly adopted, and had the desired effect. The militia, beholding as they thought, the heads of their opponents elevated above the ditch, emptied their muskets with a hasty volley, which, of course, proved quite harmless.

Having halted to deliver this volley, the soldiery again advanced at a less hurried pace, loading their muskets the while. But twelve of the insurgents were armed with guns. Six of these now rose, and resting the barrels of their muskets upon the ditch, delivered their fire with deadly accuracy upon their assailants. Six of the militia fell, and their comrades in dismay and confusion returned the fire with another hasty and ineffectual volley. Again six of the insurgents rose and poured in another fatal volley. This second volley deprived the unfortunate red-coats of whatever little courage the first had left them, and being now charged by the pikemen, they did not withstand for five minutes' space their furious and determined onset. Disorganised and terror-stricken, they soon broke their ranks, and fled down the slope of the hill by the way they had advanced. But they had small chance of escape from the swift-footed peasantry, who, nimble as deer, pressed upon their footsteps. Their destruction, strange to say, was rendered more complete by the presence of the mounted yeomen, for a panic had seized the crowd in the rear of the defenders of the ditch on their approach, and they had actually begun their flight down the northern side of the hill, when perceiving the mounted yeomen they retraced their steps, returning just in time to join in the pursuit. Many of the routed soldiery were piked before they could gain the foot of the hill; some, when hard pressed, turned to resist; others threw down their arms and begged, but in vain, for mercy. Some of the more agile of the fugitives reached the fields that stretch between the fatal hill and Bólábwee, but all of the rank and file perished in the pursuit.* The last was slain at the distance of

---

* Hay and Gordon both agree in their estimate of the losses sustained by the insurgents and the king's troops in this engagement, but I prefer to adopt the traditional account of the matter. The above narrative of the Battle of Oulart I have heard from the lips of those who were engaged in it.

about a mile from the hill. Lieutenant-Colonel Foote fled in time, and, mounted on a good horse, reached Wexford in safety. Upwards of one hundred of the common men fell in this action.*

Six officers were killed, viz. :—Major Lombard (already mentioned), the Hon. Captain De Courcy (a brother of the then Lord Kinsale), three lieutenants—Williams, Ware, and Barry, and Ensign Keogh. Concerning this engagement, the Rev. Mr. Gordon observes:—

"About 300 of the insurgents, rallied by their sacerdotal commander, made so furious, close, and sudden an onset with their pikes, that with the loss of only three killed and six wounded, they slew the whole detachment, except the lieutenant-colonel, a sergeant, and three privates."

Meantime the mounted yeomen remained passive spectators of the conflict, and saw with the utmost surprise and dismay the sudden and total defeat of their comrades. Their sympathy with their unfortunate allies was, however, soon changed into fear for their own safety, for one of their foes on the hill, armed with a long shore-gun, brought down one of their own body with a fatal aim. On seeing their comrade fall from his horse dead upon the field, they put spurs to their horses, and galloped off with all speed in the direction of Wexford. All the militia men were not slain on the hill, but many of them, flying in terror from the fatal hill, and seeking to escape through the adjoining fields, were pursued, overtaken, and slain.

The fugitive yeomen, when out of sight, and safe from the pursuit of the now terrible† pikemen, took a

* See in Appendix various incidents relative to this action.
† Sir Jonah Barrington's "Rise and Fall of the Irish Nation," p. 432.—"The extreme expertness with which the Irish handled the pike was surpassing; by withdrawing they could shorten to little more than the length of a dagger, and in a second dart it

dastardly revenge, by slaughtering all the " croppies" they encountered, and setting fire to many houses. While these cowards are making their way towards Wexford, murdering as they go, the victorious insurgents, under their indomitable leader, not being able, for lack of cavalry, to pursue their flying enemies, set forth for the hill of Carrigrew, on which they encamped for the night. Next morning at an early hour they marched in some sort of military order to Camolin, where they were to find some arms that had been lately deposited there for the use of the yeomen. From Camolin they continued their march to Ferns, and there learned that the royal troops had retreated to Gorey and Enniscorthy. Father John now led on his gallant little band towards the latter town, taking a circuitous route thither by the bridge of Scarawalsh in order that the people of that district might have an opportunity of joining his forces. The glad tidings of these successes had spread rapidly over the county, and numbers of gallant young peasants, for the most part of the better class, came flocking to join the victors, prepared to fight to the death under such a brave and successful leader. The small force wherewith Father John had so boldly begun the insurrection being by this time augmented to some 5,000 men, about 500 of whom carried fire-arms, chiefly long fowling-pieces, it was thought expedient to hold a council of war to deliberate on their further proceedings. At this council it was decided to march without delay to attack Enniscorthy.

out to its full extent. At old Kilcullen they entirely repulsed General Dundas, and the heavy cavalry, in a regular charge, killing two captains, and many soldiers; the General escaped with great difficulty, by the fleetness of his horse. At New Ross they entirely broke the heavy horse by their pikes. . . Colonel Foote's detachment of infantry was nearly annihilated by the pike at Oulart; only the major and two others escaped."

On their way to that town they came to a halt on the hill of Balliorrell, both to rest after their long march and to deliberate concerning the intended attack. While they were halted on Balliorrell they were joined by the Rev. Michael Murphy, at the head of some young men of his parish of Ballycanew, full of ardour for the fight, but, like their comrades, ill-armed.

The plan of the intended attack on Enniscorthy being finally arranged, the insurgents descended the hill, and advanced towards the town. Two hundred men, armed with fire-arms, preceded the main body, which consisted chiefly of pikemen, on whose flanks, and in whose rear some marksmen were placed. Moving onward in this order, they soon came in sight of the enemy, whose force consisted of several corps of yeomanry, mounted and on foot, and a body of the North Cork Militia amounting to about 500 men. This disciplined and well-armed force were strongly aided in the engagement that ensued by the loyalists of the town, who now took their stand on the nearest part of the town wall, or remained more safely ensconced within their houses, prepared to assist as much as they could the King's troops against their common foe. Besides these loyalist Orangemen, many "respectable Catholics" had offered their services, begging to be supplied with arms, that they might evince *their* loyalty by firing upon their countrymen and co-religionists, but, being regarded as untrustworthy in this crisis, they were refused, and harshly threatened for their temerity in daring to proffer their despised aid.

The advanced guard of the insurgent army now had advanced to within musket shot of the Duffery gate, the principal entrance to the town. In front of the entrance several corps of yeomanry were drawn up. Their left flank was protected against attack by the River Slaney, which runs through the town, and their right flank and rear by the strong walls of the town and the houses that overtopped it, garrisoned with armed loyalist citizens. They were thus secure on either flank, and in the rear. Captain Snowe, with his company of North Cork, was stationed at the bridge, to secure the retreat of his comrades, in case they suffered a defeat. The road by which the assailants advanced to the attack was one of the three leading to the Duffery gate, and on their advance being perceived by its defenders, they were charged with great fury by the cavalry. When the insurgents beheld their enemy approaching swiftly towards them they quitted the road, and posted themselves behind the ditches that bounded it on either side, and, resting their guns on them, poured upon their advancing foes a deliberate and deadly fire, which cooled their ardour, and made them retreat more quickly than they had advanced. However, on being reinforced, they again advanced, but with no better success, being forced to fly before the fire of the deliberate gunsmen.

While the gunsmen thus keep their mounted enemies at bay and exchange a distant and scattered fire with the hostile infantry stationed at the Duffery gate, and the townspeople on the walls and in the houses, the main body of the insurgents, being come to a halt at a short distance from the town, hold a brief consultation as to the best mode of attacking troops so well armed and so advantageously posted as their enemies.

Father John, who on every occasion evinced a military genius, suggested that the best plan, and that most likely to be attended with success, was to drive a number of cattle, that were herded in the rear of the column, to the front, and thence to goad them onwards towards their enemy's ranks by a chosen body of pikemen, and that they might themselves safely follow in the rear of the maddened herd.

This stratagem was tried and proved completely successful. The cattle used for this purpose—the youngest and wildest of the herd—were driven quickly to the front, and thence onwards towards the gate.

They no sooner heard the wild shouts of those who drove them than they set forward at a rapid pace in the required direction, the agile pikemen following closely upon their heels, and thus approaching unharmed the line of their armed foes. The latter, perceiving the wild herd advancing furiously upon them, and hearing from the rear, above the bellowing of the maddened beasts, the louder and fiercer shouts of their dreaded foes, endeavoured with all their might to check the cattle in their furious advance. To effect this some of the soldiery rushed forward to drive them back with the bayonet, while others fired their muskets into the midst of the herd. But all their efforts were unavailing to arrest that furious onset, for the cattle, goaded to madness by the yells of the men in the rear, and, when they attempted to turn back or slackened their pace, feeling the sharp points of the pikes, charged furiously forward into the ranks of the dismayed soldiery, and opened the way for a yet more dreaded foe—for, with a wild cheer of revenge and hatred, the pikemen were amongst them. Not a moment's stand did they make against the peasants whose destruction they had but lately sworn to accomplish. The remembrance of the fearful wrongs they had endured—their burned homesteads—their tortured or murdered friends—nerved the peasant's arm, and heightened the courage of his brave heart. Success, too, had given him confidence in himself, and days of hard fighting had given him something of the soldier's heedlessness of life.

The King's troops, completely routed, fled with the utmost precipitation into the town, with their victorious foes at their heels in close pursuit. The impetuous advance of the insurgents was, however, checked by a most destructive fire directed against them from those houses near the gate, whose doors opened to receive and shelter their routed foe. Those of the late defenders of the Duffery Gate, who succeeded in escaping the fury of the insurgent assault, having now joined their adherents already posted within the houses—both united, poured a terrible fire on their unsheltered assailants. However, the undaunted peasantry sustained this terrible fusillade with the resolution of veteran soldiers, and straightway proceeded to force an entrance into those houses that proved so advantageous to their enemies, and so destructive to themselves. This combination of valour and stubborn perseverance finally won the day. Consternation seized the foe on seeing such a display of heroic resolution in those frieze-coated men on whom they had so long trampled with impunity. Alas! they, too, were Irishmen, and in a good cause might have fought valiantly, but having chosen to become the hired cut-throats of a foreign Government, and employed to butcher their fellow-countrymen, they lacked that generous determination to conquer or die that men who fight in a good cause alone can feel. At length the sight of the suburbs in a blaze (set on fire by the patriotic inmates), together with that of a multitude suddenly appearing on the summit of Vinegar Hill, completely disheartened the loyalists.

Thomas Sinnott, of Kilbride, contributed much to the insurgent success by leading a large body across the Slaney, about a mile above Enniscorthy, and unexpectedly pouring into the town from the northern direction. Assailed thus on all sides the dispirited loyalists gave way. Orders were hurriedly given to sound a retreat, and in a short time the garrison of the town with their families and a large number of their civilian adherents, were on their way to Wexford. A panic-stricken and disordered crowd they were—soldiers and civilians, women and children, forgetting every distinction of rank in their terrified eagerness to escape. Mr. Hay thus describes the confusion of their flight:—" Officers had been induced to tear off their epaulets, and every other mark that could distinguish them from the privates, considering themselves in more danger if they were recognised as officers. However, not being attacked, there was sufficient leisure to escort those that accompanied them, and who were in such a piteous plight as to excite on their arrival the hearty commiseration of all the inhabitants of Wexford, who invited them indiscriminately to their houses, and supplied them with every comfort and necessary in their power—and of which they stood in so much need . . Some had their clothes scorched about them, others wanted their shoes and other parts of their dress which had been lost or torn off; besides the great heat of the day made it doubly distressing to delicate females—many of whom had the additional charge of the burden and care of their children."

While the retreat was being sounded a party of Orangemen approached the castle with the fell intent of putting all the " Papists " therein confined to death, and thus revenging in some degree their defeat. But fortunately for those whose lives they had determined to take, the keeper of the prison had already fled, taking the key with him, and as the intended murderers had not sufficient time to force the strong door of the prison, they were forced to depart, their cruel intent unfulfilled. So utter was the disorganisation of the routed royalists that had they been pursued by their victorious enemies they must all have been slain or taken prisoners, but the pikemen who on that day had marched thirty miles, and fought, as we have seen, for several hours afterwards without partaking of any food whatever, were far too weary to pursue fresh men, who fled as those only can fly who fear that death pursues. The insurgents used their victory with a moderation that adorned their valour, for no house was set on fire and no person maltreated or put to death—and this although many of the townspeople had taken an active part against them.

And yet these men have been branded as cruel and ferocious, because isolated deeds of revenge were perpetrated by individuals amongst them.

I defy the base defamers of a race, who are generous and forgiving almost to a fault, to substantiate the charges of cruelty and ferocity they had so unscrupulously made against the insurgents in the brief and disastrous but heroic struggle of the Irish of one county against all the military resources of England!

In this action the English lost upwards of a hundred men of the rank and file and three officers, amongst the latter Captain Pounden, of the Enniscorthy Infantry, who fell at the Duffery Gate.

The insurgents, now masters of Enniscorthy, having possessed themselves of whatever arms and ammunition they found therein, deemed it prudent to quit the town, and encamp on the rocky eminence called Vinegar Hill, that overlooks, and stands like a huge sentinel to guard it.

While the insurgent army were encamped on and around Vinegar Hill, their number was hourly augmented by fresh arrivals, for the news of their success had spread far and wide during the night.

Amongst the brave men who thus came to share the danger and glory of the contest were some whose position and education caused the insurgents to hail their arrival with joy. Garret Byrne, of Ballymanus;

Thomas Clooney, of Moneyhore; and Barker, of Enniscorthy, arrived at the camp during the day to aid, to the best of their power, their countrymen in the struggle for freedom. Vinegar Hill was now the centre towards which the insurgents from the surrounding districts came flocking, and there were gathered the materials of as brave an army as ever bore arms in the cause of an oppressed country. They needed but unity of counsel and competent leaders to crown their cause with the most glorious success. Unity, however, was wanting, for every leader held his own view as to what course they should pursue, and the insurrection had nearly come to a premature end when a fortunate incident occurred, which fixed their wavering thoughts, and made them resolve to march on Wexford.

This was the arrival of a deputation from the Wexford loyalists summoning them to surrender and disperse. The arrival of the liberated prisoners was hailed with the greatest enthusiasm by the people still remaining, and the joyful and surprising event, in a brief while spreading far and wide, had the effect of recalling to the scene those who were already quitting it.* When the gentlemen of the deputation informed their excited audience that they had been sent by the loyalists to dissuade them from advancing upon Wexford, the multitude burst forth into loud shouts of

* The Rev. Mr. Gordon in his History of Ireland thus describes the effect of the embassy:—
"The insurgents were found by the two gentlemen on the afternoon of the 29th in a state of confusion, distracted in their councils, without leaders of general influence, and without a plan; the greater part were dispersing to defend their houses from Orangemen. But when shouts repeated from group to group announced the arrival of the *gentlemen prisoners,* as they were styled, from Wexford, the straggling bands collected from all sides into one body, and retaining Fitzgerald as a leader formed immediately the resolution of marching to Wexford.

exultation, justly regarding the embassy in its true light as an evidence of the weakness of their enemy and of their own strength, which they themselves had not fully estimated. It inspired them with a confidence in themselves and their cause that hitherto they had somewhat lacked. Unable to agree before, they now demanded with unanimous voice to be led without delay against the town. Mr. Colclough was immediately sent back (Mr. Fitzgerald being detained) to announce their determination. That very evening the insurgents set out for Wexford, and encamped for the night on the "Three Rocks," a ridge of the Forth Mountains so called—which are situate about three miles from the town.

Upon these barren and lofty hills the insurgents pitched their camp, and having posted sentinels, retired to rest for the night, which was of unusual darkness. Early the next morning the watchful sentinels aroused their slumbering comrades with intelligence that they had descried a large force of royal troops on the march, from the direction of Duncannow, towards Wexford. On the receipt of these tidings a body of men was despatched, under the command of Clooney, and Kelly of Killane, to intercept and give battle to the advancing force. Well did these brave men execute their orders. Having descended the hill they sought a convenient ambush at its foot, and there awaited the approach of the loyalist force, who continued to advance in fancied security, till the insurgents, starting from their place of ambush, attacked them at once both in front and rear. The struggle was brief and soon decided. In this, as in subsequent engagements, the soldiery proved no match for their peasant foe, whose strength and activity set at nought the resistance of England's trained hirelings.

After a fight of about ten minutes' duration, the

entire detachment, amounting to about one hundred men and three officers of the Meath Militia, were either slain or made prisoners, and two pieces of cannon became the prize of the victors. The main body, of which the detachment thus signally defeated formed the advanced guard, had advanced from Duncannon Fort as far as Taghmon on their way to Wexford, but on hearing of this defeat, General Fawcett, their commander, gave orders to retreat with all speed whence they had come.

The following is the official account of the affair:—

"*Dublin Castle, June 2nd, 1798.*

"Accounts have been received from Major-General Eustace at New Ross, stating that Major-General Fawcett having marched with a company of the Meath regiment from Duncannon Fort, this small force was surrounded by a very large body between Taghmon and Wexford, and defeated. General Fawcett effected his retreat to Duncannon Fort."

We now leave the valiant and victorious insurgents to enjoy their latest triumph, in order to recount as briefly as we may the chief events that took place within the county town since the battle of Oulart.

CHAPTER VIII.

Consternation produced amongst the loyalists in Wexford by the defeat of the militia at Oulart.—Attempt of the militia to put the prisoners to death.—Their design defeated by the governor of the jail.—Arrival of fugitive loyalists from Enniscorthy.—Wexford a hot-bed of Orangeism. —Preparations made by the loyalists for the defence of Wexford.— Arrival of reinforcements.—Terror of the Orangemen.—Precautions taken for the security of the town.—Loyalists resolve to send a deputation to the insurgents.—Arrival of Mr. Colclough in Wexford.—Delivers his message.—Sally headed by Colonel Watson.—Its results.—The loyalists hold a council of war and resolve to evacuate the town.—The dishonest stratagem employed by the loyalists to retard the approach of the insurgents.—Strange scene of confusion exhibited in the flight of the military.—Entrance of the insurgents from Ferrybank.—Rage of the insurgent army on discovering the deceit practised upon them by the soldiery.—Altered aspect of Wexford on the entry of the insurgents.— Two Orangemen put to death on the Quay.—Excesses of the fugitive garrison.—Tranquillity in Wexford.—Departure of the insurgents.

WHEN the tidings of the destruction of the North Cork reached Wexford, the loyalists there were filled with the greatest consternation. The comrades of the slain men vowing to avenge or perish with them, hurriedly assumed their arms and set out for Oulart. However, on arriving at the bridge they were met by a number of the loyalist townsmen, who succeeded in persuading them to defer for the present the execution of their purpose, and return to their barracks.

The widows and orphans of the fallen soldiers ran through the streets loudly bewailing the loss of their husbands and fathers, and mingling with their lamentations the bitterest execrations of the yeomanry, to whose cowardly conduct they attributed their destruction. The militia, not finding any other means of gratifying their vengeance, determined to put to death the prisoners in the town-jail—singling out in particular Messrs. Harvey, Colclough, and Fitzgerald. But the governor of the jail, Joseph Gladwin, resolved to protect his charge against the violence of these desperate men. Having contrived to get the military guard outside the prison, he locked the door, and proceeded to warn the prisoners of their danger, furnishing the three gentlemen with weapons, that in case the militia succeeded in obtaining an entrance they might not perish without a struggle. The enraged militia, thirsting for blood, soon after arrived at the gates, and loudly demanded entrance. This being refused, they essayed to burst in the door, but its great strength defied all their efforts. At length, unable by force or stratagem to effect an entrance, these baffled banditti departed and returned to their quarters. But yet greater reverses than any which had hitherto befallen them awaited the loyalists of Wexford. Next day they heard that the victors of Oulart had attacked Enniscorthy, and from the dense clouds of smoke that could be discerned hanging over that town, they concluded that it had been set on fire, and their terrified imagination added horrors to the catastrophe they had divined. The arrival of the fugitives from the captured town in the most miserable plight imaginable, and the exaggerated accounts they gave of what they had witnessed and what they believed had taken place after their departure, inspired their woe-begone brethren of Wexford with the utmost dread. The town of Wexford was at this period a hot-bed of Orangeism, and the members of that baneful organisation, upheld and fostered by English influence, had hitherto been absolute masters of the lives and properties of their Catholic fellow-townsmen. They had ruled in the fiercest spirit of hatred the unfortunate professors of a creed banned by the laws of England, and evinced to the utmost the detestation they bore to any Protestant who discountenanced their villainous tyranny. They now beheld with terror the long down-trodden helot rising up in the energy of his manhood and threatening to shake off the galling yoke he had so long borne, not indeed with patience, but with the hapless resignation of despair. In their days of power they had shown no mercy, and they now believed that if they fell into the hands of their enemy they might expect none. To secure themselves against such a calamity they resolved to use every possible precaution.

The ancient town of Wexford now bristled with warlike preparation. Every avenue was strongly barricaded, and cannon were planted in the most advantageous positions. The loyalist inhabitants, including most of the wealthier class, came forward in this emergency to proffer their aid in the defence. Two hundred of their number were furnished with weapons and employed in guarding the walls (at the time entire), conforming in every respect to military discipline. Messrs. Harvey and Colclough, though still detained in prison, began to be treated with some consideration, being regarded in the light of valuable hostages. A numerous deputation of magistrates and military officers waited upon them in their place of durance, and besought them to exert their influence with their tenantry in the baronies of Forth and Bargy, to deter them from taking part in the insurrection. With this request the imprisoned gentlemen complied—in truth they had no option, being quite at the mercy of their enemies. The loyalists of Wexford, deeming that town would be selected by the insurgents as the next object of attack, despatched messengers to obtain reinforcements from the nearest garrisons, all the while prosecuting with the utmost vigour their defensive preparations. At an early hour on the 29th of May, the first of the expected reinforcements arrived. It consisted of two hundred of the Donegal Militia, under Colonel Maxwell, accompanied by the Heathfield yeomen cavalry, commanded by Captain John Grogan. With these came several officers of the 13th regiment of Meath Militia, who announced the approach of that force under General Fawcett. At a later hour the Taghmon cavalry, under Captain Cox, rode into town. Notwithstanding the vigorous preparations they had made, and the presence of such a large number of armed defenders, the loyal burghers of Wexford could not shake off the terror that had seized them when the idea of an insurgent attack upon the town had first entered their minds. Nothing could exceed the terror now displayed by the Orangemen, arising, as it may naturally be supposed, from the consciousness of the outrages they had committed, of the houses they had burned, of the innocent people they had tortured and put to death. Filled with the most direful apprehensions, many of them hastened to take refuge on board the ships that lay moored within the harbour, intending to sail for England in case the insurgents became masters of the town. Others shut themselves up in their houses and awaited in anxious suspense the further course of events. In addition to the precautions already adopted for the security of the place, an order was issued commanding that all fires should be extinguished, even those used for baking purposes, and that all thatched houses should be stripped of their covering. Scouts were despatched to explore the country in all directions, and to bring in whatever intelligence they could gather of the enemy's movements. To add to the feelings of depression that weighed so heavily on the inhabitants, the bodies of the officers who had been slain at Oulart were brought into town in mournful procession, the first victims to hostile rage seen in Wexford on the loyalist side since the contest between the people and their rulers was entered upon.

Mr. Hay being thought a favourite among the insurgents, though a loyalist, was now appealed to and entreated to use his influence with the latter, and, if possible, to induce them to disperse. He himself gives the following account of the transaction, which exhibits a strange mixture on the part of the Orangemen of dread of the insurgents, and distrust of the "Papists," of the most overweening arrogance and most arrant cowardice curiously combined. He says:—

"No magistrate being found, as I suppose, that would venture on this dangerous service, it was then inquired whether the liberation of Messrs. Harvey, Fitzgerald and Colclough might not appease the people? On this question I declared myself incompetent to decide. I was then asked whether, if enlarged on bail, they, but particularly Mr. Fitzgerald, whose residence lay in the country then disturbed, would undertake to go out to the insurgents and endeavour to prevail on them to disperse? On this inquiry my opinion was that as the lives of these gentlemen were in danger from the fury of the soldiery, while they continued in prison, I thought they would comply with this requisition. The matter now became public, and the prisoners were accordingly visited by the most respectable gentlemen in the town; several requesting of me to accompany them to the prison, for the purpose of introduction. Indeed, so marked was the attention paid to them on this occasion that an indifferent spectator would be led to consider them rather as the governors of the town than as prisoners. On the 28th and 29th, I had many conversations on this subject with the officers and gentlemen of the place, and at length I was myself, together with five other gentlemen (two for each of the three prisoners), bound in five hundred pounds severally; and Messrs. Harvey, Fitzgerald, and Colclough themselves individually, in one thousand pounds security for their appearance at the next assizes. It was further conditioned that, although they were all three bailed, two only should be at large at any one time; but that they might take their turns of going abroad interchangeably at their discretion, provided 'one should always remain in gaol as a guarantee for the return of the rest.'" How this embassy fared will appear in the sequel. The force of royal troops that now held possession of Wexford amounted to about 1200 men, including regular troops, yeomanry, militia, and armed citizens.

Of this large force, Ex-Colonel Watson, though not formally appointed, undertook the command, to which important trust the energy and courage he so signally displayed very justly entitled him. But the brave old veteran did not seem quite successful in inspiring his own spirit into his followers. The hopes of turning the tide of insurgent warfare from the town, which had for awhile upheld their sinking spirits, were quite dispelled on the arrival of Mr. Colclough that evening to announce the final determination of their enemies. The gentleman in question, without dismounting from his horse, proceeded straightway to the "bull-ring," and there announced, in a loud voice to the people who anxiously gathered round him, the answer returned by the insurgents to the deputation, and their resolve to attack the town.

Having delivered this unwelcome message, he proceeded to visit Mr. Harvey, who was still detained in prison, and, having had a short interview with that unlucky captive, rode off to his own residence at Ballyteigue. The tidings brought by Mr. Colclough completed the dismay of the loyalists. The ships in the harbour, before quite sufficiently filled with people, were now overcrowded. The places of business were all closed as on a holiday, but there was no appearance of Sabbath calm or tranquillity in Wexford. Every loyalist beheld his own feelings of terror and anxiety reflected upon the pallid faces of his brethren. As night fell the scouts came in announcing the approach of the enemy. Meantime the military stood to their arms alert and watchful. Fearing lest the insurgents might enter by the bridge, its portcullis was raised, and all means of approach from that side cut off. At day-break the tarred piles of that structure were discovered to be on fire, nor could the conflagration be extinguished till the foot-boards were quite consumed. All night long the streets echoed to the heavy tramp of the military as they passed to-and-fro between the different posts, while the only other sound that invaded the silence of the night was the wailing of women and children, terrified by the anticipation of coming evil. At length morning broke, and its light showed the loyalists a great multitude of people assembled at Ferry-bank, at the farther end of the bridge, evidently with no friendly purpose.

The 13th regiment, under General Fawcett, being expected to arrive on this day, Colonel Watson resolved to make a diversion in their favour, and by engaging the attention of the insurgents to facilitate the entry of the royalist general.

With this intent he led out a force of some three hundred of the garrison, taking his route in the direction of the Three Rocks. More zealous in the cause than his men, the veteran pushed on before them to reconnoitre, but being descried by one of the wary insurgent sentinels, when he had advanced as far Belmount, he was fired at, and fell pierced with a mortal wound.

On seeing the fall of their leader, the troops, who were following at a safer distance, took to flight, the yeomen cavalry, as they galloped into town, well nigh riding down the infantry. Their arrival but served to complete the dismay of the inhabitants. Immediately upon the return of this fruitless expedition, a council of war was held, in which it was decided to evacuate the town forthwith. Before quitting the place, the yeomen determined to murder the prisoners in the gaol. But the resolute and wary governor, true to his trust, foiled them on this occasion, as he had done on the previous one, to which we have referred. In the present perilous situation, Mr. Harvey's supposed popularity gave him no little importance in the eyes of the Orange gentry. A number of them waited upon that worthy, but it must be acknowledged not very heroic personage. They found him hiding in the chimney of his cell, up which he had clambered on hearing that the yeomanry designed to attack the prison. Being hauled down from that undignified retreat, with no small exertion on the part of his visitors, in a very begrimed condition, he was politely informed of their object in seeking him. His fears abated on being told that instead of coming to take his life his visitors only desired him to try and save their own by proceeding to the insurgent camp and using his influence there to obtain as favourable terms as possible for the loyalists.

He could not, however, be induced to undertake this commission, but consented to write a letter to the insurgents. The epistle penned by Mr. Harvey on this occasion is as follows :—" I have been treated in prison with all possible humanity, and am now at liberty. I have procured the liberty of all the prisoners. If you pretend to Christian charity, do not commit massacre, or burn the property of the inhabitants, and spare your prisoners' lives.—B. B. HARVEY. *Wednesday, May 30th,* 1798." To find some trustworthy person to bear this missive to its destination was the next step to be taken. A Catholic yeoman named Doyle presented himself, but his offer was contemptuously rejected—he was a 'Papist,' and therefore quite unworthy in the eyes of the senders to undertake any important commission on their behalf. At length two brothers named Richards—both counsellors—were pitched upon, and despatched immediately to the 'Three Rocks.' No sooner had these gentlemen set out on their mission than the military began to make the hastiest preparations for flight. The sending of the embassy was in truth nothing but a wily and dishonest stratagem to engage the attention of the insurgents and to retard their advance till all the sinister designs of the royalist garrison had been effected. The town now presented an extraordinary spectacle. The military having thrown off all discipline, presented the appearance of an armed mob, confused, disorderly, and terrified, but cruel and truculent even in the extremity of their terror. The North Cork were the first to quit the town, setting fire to their barracks as they abandoned it.

The yeomanry delayed their departure for some time, employing the interval in destroying such ammunition as they could not carry away with them—plundering some houses and setting fire to others. All ranks seemed equally affected by the disgraceful panic of the moment—the royalist officers displaying no less cowardice than the common men. Some of the gentlemen in question tore off their epaulets and other insignia of rank, while others, thinking this precaution insufficient, divested themselves of their uniforms, and replaced them with such tattered and beggarly garments as they could procure, and thus metamorphosed, hurried down to the quay, and threw their swords and pistols into the river. Mr. Hay, a witness of this scene, thus describes it :—"The confusion and dismay which prevailed was so great, as no kind of signal for retreat had been given, that officers and privates ran promiscuously through the town, threw off their uniforms, and hid themselves wherever they thought they could be best concealed. Some ran to the different quays in expectation of finding boats to convey them off, and threw their arms and ammunition into the river. All such as could accomplish it embarked on board the vessels in the harbour, having previously turned their horses loose. Some ran to the gaol to put themselves under the protection of Mr. Harvey . . . In short, it is impossible that a greater appearance of confusion, tumult, or panic could be at all exhibited."

This scene of confusion and terrified preparation for flight did not escape the vigilant eyes of the multitude assembled since early dawn at Ferrybank. Aware of the intentions of the loyalists, they strove hard to repair the bridge, so as to be enabled to cross over and hinder their escape. While these transactions were going forward within the town, and in its immediate vicinity, the two brothers despatched to the Three Rocks by the loyalists were engaged in endeavouring to obtain terms of capitulation from the insurgents. They stipulated on the part of those who sent them that the town, together with all the arms and ammunition it contained, should be delivered up to the captors, on the sole condition that the lives of the garrison should be spared. To these terms the insurgents at length agreed, and, detaining one of the brothers, sent the other, in company with Mr. Fitzgerald, to see that the conditions were faithfully carried out. When they arrived at the town they found, to their great surprise, that it had been already evacuated by the military.

Meantime the insurgents at Ferrybank having succeeded in repairing the bridge, though too late to prevent the escape of their treacherous enemy, came pouring into the town, rending the air with shouts of triumph. Immediately on entering, they proceeded to the gaol, and liberated the prisoners, many of whom were their friends and relatives.

The town now threw off its mourning aspect, and assumed a gay and lively air to correspond with the feelings of its new occupants and masters.

In a marvellously brief space of time the quaint old houses of the sober town were profusely decorated with boughs of all sizes, and of every shade of the same pleasant hue. All the doors were thrown open, and the freest hospitality offered to the new-comers, which, though no doubt, quite sincere on the part of some of the inhabitants, was more than doubtful on that of others. So suspicious were the peasantry of the sincerity of this welcome when proffered by known loyalists, that they required of them to taste the liquor they offered them before partaking of it, for they believed these worthies were quite capable of poisoning the draught, not being in the least deceived by the false colours they had hung out.

None were at this juncture more demonstrative in their exhibitions of affectionate welcome than those adherents of the Orange faction who remained in town.

No houses were decorated with a greater profusion of green boughs—no hats displayed the green cockade more conspicuously than theirs. Shortly after the arrival of this body of peasantry, the insurgent army from the Three Rocks marched in and halted at the Windmill Hill. On being informed of the treacherous ruse played upon them by the garrison, they gave way for a time to violent rage, and could with difficulty be dissuaded by their leaders from setting fire to the town, for they deemed the inhabitants accomplices in the deception practised upon them. However, the anger of the duped insurgents confined itself to the pillage and burning of but one house, that of Captain Boyd of the Wexford yeomanry, a notorious persecutor—with this exception, the town sustained no injury at their hands. Those Orangemen who had taken refuge on board the shipping in the harbour, were now led back to town.

Two of their number were sacrificed to popular vengeance. These were John Boyd, brother of Captain Boyd above-mentioned, and George Sparrow, an Enniscorthy butcher, both Orangemen, and both of infamous character. They were piked on the quay soon after landing. While these transactions are in progress in the captured town, the fugitive military are on their way to Duncannon Fort.

They marched rapidly through the country till they had gained what they deemed a safe distance from Wexford, and then began to advance at a more leisurely pace till they reached the village of Mayglass. Here they first began to glut their brutal rage by the slaughter of a number of unoffending people, who had come out from their houses to gaze upon them as they marched past.* They also found time to set fire to the Catholic church of Mayglass. In their further progress no one they encountered escaped their fury, not even the women and children. On the ensuing morning, these murderous banditti, exhausted by their long march, reached Duncannon Fort.

This eventful day at length came to a close, and night fell upon the liberated town as peacefully as if nothing had occurred to disturb its wonted tranquillity. But on the ensuing morning the streets were thronged with a busy and excited multitude. An eager search was instituted for ammunition, of which the insurgents stood sorely in need, and their chagrin was excessive at finding only three barrels of gunpowder. The mar-

* "Their course through a country, which had as yet remained perfectly quiet, was marked with devastation, the burning of houses, and the shooting of unarmed peasants."—Rev. Mr. Gordon's "History of Ireland."

tial spirit of the victorious insurgents did not suffer them to rest while an enemy trod the soil of their country, nor were their leaders less prompt in action, than the men who marched under their command.

Early on the morning succeeding the capture of the town the insurgent leaders issued orders to their men to march out and encamp on the Windmill Hill, leaving behind only such a force as they judged sufficient to garrison the town.

CHAPTER IX.

Two divisions of the Insurgent army march from Windmill Hill, taking separate routes.—Force under Father John Murphy joined by that under Fathers Roche and Kearns.—Attack on Newtownbarry.—March of the royal troops from Gorey and Carnew against the insurgents on Carrigrew.—Defeat and death of Colonel Walpole.—Flight of General Loftus.—Mr. Plowden on the above-mentioned affairs.—Esmond Kyan's services.—Joyful surprise of the people of Gorey.—Results of these victories.—Speech of Mr. Fox in the British House of Commons.—Loss sustained at this period by the English.

MEANTIME the armed thousands posted on the Windmill Hill were told of the final determination of their leaders to divide their force into two divisions, each of which would take a different route. Accordingly, General Harvey and the corps under his immediate command, who were chiefly men from Forth and Bargy, took the direction of Taghmon, and encamped there for the night. The second division, comprising those gallant men who had won the battles of Oulart and Enniscorthy, and were for the greater part from the northern parts of the county, set out once more in the direction of Gorey, passing on their way the scenes of their former victories. Though they had consented to the appointment of Harvey as commander-in-chief, they had formed a true estimate of his capability, and justly placed far more confidence

in the man who had often led them to victory,
Father John, their own brave Soggarth. On the first
day's march of what we may call their second campaign, they were joined by the Rev. Philip Roche
and the Rev. Father Kearns. Father Roche possessed
in an eminent degree those personal advantages so highly
prized by his countrymen. He was brave and handsome, of pleasing manners, and well fitted in every way
to be a popular leader. Father Kearns was a man of
great size and strength, whose scorn of danger, and
confidence in his own strength and activity, were evinced
by his going into action armed only with a heavy riding
whip. However, his courage degenerated into rashness,
and his self-reliance was unallied with other qualities
as indispensable in a leader.

Soon after his arrival, Father Kearns proposed that
an attack should be made on the soldiery stationed at
Newtownbarry, with the design of driving them thence,
and thus opening communication with the counties of
Wicklow and Carlow, affording their inhabitants, who
were at the time being hunted down like wild beasts,
an opportunity of finding a rallying place among the
conquering Wexford men. This proposal was joyfully
consented to, and Father Kearns himself being chosen
leader of the enterprise he had suggested, soon found
himself at the head of about two thousand men, chiefly
armed with pikes, for even at this period firearms of any
description were rare among the insurgents.

These soldiers of freedom proceeded without delay
towards their destination, preserving, in their progress,
as much appearance of military order as could have been
expected. They encountered no enemy on their march
save some bodies of mounted yeomanry, who fled as they
approached, or if they attempted to make a stand it was
but for a moment, being unable to withstand the impetuous charge of the determined pikemen. It is an ad-

mitted fact that in few instances could those well-armed and well-mounted men be brought to face the undisciplined and ill-armed insurgents, who had little to rely on but their native valour, heightened by the sense of wrong, and the consciousness of fighting in a just cause.

When this division arrived within sight of the town, they halted, in order to repose for a brief while after their long and rapid march. During this halt one of the men approached Father Kearns, and modestly suggested that it would be prudent, in case the attack succeeded, to occupy a similar position on the opposite side of the town as a precaution against any possible surprise. Unfortunately Father Kearns slighted this wise counsel, and thereby, as we shall see, lost the town, though successful in the first assault. After a short interval of rest, Father Kearns, having first invoked, aloud, the Divine aid, gave the signal for attack. The insurgents rushed down the slope of the hill on which they had halted, with their customary impetuosity, and in a few minutes reached the town. Their confident courage was nothing daunted by the sight of five hundred regular troops, under the command of Colonel L'Estrange, arrayed against them, together with several corps of the despised yeomanry; for the people had so often defeated both soldiery and yeomanry that they began, as a natural consequence, to hold them in contempt.

On this occasion, as on others, the united charge of the stalwart peasantry, their semi-military line bristling with the formidable pike, carried all before it. After a brief and feeble resistance, the regular troops retreated with the greatest precipitation; and, as for the yeomen, they galloped off, after making a feint of resistance, to seek revenge for their defeat in burning the houses and slaughtering the defenceless friends of their peasant foemen.

However, all the advantages thus gained by the gallant onset of the insurgents were lost by the neglect of the precaution above mentioned; for the flying soldiery were encountered, when only a short distance outside the town, by a detachment of the King's County Militia despatched to their aid. On receiving this timely reinforcement they rallied, and soon determined to return to the town, reckoning on their taking the enemy by surprise.

Acting on this resolve, they returned once more and found their lately victorious enemy dispersed here and there through the place, and, as might be supposed, had little difficulty in driving them outside the walls. Thus what valour had so lately won, lack of prudence now lost.

However, though surprised and divided, they fought bravely, and inflicted, in their retreat, considerable loss on the enemy. In this way was Newtownbarry lost and won, and with it all the advantages that would have accrued to the insurgent cause from its possession.

Thus were all the efforts of these valiant peasants rendered unavailing by the neglect of an ordinary precaution. But, while we regret the error and its consequences, we can hardly blame such novices in the art of war for an error into which trained troops have often fallen.

The men whose enterprise had thus failed were now forced to march by small detachments to reach the only rallying place known to them—the camp on Vinegar Hill. The greater number of them reached that rendezvous the same night, and early on the following morning set out to rejoin their comrades, whom they found encamped on the hill of Carrigrew. They were received kindly by them, and found them busily engaged in acquiring some knowledge of military manœuvres, under the direction of such patriotic yeomen as had left their corps, or had been expelled therefrom on suspicion of being United Irishmen. While the insurgents are thus wisely endeavouring to acquire that training which, united to their dauntless valour, would have rendered them invincible, the English commanders were not idle, but were making preparations to attack, with an irresistible force, the foe they had at first despised, but had now learned to dread.

On the morning of the 4th of June tidings reached the insurgent camp at Carrigrew that two divisions of the regular army were on the march from Gorey and Carnew to attack them; moreover, that each division of this formidable force was furnished with artillery, and accompanied by several corps of mounted yeomanry. They were to meet near the insurgent position, and unite for a combined attack.* Of the large forces thus acting in concert against the insurgents, General Loftus and General Walpole were the commanders.

To oppose such a formidable array of trained troops, provided with every warlike munition, and led on by officers of high rank and experience, the means at the command of the insurgent leaders seemed but too inadequate. They were strong, indeed, in numbers, and in the possession of a brave and determined spirit, but destitute of all else that render men formidable in war. They had neither cavalry nor artillery, their fire-arms were but few, and their supply of powder and ball extremely scanty.

Greater part of the men were, it is true, by this time possessed of pikes—admirable weapons when used in a close fight, but otherwise useless. Yet, notwithstanding

* "The royal army marched from Gorey in two divisions; one under the immediate command of General Loftus, by a more circuitous route; the other was led on by Colonel Walpole direct for the camp. The troops were in high spirits; their number, discipline, and well-concerted arrangements, left no room to doubt of success."—"Personal Narrative of the Irish Rebellion," by Charles Hamilton Teeling, p. 163.

all these disadvantages, which would have been quite
sufficient to induce any but Irishmen to abandon the
contest as useless, the men on Carrigrew, confident of
their own courage, and proud of their heroic leaders,
resolved to meet their enemies once more in battle. The
insurgent leaders having consulted together in this perilous
and critical situation, concerning the best course
to be adopted, resolved to march without delay and attack
that division of royal troops just then advancing
towards them from Gorey, and having, as they hoped,
defeated them, to proceed to the release of the unfortunate
men confined and awaiting execution in that town.

Having come to this resolve, the insurgents once more
quitted Carrigrew, and, halting at a short distance from
that eminence, on level ground, proceeded, under the
direction of their chiefs, to put in practice some of the
lessons they had received in the art-military a little
while before.

They soon fell into fair marching order, and, at the
word of command, set off at a pace that few armies
could have maintained.

A body of two hundred chosen pikemen, with gunsmen
interspersed, preceded the main body at the distance
of a mile. In the meantime Colonel Walpole,
against whose division they were on the march,* had

* Walpole had been warned of the approach of the insurgents
by a loyal Protestant named Thomas Dowling, whose intelligence
he slighted.—Gordon.

"This gentleman was a relative and favorite of Lord Camden's.
He was no soldier; but being ambitious of signalizing himself in
the rebellion, had, through importunity at the Castle, where favor
had too frequently outweighed merit, procured the command of
five hundred men. He had only one quality of a soldier—courage,
which without discretion in a commander becomes rashness. He
refused to employ scouts or flanking parties, and was not aware of
the enemy till they were within gun-shot. He was conspicuously
mounted on a white charger in full uniform and plumage."—
Plowden, "Historical Review," p. 728.

information of their advance, and led out his men to meet them.

Having advanced a short distance beyond the village of Tubberneering, he halted at a spot where the road takes a sharp turn to the right in the direction of Carrigrew, so that a body of men advancing from that direction would be likely to march right into sudden view of the enemy, and, consequently, surprised and panic-stricken, would fall an easy prey. Thus reasoned the English chief, and thus, with his chosen troops drawn up in line of battle, his powerful and numerous artillery in good position to sweep the insurgent ranks with a discharge of ball and canister, his cavalry all impatient to make havoc among the peasantry, routed and disordered by the fire of musketry and cannon, the royalist officer awaited the approach of the insurgent army.

He was not long kept in expectation.

The advanced guard of the insurgents arrived at the point where the road made the sharp turn described, and, marching in a compact body, and with quick step, came suddenly in the presence of their red-coated foes, who instantly welcomed them with a combined and terrible fire of artillery and musketry.

The insurgents, on receiving this unexpected salutation, halted, and one of the few horsemen who accompanied them was instantly despatched by their leader to apprise the main body of the presence of the enemy. During this brief halt the insurgent vanguard had kept their ranks manfully, and now advanced amid a storm of death-dealing missiles to take up a less exposed position behind a ditch that lay at some distance on their left. While crossing a large field which extended between them and the shelter they sought, they suffered great loss from the enemy, who continued to pour into their thinning ranks a deadly discharge of all arms.

The insurgents at length gained the ditch, which, as they had hoped, afforded them protection from the enemy's fire, and thence in their turn commenced and maintained a telling fire on the hostile ranks. The insurgent fire was extremely destructive, for those of them who were armed with guns were for the most part practised sportsmen, and the ditch behind which they lay was but half musket shot from the royal troops. Thus the insurgent advanced guard galled the royalists and kept them in check, for the latter feared to advance and drive the gunsmen from their shelter, for though insignificant in number, they knew them to be accompanied by the pikemen, who had ever proved such terrible foes at close quarters.

The main body of their dreaded enemy now appeared in swift and impetuous advance, drawn up in the form of a crescent, and bristling all over with the formidable pike. The advancing insurgents avoided the open ground on which their advanced guard had suffered such severe loss, and, keeping towards the left, seemed determined to assail the royal troops on their left flank, while the gunsmen engaged them in front.

On seeing this large body advancing to attack his division, already disheartened by the loss they had sustained from the persistent and fatal fire of their sharp-shooting foes, the royalist commander gave orders for retreat.

But while the royal gunners, in obedience to this welcome command, were engaged in harnessing their horses to the gun-carriages, they were surprised and taken, together with their iron charges and all that appertained to them, by the advanced guard, who now sallied from behind the ditch they had so defended.

The insurgents, who were as merciful as they were brave, treated their prisoners kindly, and soon applied themselves to learn from them the management of the destructive weapons they had so gallantly captured.

Colonel Walpole, though thus forced to retreat before his peasant foe, resolved, like a brave soldier, to make a final stand, and thus decide the contest. With this determination he halted at Clough, a village between Gorey and Tubberneering. Here he was reinforced by a company of grenadiers, despatched by General Loftus to his aid—until that officer should arrive with his whole division. The rallied troops of Walpole, reinforced by the grenadiers of Loftus, were not long awaiting the second attack from their determined foe, who soon appeared in sight, advancing at a running pace, with the evident design of coming immediately to close quarters, and thus avoiding the sustained and destructive fire of their opponents. The English troops had just time to pour a few hasty volleys into the rapidly advancing ranks, and then the pikemen closed with them.

The clubbed musket and the bayonet proved in this as in all former contests, but a poor defence against the long pike borne by the insurgents.

In addition to the advantage the peasantry derived from such an effective weapon as the pike in such contests as we describe, they were themselves in strength and agility superior to the royal troops; and, practised in every athletic exercise, they wielded their arms with resistless force. The issue of the combat might have been foreseen once the insurgents closed with their foes. The regular troops were completely routed, and fled in the utmost confusion and terror, throwing away their arms and accoutrements to facilitate their escape. Yet with all this they were captured in great numbers by their swift-footed pursuers, who, as usual, treated them with kindness, contrary, as it seemed, to the expectation of the fugitives, many of whom were found with their coats turned inside out, to denote, doubtless, a corresponding change in their sentiments sufficiently great to incline the victors to mercy.

When the contest was over, the gallant Walpole was found lying dead beside his charger on the field, while stretched around were numbers of killed and wounded. Thus ended the engagements at Tubberneering and at Clough.*

Of the above described actions, Mr. Plowden says:†—

"The rebels surprised a division under Colonel Walpole, at a place called Tubberneering. The rebels instantly poured a tremendous fire from the fields on both sides of the road, and he received a bullet through the head from the first fire. His troops fled in the utmost disorder, leaving their cannon in the hands of the enemy. They were pursued as far as Gorey, in their flight through which they were galled by the fire of some of the rebels who had taken station in the houses. The unfortunate loyalists of Gorey once more fled to Arklow with the routed army, leaving all their effects behind. While Walpole's division was attacked by the enemy, General Loftus being within hearing of the musketry, detached seventy men, the grenadier company of the Antrim militia, across the fields to its assistance, but they were intercepted by the rebels, and almost all taken or killed. The General still ignorant of the fate of Colonel Walpole's division, and unable to bring his artillery across the fields, continued his march along the highway, by a long circuit, to the field of battle, where he was first acquainted with the melancholy event. For some way he followed the rebels towards Gorey, but finding them posted on Gorey hill, from which they fired upon him the cannon taken from

---

* The official accounts of these engagements were suppressed—why it is not difficult to divine.

† Historical Review of the State of Ireland, p. 128.

Colonel Walpole, he retreated to Carnew; and still, contrary to the opinion of most of his officers, thinking Carnew an unsafe post, though at the head of twelve hundred effective men, he abandoned that part of the country to the rebels, and retreated nine miles farther, to the town of Tullow, in the county of Carlow."

The insurgents, though wearied by their long march and subsequent hard fighting, pushed on rapidly towards Gorey, resolved to allow their routed foe no time to put into execution the vengeance they were well aware they meditated on the prisoners there confined. So closely did they press on their flying enemy that the latter had no time to rally their broken ranks, or to put into execution their cruel purpose. They had barely time to fire in through the window of the prison on those confined therein, who, at the suggestion of Esmond Kyan, one of their number, by throwing themselves on the ground, avoided the otherwise fatal volley. On the arrival of the insurgents at Gorey, the prisoners who had thus narrowly escaped death were set at liberty.

Esmond Kyan, who understood the management of artillery, was placed in command of the pieces lately captured. The insurgents now pitched their camp on a hill outside the town, and there awaited the appearance of General Loftus, who, as they were aware, was then on his way to join the troops of Walpole, of whose defeat he was yet uninformed.

On the appearance of this officer, he was received with a well-directed discharge from the captured cannon.

This unexpected salute proved too much for the courage of Loftus and his soldiery. Seized with panic, they took to their heels, and were perceived by some of the mounted insurgents sent after them to ascertain their route, in full flight in the direction of Carnew.

The insurgents, well nigh exhausted by their previous

exertions and want of food, did not feel inclined to pursue them, and, having no cavalry, were forced to allow them to escape unmolested.

The success of these engagements was chiefly due to the prompt advance of the insurgents to meet Walpole while on his march to Carrigrew, instead of waiting to be attacked by that officer and Colonel Loftus at their encampment on the hill.

By this energetic movement, they disconcerted the plan agreed on by two English leaders, and, as we have seen, put them both to flight in separate engagements.

Loftus seems to have entertained a salutary dread of the pikemen, for it is evident that had he wished to reinforce Walpole, he could easily have arrived in time as well as the detachment of grenadiers that bore a part in the contest.

The inhabitants of Gorey and of the surrounding district, so many of whom had been rescued from death by the success and timely advance of the insurgent army, now came flocking around their deliverers, testifying in every possible way their gratitude for a boon as great as it was unhoped for. Many of them declared that on beholding the formidable array of foot, horse, and artillery that marched out of the town with the joyful and proud confidence of men who go to certain victory, they entertained but little hope of their ill-armed and undisciplined countrymen offering any effectual resistance.

They moreover affirmed that Walpole felt so confident of victory that he had received several wagers that the "rebels" would not sustain for twenty minutes the combined onset of the royal forces, aided as they were by more than a dozen corps of yeomen cavalry.

The insurgents, remembering their surprise at Newtownbarry, resolved to take precautions against a similar misfortune, and to this effect they took care to post sentinels at all the advances to the town.

They adopted, moreover, the further precaution of posting a strong guard on the road to Arklow, whence they deemed an attack most likely to be made. However, the arrival of a large body of Arklow men at the insurgent camp, with the tidings that the royal troops had evacuated the town in question, set them at ease on that point.

The night of the 4th of June passed away quietly in the camp of the brave insurgents, whose dauntless courage success had so happily crowned.

Here we may mention that such as escaped of the routed troops of Walpole, after passing through Gorey, continued their flight to Arklow, which they also left behind them, nor finally halted till they reached Dublin. The troops commanded by Loftus ended their flight at Tullow.

These decisive victories made the insurgents masters of the entire county of Wexford, with the exception of Newtownbarry, New Ross, and Duncannon Fort, which are situate on its borders. They had also possession of that part of Wicklow which lies between Arklow and the Wexford boundary. The gallant Wicklow men had greatly aided their Wexford neighbours; and had other counties acted such a noble part English rule in Ireland would now be a thing of the past. "It was now," says Mr. Teeling, "that the Irish government became seriously alarmed. They had kindled a war in the heart of the country, and it was doubtful whether they possessed the power of extinguishing it. The incessant marching and counter-marching of the troops, the fatigues they encountered, the losses they had sustained, the several posts they had been forced to abandon, all tended to lower that spirit with which they were animated on first taking the field . . Intemperate counsels had placed the country on the brink of ruin, and the more reflecting on both sides looked with awful suspense to the result. Mr. Fox, ever sensitively alive to the honour of his country and the feelings of humanity, again appealed to the British senate, and implored the minister to halt in his desperate career, and extend, ere it should be too late, the hand of conciliation to Ireland. 'I hold,' said he, 'documents incontrovertible which show that this sanguinary contest has already cost his Majesty's forces the loss of *ten thousand men;*' and, in the name of justice and humanity, he moved for an inquiry into the state of Ireland. The feeling and energetic appeal of Mr. Fox was ineffectual, and with it the last hope of conciliation fled."

CHAPTER X.

Preparation made by the insurgents under General Harvey for the assault upon New-Ross.—Harvey sends an officer with a flag of truce to demand the surrender of the town.—Death of the envoy.—Letter found upon his person.—Death of Lord Mountjoy.—New-Ross, its situation.—Dispositions for its defence made by General Johnson.—Various accounts of the battle.—How it began.—Marvellous courage displayed by the insurgents, acknowledged even by their enemies.—Colonel Clooney's attack upon the loyalists posted in the market-place and at Irishtown.—Return of the loyalists.—Their subsequent success.—Real cause of the insurgent defeat.—Number of killed and wounded on both sides.—Accounts given by various writers.—Heroism displayed by a boy of thirteen.—A heroine.—The burning of Scullabogue.—Further details of this massacre.—Examination of Mr. Frizel at the bar of the House of Commons.—Last proclamation issued by General Harvey.—His resignation.—The insurgents quit Carrickburn and arrive at Sleive-Keolter—The forging of false despatches by loyalist officers proved.

THE division of the insurgent army, under the immediate command of General-in-Chief Bagnal Harvey, having bivouacked for the night of the 30th near Taghmon, arrived at Carrickburn on the next day, where they remained till the 4th of June, when they set out for Corbet Hill, within a mile of Ross, which town it was decided should be attacked on the morning of the ensuing day. The insurgent leaders decided that a simultaneous attack should be made on the town at three different points.

Before General Harvey issued orders for the assault he despatched an aide-de-camp named Furlong with a flag of truce to summon the garrison to surrender.

This commission proved fatal to the bearer; for scarce had Furlong approached within view of the outpost, bearing aloft the flag of truce, than he was fired on by a sentinel and fell mortally wounded. In his pocket was found the following letter from Harvey to General Johnson:—"SIR—As a friend to humanity, I request you will surrender the town of Ross to the Wexford forces now assembled against that town. Your resistance will but provoke rapine and plunder, to the ruin of the in-

K

nocent. Flushed with victory, the Wexford forces, now innumerable and irresistible, will not be controlled if they meet with resistance. To prevent, therefore, the total ruin of all property in the town, I urge you to a speedy surrender, which you will be forced to in a few hours, with loss and bloodshed, as you are surrounded on all sides. Your answer is required in four hours. Mr. Furlong carries this letter and will bring the answer.— I am, sir, B. B. HARVEY, General Commanding-in-Chief. *Camp at Corbet Hill, half-past three o'clock in the morning. June 25th, 1798."*

This shooting of bearers of flags of truce seems to have been quite a matter of course with the military. It however taught the insurgents that they should neither show mercy to, nor expect it from, such a faithless foe, and doubtless led to the death of Lord Mountjoy soon after, as he advanced before his regiment with the intention of parleying with them while advancing.

The town of Ross,* about to be the scene of a bloody

---

* " The battle of Ross, with respect to its incidents and extensive results, was one of the most important of the insurrection. Ross is surrounded on three sides by steep hills, and on the fourth by a river, dividing it from the southern counties, and having a long wooden bridge. The possession of Ross, therefore, would open a communication with the southern insurgents, who were prepared to rise *en masse* the moment their friends should occupy that town; and the city of Waterford, and probably the whole of the western and southern counties, would have risen in their favour."

" Their General, Beauchamp Bagenal Harvey, was of all men probably the most unfit for so desperate an enterprise; his figure diminutive, his voice tremulous. He was a Protestant barrister of fortune; good tempered and of good private character; and was selected from being Lord of Bargy Castle and of considerable demesnes in the county of Wexford.

" Of individual courage he had sufficient, but of that manly heroic intrepidity which converts danger into enthusiasm and is indispensable to the leader of such an army and such a cause, he was altogether unsusceptible . . . Harvey and his aide-de-camp, contest, was garrisoned by about two thousand regular troops under the command of General Johnson, in addition to which large force there were several corps of yeomanry. Ross was at this time a walled town, and the principal entrance from the southern side was by the *Three-bullet* Gate. Towards this gate the road by which the insurgents were about to advance led in nearly a straight line with a high ditch at either side. The fields extended to within a few perches of the wall, and were enclosed by ditches similar to those which bounded the road. General Johnson, rightly judging that the principal attack would be made on this gate, had posted thereat a strong force in the most advantageous positions within and without, while two six-pounders were planted so as to pour their fire upon any body of men advancing along the road before mentioned. Behind the ditches on either side of the road, and in every other available cover, soldiers were placed to gall with their fire the expected assailants. It must be admitted that to force an entrance through a post so well guarded was an enterprise of no easy nature, but yet the undisciplined and ill-armed insurgents undertook and effected the task. All who have written of the eventful period vary materially in their accounts of the battle of Ross. Hay, who seems to have been at much pains to obtain accurate information, gives what he, no doubt, believed to be a correct account of the engagement, while Clooney,

Mr. Gray, a Protestant attorney, remained upon a neighbouring hill, inactive spectators during ten hours' successive *fighting*."— Sir Jonah Barrington's " *Rise and Fall of the Irish Nation*," p. 450.

Mr. Harvey was reputed by his contemporaries a man of courage, yet he displayed undoubted cowardice during this desperate battle. His reputation was founded upon the fact of his having fought several duels. A similar anomaly appeared in the conduct of such of the peasantry as had been noted before the insurrection for their excessive pugnacity at rural gatherings. When it came to real fighting, these 'bullies' generally made a poor figure,

who took an active part in the affair, differs from him
in many important particulars. Both these impartial
writers concur, however, in stating that the greater
number of the men who formed the camp on Corbet Hill
took no part in the battle, and that one of the divisional
leaders deserted his post at the very beginning of the
assault. It appears that not more than three thousand
men took part in the assault, and that great part even
of these left before the battle was finally decided.*
While the insurgents' officers were marshalling their
men as best they could preparatory to the attack, they
were much annoyed and sustained some loss by a sharp
fire, maintained by the enemy's outposts. Seeing this,
General Harvey ordered Colonel Kelly to charge, and
drive in these outposts with the battalion of Bantry-men †
under his command. This order the brave young colonel
so well obeyed that he drove them before him in confusion to the very walls of the town. Kelly found it
much easier to lead his men to the charge than to withdraw them from it, and they were soon hotly engaged
with the defenders of the gate. Clooney, who had commanded a similar battalion of Bantry-men, and had been
ordered by Harvey to support Kelly, now rushed forward
to join in the fray. The main body of the insurgents,
seeing their comrades in actual conflict with the enemy,
could no longer be restrained, and, despite the efforts of
their leaders, poured down swiftly towards the scene of
strife. This ardour, so natural in undisciplined men,
entirely disconcerted the original plan of assault. The
entire battle was now fought between the defenders of
the gate and their assailants. From the gates, from the
walls, and from the ditches, the military poured a close
and terrible fire on the fierce assailants, who, though

---

* Mr. Gordon says: "Of the insurgents on Corbet Hill not
more than a half or perhaps a fourth descended to the combat."

† From Bantry, a Wexford barony.

they fell in great numbers under a withering fire, still kept rushing forward with matchless intrepidity* to supply the place of their fallen comrades. Even those who write in the bitterest spirit of hostility to the insurgents, speak of their conduct on this occasion in the following terms:—"Such was their enthusiasm that, though whole ranks of them were seen to fall, they were succeeded by others, who seemed to court the fate of their companions by rushing on our troops with renovated ardour." (Sir Richard Musgrave).

An English officer, forced into an involuntary admiration of the reckless bravery with which these devoted people fought, exclaimed, "that the devils out of hell could not resist them." After half an hour of this desperate fighting the soldiery began to fall back inside the gate, while their assailants took possession of the barracks, which stood a short distance from the wall. Here it was that the young hero, Colonel Kelly, was disabled by a shot in the thigh. At this period of the fight a strong squadron of the Fifth Dragoon Guards made a sally from the town by a lane, hoping to take the insurgents in the rere. This, however, they failed to do, and were themselves charged by the fierce pikemen, who in a few minutes slew twenty-

* Of the courage displayed by the insurgents in this action we have more than sufficient testimony. We give that of two witnesses. An old gentleman named Harris, who died since the first edition of this work was published, was present at the battle of Ross as captain of yeomanry, and was wont to tell of the extraordinary bravery exhibited by the insurgents in endeavouring to force a passage over the bridge, though it was swept every moment by chain shot, which literally mowed them down by dozens at each discharge. Counsellor Lundyfoot, a friend of Sir Jonah Barrington, was also present, and described to him "the desperate valour of the peasantry." Had these brave men a competent leader instead of the imbecile Harvey they would have driven the English into the sea.

eight of their number, together with their cornet, Dodwell. An amazon named Doyle, who marched with the insurgent army and bore herself as gallantly as the most courageous man, now made herself useful by cutting off with a bill-hook the cross belts of the fallen dragoons, and handing them, together with the cartouche boxes, to her comrades. The insurgents having by this time won the gate, General Johnson judged it time to sound a retreat, which signal was obeyed by his troops with more speed than dignity, while their successful opponents, with shouts of triumph, poured into the town for whose possession they had so bravely contended.

Though General Johnson, with the main body of his troops, had evacuated the town, yet the insurgents could not be considered complete masters of it, for the main guard of the hostile army, with two swivel guns, still kept possession of the market-place, while Major Vandeleur, with the Clare Militia, still maintained his ground at a suburb called Irishtown. Great numbers of the insurgents were now dispersed throughout the town in search of some refreshment, which they sorely needed. Some writers assert that on this occasion the peasantry gave way to intemperance, and thereby lost the battle, but their fault, if any, has been greatly exaggerated, and it is clear that the subsequent loss of the town was owing to other causes than intemperance. Many of the peasantry who had taken part in the attack upon the town had already departed for their homes, great numbers of the bravest men had been slain, and those that remained in partial possession of the town were well nigh exhausted by continued exertion, that proved too much even for their hardy, vigorous frames. The town remained in possession of its new masters for some four hours. During this time Colonel S. Clooney collected all the men he could to follow him, and,

strange to say, he could not find more than forty, and
led them first to dislodge the guard that still kept
possession of the market-place, but he was received
with so hot a fire from the men that held the building,
and their adherents in the neighbouring houses, that
he was forced to retreat. Foiled in this attempt, the
same brave and energetic chief proceeded, with his
small body of men, to drive the Clare Militia from their
position at Irishtown. This was evidently an enterprise of a desperate nature, but Clooney, who seems to
have been a man of extraordinary daring, did not seem
to think so. He led his handful of wearied men across
two fields, all the while exposed to the fire of the
enemy, but naively confesses that he could not get them
to mount a ditch that separated them from their far
more numerous foes. Meantime General Johnson who,
with the main body of his army, had been compelled, as
we have seen, to beat a hasty retreat from the town,
finding himself unmolested in his retreat, altered his
previous determination of altogether abandoning the
place to the insurgents, and resolved to make a final
effort to regain possession of it. The County of Dublin
Militia, burning to revenge the death of their Colonel,
Lord Mountjoy, led the advance. The result might have
been anticipated; they found their enemies dispersed
through the town, unprepared for the attack, and succeeded in driving them out. The insurgents, whom defeat
had once more united, soon renewed the attack with
marvellous courage.* Once more these dauntless men

* Concerning this renewed attack, Mr. Hay says:—"Having
respired a little from their hasty retreat, which in a great degree
made them sober, they again returned to the charge, and the contest which now ensued was maintained on both sides with great
obstinacy, both parties being induced by experience of the former
encounter not to relax their exertions. The intrepidity of the
insurgents was truly remarkable, as, notwithstanding the dreadful

rushed upon their disciplined foes, and, despite the fearful carnage made in their ranks by the terrible fire poured upon them, they charged pike in hand to the very muzzle of the musket and the mouth of the cannon, and drove the soldiery in precipitate flight from the town. Hay states that on this occasion, as on that of their previous success, the victorious insurgents indulged in intemperance. But this statement must be regarded as at least doubtful, and the victory finally won by the king's troops must be attributed to the havoc made in the insurgent ranks by the long continued fire of the artillery and musketry. Soon after this repulse the troops returned once more to the assault, and victory crowned their persevering bravery. After an almost continuous fight of thirteen hours' duration, victory finally rested upon the royal standard. This contest, though it may be deemed inconsiderable with regard to the numbers therein engaged, has never been surpassed in the annals of war for the bravery and determination displayed by the combatants on both sides. Clooney, who is a truthful and impartial writer, estimates the loss of both contending hosts to have been nearly equal, that is about three hundred killed and five hundred wounded on either side. As for the accounts given by such writers as were professed partizans of the Government they are utterly unworthy of credit, as they are proved to have been guilty of systematic and deliberate falsehood and exaggeration.

I am inclined to believe that Mr. Clooney, in his desire not to exaggerate, greatly underrates the loss

havoc made in their ranks by the artillery, they rushed up to the very mouth of the cannon, regardless of the numbers that were falling on all sides of them, and pushed forward with such impetuosity that they obliged the army to retire once more and leave the town to themselves." p. 152.

sustained in this action. Taking into account the fierceness of the struggle and its duration, it is impossible to place it so low. Sir Jonah Barrington estimates the loss on both sides to have been far greater, and is of opinion that upwards of 5000 men were either killed or consumed by the conflagration. The same author relates a singular incident that occurred during the battle:—The insurgents were on the point of being finally repulsed, when a young gentleman of thirteen years of age, from the town of Wexford, of the respectable family of Lett, in that town, who had stolen away from his mother and joined General Harvey on Corbet Hill, saw the disorder of the men and the incapacity of their leaders, and with a boyish impulse he snatched up a standard, and calling out, "Follow me who dare!" rushed down the hill, two or three thousand pikemen rapidly followed him in a tumultuous crowd, and uttering the most appalling cries. In a moment he was at the gate, rallied his party, and with his reinforcement, rushed upon the garrison, who, fatigued and astonished at the renewed vigour of their enemy, were again borne down and compelled with much loss, fighting step by step, to retire towards the bridge.

This was, perhaps, the most important engagement of the entire insurrection, and, had the insurgents succeeded, the final event might have been far different. General Harvey now ordered a retreat to be sounded, and the dispirited insurgents marched off to their former encampment on Carrickburn, unmolested in their retreat by the enemy, who were content with the success they had achieved. The intrepid woman Doyle, before mentioned, seeing the insurgents about to quit the scene of their late combat, and leave a gun they had brought with them behind, seated herself upon it, and spiritedly declared that if "they did not bring her dear little gun with them she would remain behind also at all risks." Ashamed not to comply with the request of the heroine, some of the weary men gave her their aid in conveying away her strange favourite. We must now proceed unwillingly to record a deed of savage cruelty perpetrated by some of the dastardly runaways from the battle of Ross. That the brave men who took part in that combat had no share in the savage deed is distinctly stated by Clooney. Alas! that such recreants had power to stain the otherwise unblemished laurels of the brave insurgents of Wexford.

The burning of Scullabogue has often been cited as an instance of fiendish cruelty. We seek not to paint it otherwise. If it proves anything, it is that there were men amongst the insurgents as cruel and cowardly as amongst their enemies, but their number must have been far smaller in proportion, nor do we find that the insurgent leaders encouraged their followers to the perpetration of such excesses, but, on the contrary, that they did all in their power to prevent them. Can the apologists or panegyrists of the English soldiery or of their more savage allies say with truth as much in their defence?* For one black deed such as the one in question, we can cite hundreds on the part of the partizans of English rule, committed, not in the madness of passion, but with cold-blooded deliberation. For instance, the insurgent depot of wounded men burned in New Ross by the military, the insurgent hospital at Enniscorthy by the yeomen, and the murder by the militia and yeomanry of the sick and wounded insur-

---

* To prove that we do not exaggerate when making mention of the conduct of the loyalists, we give the testimony of the Rev. Mr. Gordon, a Protestant minister, whose son was an officer of yeomanry, and himself a loyalist. "Indeed, it was their settled practice (speaking of the loyalists) to shoot all men they met."—See History, p. 113.

gents in the hospital of Wexford, when the royalists took possession of that town.* An entire chapter might be filled with instances of similar ruthless deeds perpetrated by military, militia, and yeomanry. We must now proceed to describe what occurred at Scullabogue. Before the insurgents marched to the attack on Ross, they despatched their prisoners, to the number of about one hundred, to be confined in the barn of Scullabogue House, at the foot of Carrickburn, and there stationed a guard over them. Of these prisoners we may mention that some twenty were Catholics, and when we say that the remainder were Protestants, it must be remembered that the majority of persons professing Protestantism had manifested by every means in their power the bitterest hostility to their insurgent countrymen in their desperate struggle for liberty, so that they were confined, not as Protestants, but as persons who in a life and death struggle had ranged themselves under a hostile standard. While the battle was raging at Ross, runaways from both armies filled the country around with the most contradictory rumours. At length it was known that the day had gone against the insurgents. The minds of the people were much inflamed by the account of the shooting of the bearer of the flag of truce, the burning of houses with their inmates, and the indiscriminate slaughter by the soldiery.

Popular fury is wild and unreasoning, and destructive in its course as the hurricane, and only required an object on which to wreak its vengeance; in this instance unhappily the object was at hand—the unfortunate prisoners in the barn of Scullabogue. Thither rushed an infuriated crowd, composed mainly of runaways from the battle of Ross, and others who were driven by a

* For the truth of this statement see Hay, Gordon, Clooney, and Plowden's Histories.

thirst for vengeance for their own wrongs to take part in the cruel deed.* In vain Murphy, the captain of the guard, resisted at the peril of his own life—he and his men were fiercely thrust aside, and fuel was immediately applied to the walls of the barn. In vain did the victims endeavour to escape; they came forth from the burning fabric but to fall by the pikes of the savage mob. Those who remained within screamed and implored mercy in piteous accents. But why prolong the description of such a revolting scene? The barn, with all the unfortunate beings it contained, was consumed in the flames. Their terrible revenge being accomplished, the murderers dispersed. The brave men who had fought at Ross heard on their return to Carrickburn with horror and regret of this detestable act of cruelty, and, without doubt, had they then discovered the murderers, they would have inflicted on them such punishment as they deserved.

Of this horrid transaction, Mr. Plowden discourses as follows:—

"Bloody as was the carnage at New Ross, where the rebels were said to have lost between two and three thousand men, the horrors of that scene vanish before the inhuman massacre of a number of unfortunate prisoners, men, women, and children, mostly Protestants, burned to death in a barn at Scullabogue, on the evening of that same day. Scullabogue House, which is the property of a Mr. King, was situated at the foot of Carrickburn Mountain. When the rebel army marched to Corbet Hill, their prisoners had been left under a guard, commanded by John Murphy of Loghnaghur. The runaways declared, that the royal army in Ross

* "A body of fugitives from the battle forced the guard."— Rev. Mr. Gordon.

were shooting all the prisoners, and butchering the Catholics who had fallen into their hands, and feigned an order from Harvey for the execution of those at Scullabogue. This order which Harvey, himself a Protestant and a man of humanity, was utterly incapable of giving, Murphy is said to have resisted, but this resistance was vain. Thirty-seven were shot and piked at the hall-door; and the rest, a hundred and eighty-four in number, according to report, crammed into a barn, were burned alive, the roof being fired, and straw thrown into the flames to feed the conflagration."

In the same year in which the above detailed massacre was enacted, a gentleman named Frizel, who was amongst the prisoners, was examined at the bar of the House of Commons concerning the affair. He was asked every question that could be suggested relative to the massacre, to which his answers were substantially as follows :—

" That having been taken prisoner by a party of the rebels, he was confined to a room on the ground floor in Scullabogue House, with twenty or thirty other persons; that a rebel guard with a pike stood near the window, with whom he conversed; that persons were frequently called out of the room in which he was by name, and he believes were soon after shot, as he heard the reports of muskets, shortly after they had been called out; and that he understood that many were burned in the barn, the smoke of which he could discover from the window; that the sentinel pikemen assured him that they would not hurt a hair of his head as he was always known to have behaved well to the poor; that he did not know of his own knowledge, but only from the reports current amongst the prisoners, what the particular cause was for which the rebels had set fire to the barn." Upon which Mr. Ogle rose with precipitancy from his seat, and put this question to him with great eagerness; " Sir, tell us what the cause was?" It having been suggested that the question would be more regularly put from the chair, it was repeated to him in form, and Mr. Frizel answered, that the only cause he, or he believed the other prisoners, ever understood induced the rebels to this action was, that they had received intelligence that the military were again putting all the rebel prisoners to death in the town of Ross, as they had done at Dunlavin and Carlow. Mr. Ogle asked no more questions of Mr. Frizel, and he was soon afterwards dismissed from the bar.

With a view to put a stop to any repetition of such disgraceful and barbarous deeds, General Harvey immediately issued a proclamation, in which he threatened death to all who should, under any pretext, be guilty of outrages to person or property. This proclamation was as follows:—

"At a meeting of the general and several officers of the united army of the county of Wexford, the following resolutions were agreed upon:—

"Resolved, that the commander-in-chief shall send guards to certain baronies, for the purpose of bringing in all men they shall find loitering and delaying at home, or elsewhere; and that if any resistance be given to those guards so to be sent by the commanding officer's orders, it is our desire and orders that such persons so giving resistance shall be liable to be put to death by the guards, who are to bear a commission for that purpose; and all such persons found to be loitering and delaying at home, when brought in by the guards, shall be tried by a court-martial, appointed and chosen from among the commanders of all the different corps, and be punished with death. Resolved, that all officers shall immediately repair to their respective quarters, and remain with their different corps, and not depart therefrom under pain of death, unless authorized to quit by written orders from the commander-in-chief for that purpose. It is also ordered that a guard shall be kept in the rear of the different armies, with orders to shoot all persons who shall fly or desert from any engagement, and that these orders shall be taken notice of by all officers commanding in such engagement. All men refusing to obey their superior officers, to be tried by court-martial and punished according to their sentence. It is also ordered that all men who shall attempt to leave their respective quarters where they have been halted by the commander-in-chief, shall suffer death, unless they shall have leave from their officers for so doing. It is ordered by the commander-in-chief, that all persons who have stolen or taken away any horse or horses, shall immediately bring in all such horses to the camp, at head-quarters, otherwise for any horse that shall be seen or found in the possession of any person to whom he does not belong, that person shall, on being convicted thereof, suffer death.

"And any goods that shall have been plundered from any house, if not brought into head-quarters, or returned immediately to the houses or owners, that all persons so plundering as aforesaid shall, on being convicted thereof, suffer death.

"*It is also resolved, that any person or persons who shall take upon them to kill or murder any person or prisoner, or burn any house, or commit any plunder, without special written orders from the commander-in-chief, shall suffer death.* By order of

"B. B. HARVEY, Commander-in-Chief.
FRANCIS BREEN, Sec. and Adj.

"*Head Quarters, Carrickbyrne,
Camp, June 6, 1798.*"

In Wexford town a similar proclamation was issued about the same time.

The above-given proclamation was the last issued by Bagenal Harvey, for there were loud murmurs against him arising from his conduct at the battle of Ross. He soon after resigned his command, and was succeeded therein by the Rev. General Philip Roche.

On the third day after the disastrous battle of Ross, the insurgents quitted Carrickburn Hill, and proceeded to that of Slieve Kielter, near which eminence flows the River Barrow. On the first day of their encampment on this hill, they captured a gun-boat which, with two others that escaped, was on its way to Waterford. On board they found, amongst other things, despatches from military officers concerning various engagements that had taken place between the insurgents and the King's troops. These reports were found, on examination, exaggerated and one-sided in the extreme—the loss of the insurgents in every engagement was enormously exaggerated, and that of the royal troops proportionately diminished. Our readers may judge of the value of histories, such as Musgrave's and Maxwell's, compiled from such *truthful* documents.*

---

* Mr. Clooney saw these exaggerated reports himself, as he informs us in his history.

In further proof that *suppressio veri* and *assertio falsi* were systematically carried on by the English commanders, or by the Government, in case the former failed to do as they were expected, we cite the authority of Mr. Hay, who, referring to the battle of Fooke's mill, says, "But although General Moore's despatches concerning the engagement have been published, yet the list of the killed and wounded, mentioned to have been sent in the General's letter, has been suppressed." Thus, when an officer was found too upright to conceal the truth in his despatch, the Government undertook to do it for him!

CHAPTER XI.

Insurgents on Gorey hill.—Difficulty they experienced in obtaining provisions.—Burning of Hunter Gowan's house—Insurgents march towards Carnew.—General Loftus takes refuge in Tullow.—Insurgents hearing of the occupation of Arklow by the loyalists return to Gorey Hill.—Disadvantages under which they laboured.—The Insurgent leader, Father John Murphy.—Exertions made by the Insurgents to acquire military discipline.—How they progressed.—The lack of gunpowder a great obstacle to their success.—Gunsmen and pikemen.

THE second division of the insurgent army, by whom Generals Walpole and Loftus had been so signally defeated, remained during the 5th and 6th of June in their encampment on Gorey Hill, employing this interval of comparative repose in acquiring some further knowledge of military movements, and in sending out reconnoitering parties to ascertain the movements of the enemy, or in procuring such provisions as were necessary for the sustenance of their numerous army, which this time amounted to about fifteen thousand men. The latter task they found a rather arduous one, for the hordes of Orangemen, corps of yeomanry, and bodies of regular troops, had subsisted at the cost of the unfortunate people for months; and not content with taking by force what they required, they wantonly destroyed what they could not use. Under these circumstances the requisitionists from the insurgent camp found it extremely difficult to obtain the necessary supplies. It was in one of these forays that the house of Hunter Gowan, of infamous memory, was burned, an inadequate retaliation, indeed, for the fiendish deeds of cruelty perpetrated by that inhuman villain. At length the insurgent chiefs deemed the time was come when the attack on Carnew should be made, and, accordingly, they left their camp on Gorey Hill, and directed their march towards that town on the 7th, about mid-day.

L

Towards evening, the insurgents drew near Carnew and encamped on Kilcavan Hill, in the vicinity of the town. This march on Carnew had been made to satisfy the people of that town and the surrounding neighbourhood, who had suffered extremely from the cruelty of their enemies, who had long trampled on them without mercy, till, driven to madness by their unprovoked wrongs, they breathed nothing but a spirit of revenge and retaliation.

This spirit manifested itself in the burning of the houses of their persecutors, and, as Carnew was mainly inhabited by Orangemen, it was in a great measure destroyed. Yet, extraordinary to relate, though the oppressed inhabitants of Carnew had now many of their enemies completely in their power, it does not appear that any of them suffered death at their hands. This, under the circumstances, was a marvellous instance of forbearance, considering the cruel wrongs they had sustained. Some, however, of the Orange inhabitants were detained as hostages, with the intention of exchanging them for prisoners in the hands of the yeomanry. In the meantime, General Loftus, having heard of the intended advance of the insurgents on Carnew, had marched out of that town, and hastened to shut himself up in Tullow, where he thought himself at a secure distance from a foe he had now been taught to dread.

The English general could well estimate the advantage of fighting behind entrenchments, where he could use musket and cannon against men whose chief arm was the pike. The unwelcome tidings having reached the camp on Kilcavan Hill that the town of Arklow had been occupied by the royal troops in great force, it was forthwith determined by the insurgents to return to their former position on Gorey Hill, and there to prepare for an attack on the retaken town,

The insurgents rightly deemed that the crisis in their fortunes had arrived, and that to drive the formidable force of English troops out of Arklow would task their utmost energies, sadly deficient as they were in some of the chief requisites for the undertaking. They had numbers of brave men, it is true, but the greater part of them were armed with a weapon that, though unequalled in close fight, was of little use against an enemy who fought from behind an entrenched position. The artillery of the insurgents was insignificant, both as to the number of pieces and their calibre, and, though useful against an enemy in the open field, proved inefficient when the latter took shelter behind stone walls or earthen entrenchments. In addition to these serious disadvantages, the ammunition for the few smaller firearms in the possession of the insurgents was well nigh exhausted, and they had no means of obtaining a sufficient supply. This was but partially supplied by the arrival of a small barrel of powder from Wexford, sent with great reluctance, the inhabitants affirming that it was needed for the defence of the town.

Thus it will be seen that the insurgents were but poorly provided with every munition of war, and notwithstanding, relying on their own dauntless courage, they resolved to continue the contest. The continued success that had hitherto attended their army must be attributed in great measure to the excellent qualities of the gallant men who led them to fight. Amongst these may be mentioned Anthony Perry, Edmund Ryan, together with the heroic and faithful priests, Fathers John and Michael Murphy.

Father John continued to be the idol of the brave men whom he led, and who admired in him the perfection of their own courage. Always fighting in the foremost ranks, ever ready to cheer and rally those who wavered in the fight, skilful and cool after the battle to improve the victory, kind to console and warm with his own heroic ardour the humblest of his followers when their spirits, less lofty and less firm than his, drooped under the calamities of unequal war.

His matchless daring excited the admiration even of the bravest. The men fought like lions in his presence, and seeing him fearlessly exposing himself where danger was most rife, they were emulous of imitating a leader who evinced such a noble contempt for the perils of the fight.

But mere personal bravery, however great, either in the chiefs or those they led, could not fully compensate for the lack of military discipline. It is unity of action and concentration of power that form the strength of an army. This truth was keenly felt by the insurgents. To acquire this chief element of power, they had from the outset directed their efforts. To this end they conducted as closely as they could the order observed by regular troops, forming themselves into companies and regiments, appointing their captains, colonels, and generals, holding councils of war before undertaking any important enterprise, and posting outposts and sentinels around their camps.

As the insurrection went on the recruits they received from the yeomanry and militia enabled them to make a more rapid advance toward acquiring the discipline they sought.

All the time not engaged in actual combat was devoted to the practice of military manœuvres. The intelligent peasantry showed a remakable capacity for profiting by the instructions they received, so that after a short while they were able to perform, though in an imperfect fashion, the ordinary military evolutions.

In consequence, we find them every day more capable of coping with their disciplined enemies.

In one instance we see them maintaining for several hours a fight with a superior number of royal troops under a brave and able general, and retiring *unpursued* when their ammunition was exhausted. From these facts it is plain that to drive a brave people into insurrection is a dangerous experiment for any Government to make, for every day of continued warfare renders the insurgents more capable of contending with regular troops, giving them confidence in their own strength and skill in the use of arms.

This was so evident during the contest in Wexford, that many persons competent to form a correct opinion on the matter did not hesitate to affirm that had the rest of Ireland afforded any assistance to the Wexfordmen the Government would have found it impossible to quell the insurrection. The greatest obstacle to their success was the lack of gunpowder, which they did not succeed in manufacturing. The greater number of the bravest and most efficient men in the insurgent army were farmers or their sons, who being keen sportsmen, were consequently good marksmen. Many of these were provided with the long guns used in fowling upon the Slaney, excellent weapons, which sent a bullet farther than the muskets of the soldiery. The number of insurgents, however, who were furnished with firearms of any description was small compared with that of those whose only weapon was the pike. But this weapon, though excellent, was useless save in close fight. Then indeed it was irresistible. No force of cavalry could break a square of embattled pikemen, nor could any body of horse or foot long withstand the shock of their headlong onset.

A sharpened hook on one side of the pike blade was used in cutting the bridle of the cavalry soldier, and this once severed his horse became unmangeable, and he himself completely at the mercy of his opponent. The Author was informed by an old insurgent, who had fought at Vinegar Hill, Oulart, and Arklow, that all the pikemen required was "To get at the soldiery."

But this was the difficulty. To advance in the face of a body of soldiery pouring in amongst them a destructive fire, to which they could not reply, would be wanton loss of life, and was in consequence a course rarely adopted by the insurgents save when the lack of ammunition left them no alternative.

CHAPTER XII.

State of the County of Wexford.—Great increase in the number of royal troops.—Orange atrocities.—Wexford insurgents search for concealed Orangemen.—Seizure of Mr. Hunter.—Measures taken by Captain Keough as military governor.—Arrival of the Barony of Forth men.—Bagenal Harvey chosen Commander-in-chief.—His unfitness for command.—Insurgent freedom from bigotry.—Energetic preparations made by the insurgents for resistance.—Bank-notes esteemed of no value.—Provisions, their cheapness.—The Wexford "Fleet."—Capture of Lord Kingsborough and his officers.—Reinforcements sent to the camps.—Orangemen exclusively the objects of popular hatred.—Unreasonable fear displayed by the Protestants.—Pretended converts.—Instance of liberality on part of Catholics.—Hatred borne towards traitors.—Punishment inflicted upon informers.—Dixon's violence.—Requisitions.—Comparative tranquillity existing in the town.—Outrages become more frequent.—Proclamation issued against Hawtrey White and his associates.—Catholics refuse to permit the Protestant church to be used as an hospital.—Popular anger excited by the discovery of a pitch-cap.—Kingsborough's danger.—Messengers from the camp demand ammunition and reinforcements.—Good conduct of the gunsmen sent from the town.—Alarm of the loyalist prisoners in Wexford.—Kingsborough's letter to the Lord Lieutenant intercepted by Captain Dixon.—Tumult excited by the letter.—How appeased.—Severe measures of retaliation adopted by the insurgents at Vinegar Hill.

WEXFORD county was now the scene of a war which, considering the numbers engaged and the fierceness wherewith it was waged, was altogether disproportionate to its narrow area.

The royal troops within the limits of this one county could not have amounted to less than 90,000 men, including the yeomanry, whose large force was being every day augmented, while the peasantry who bore arms of any sort did not amount to more than 30,000 men.* On one side was discipline and unlimited resources, on the other was seen only the desperate bravery of men who fought for life and freedom. It had now become a struggle for victory or death—success or utter destruction between the contending parties. Scenes of bloodshed and cruelty continually exhibited were beginning to work their effect on the minds of the people, who seeing that when vanquished they received no mercy at the hands of the enemy, resolved on their part to show none.

In the school of bloodshed Orangemen were the principal masters, and against them the popular vengeance was chiefly directed. From the many deeds of cruelty and consequent retaliation, we may cite the following, which are well authenticated:

When the insurgents obtained possession of Enniscorthy, they found the dead body of a drummer of the North Cork Militia hanging in the lodgings of a Mr. Hancock, a Protestant minister and a magistrate, and having learned, on inquiry, that he had been put to death by the Orangemen for refusing to join in playing certain offensive party tunes, they naturally considered him as a martyr to their cause, and proceeded to revenge his death by shooting several of the most noted Orangemen among their prisoners. Hay also mentions that the insurgents, in revenge for the cruel murder of an

* The Wexford insurgents could not have amounted to more than 35,000 men, while their Wicklow associates hardly numbered 10,000, making in all a force of 45,000, which is perhaps too high an estimate of the insurgent forces.

idiot boy near the bridge of Scarawalsh by a party of cavalry, shot fourteen of their prisoners. If such cruel deeds were enacted occasionally under the impulse of ungovernable passion by the peasantry, they were habitually practised in cold blood and as a matter of course by their enemies.

On the departure of the great body of the insurgents on the 31st of May, those of their brethren who remained, aided by the populace of the town, instituted a search for such Orangemen as yet remained at large, with the intention of consigning them to prison.

The first they went in quest of was Mr. Turner of Newpark, a magistrate who had incurred their resentment by setting fire to some houses at Oulart previous to the battle fought at that place on the 27th.* Having found the gentleman in question at Mr. Harvey's lodgings, they seized upon him, and forthwith led him down to prison, disregarding the entreaties made by Messrs. Harvey, Hay, and Fitzgerald in his behalf. Several of the most obnoxious of the prisoners having been previously liberated through the influence of their friends, the people now insisted that no one should be freed from confinement in this irregular manner, but only on producing a certificate of their former good conduct, signed by a sufficient number of their neighbours. On the same day that the above detailed incidents occurred, Captain Keough was chosen military governor of Wexford. Under his supervision, the town was divided into wards, each furnishing a company of armed men, with officers of their own choice. Every evening these companies were paraded on the quay, while with military regularity guards were struck off and relieved, and passwords and countersigns given.

---

* The houses in question were set on fire to induce the insurgents to quit their favourable position.

In the country parishes a similar organisation was soon after adopted. While the insurgent army yet remained in deliberation on Windmill Hill, a large body of the men of the barony of Forth marched into town with Mr. Cornelius Grogan of Johnstown Castle, at their head. This aged gentleman, though entirely passive in these proceedings, did not escape the vengeance that fell on no more guiltless head, but his fate was nobler than that which befell his brother Thomas, who was slain at Arklow leading the Castletown yeomanry against the pikemen. We must not forget to mention that in the council of war held by the insurgents on Windmill Hill, before setting out on their new campaign, Mr. Bagenal Harvey was chosen commander-in-chief. This selection was most ill-judged, for Harvey, though in many respects an excellent man, was not possessed of talents to qualify him for such an important command. It must, however, be admitted by all fair-minded persons as a proof that the Catholics, who form such a vast majority of the population of Ireland, are far too generous and enlightened to entertain rancour against those who differ from them in their views of religious truth, but on the contrary, have ever shown themselves enthusiastically grateful to such Protestants as have been willing to join them in their struggles for freedom. As a further evidence of this truth we may state the fact that the greater number of their chosen chiefs were Protestants or Presbyterians,* and no voice was ever raised amongst their followers to reproach or taunt them with the fact.

---

* Of the Wexford leaders, Harvey, Keough, and Anthony Perry were Protestants; Kelly, Colclough, and Kyan Catholics, while the northerns were almost, without exception, Protestants or Presbyterians.

The Wexford insurgents, fully sensible of the desperate nature of the struggle upon which they had entered, displayed the utmost energy in the efforts they made to carry it on successfully. Every smith and carpenter in the town of Wexford and its environs was now hard at work in the fabrication of pikes and handles to that "queen of weapons."

In a short time every insurgent was provided with one of these efficient weapons, and while every hand grasped a pike, every hat displayed a green cockade.

Four oyster boats, each manned with a crew of thirty-five men, were fitted out to cruise in the offing, and by boarding passing ships to obtain provisions, which were sorely needed, as the usual markets were quite deserted. At the same time two pieces of cannon were mounted on the old fort of Roslare, to fire on any vessel of war that should attempt to cross the bar; while, to render still more difficult the entrance of the vessels in question, two sloops were sunk at the mouth of the harbour. As an indication of the hopes the people entertained at this period of severing their connexion with England and shaking off the yoke that had galled them for centuries, bank notes issued by establishments that had government security, were regarded as quite valueless, specie alone being proffered or accepted in buying or selling. Indeed, so low had paper money fallen in the common estimation, that it was no unusual thing to see men lighting their pipes with them, or using them as gun-wadding. However, money in any shape was little needed, for every kind of provision was supplied from the public stores, on the presentation of a ticket from the committee. Such persons as preferred to purchase what they needed in the market, could get good meat at one penny the pound, and other commodities at a proportionately cheap rate. The little fleet of armed oyster boats were meantime actively employed in cruising to and fro outside the harbour, and boarding such vessels as were so unlucky as to come within their reach. Captures of this kind, made by their exertions, were so numerous that a fair supply of provisions was maintained in town, and the wants of the inhabitants supplied. But on the 20th one of these little vessels alighted upon a prize of a different nature from any that had been hitherto made. This was a vessel, on board of which they found Lord Kingsborough, colonel of the North Cork, with two of his officers, who, unaware that Wexford had fallen into the hands of the insurgents, were on their way thither to join their regiment. The gentlemen in question were brought into town by their captors; and on arriving there were conducted first to the residence of Captain Keough, whence they were soon after, at the urgent demand of the people, transferred to a house in the bull-ring (an inn called the Cape of Good Hope), around which guards were stationed to prevent their escape. This happened on the 2nd of June. On the following day, a large body of the inhabitants of the barony of Forth, who had procured arms, passed through the town on their way to join the insurgents at Carrickburn; and a corps from the Faith (a Wexford suburb, inhabited chiefly by the families of sea-faring men) set off on the evening of the same day for the camp at Carrigrew. During this time, while the Catholic party in Wexford enjoyed undisputed sway, not the slightest disposition was manifested by them to injure or outrage in any way their Protestant fellow-townsmen. *The resentment of the people was directed exclusively against Orangemen.* This fact is, perhaps inadvertently, acknowledged even by Sir Richard Musgrave. But the Protestants were ill at ease, and evinced their distrust of the sincerity of their fellow-townsmen, though so unequivocally expressed, by the constant importunities wherewith they assailed the priests for admittance into the Catholic Church. However, the Catholic clergy, being well convinced of the real motive of this sudden change in religious opinions, firmly refused to comply with their request. But these strange converts were not to be put off. They followed the priests wherever they went, were constant in their attendance at the Catholic church, and showed their earnestness while there by sprinkling holy water copiously over their persons, and frequently making the sign of the cross in the most orthodox fashion. It was afterwards noticed that some of the most zealous of these converts were afterwards the most prompt in coming forward to give their testimony against those whose religious faith they pretended to adopt. Thus it is that cowardice and cruelty are generally to be found in company. The principal Catholic inhabitants of the town used their utmost endeavours to banish all apprehension from the minds of their heterodox brethren, and requested that the services which had been discontinued in the Protestant church should be carried on as usual. But to this the Protestants themselves would by no means give their consent. No truth, indeed, has been more clearly shown forth than that the Catholics of Wexford were possessed by no persecuting spirit. Traitors were punished with the same impartial justice, whether they happened to be Catholics or Protestants.

But beyond all, informers were held in such detestation that their fate excited no compassion in any breast. In bringing these wretches to condign punishment, the *famous*, or, as some may deem him, the *infamous*, Captain Dixon strenuously exerted himself. An informer named Thomas Murphy (a Catholic) had caused, by his false testimony, the transportation of

Father Dixon, a relative of the Captain's. This wretched man was the first that felt his vengeance. On Sunday the 3rd of June, while the Catholic inhabitants were assisting at Mass, the captain repaired to the gaol, from which he led out the informer, conveyed him straightway to the bull-ring, where he had him shot by three revenue officers, whom he compelled by threats to become his executioners.

This was a lawless and desperate act on the part of Dixon, but he had been deeply injured, and his conduct, though culpable, must be admitted to be far less so than that of those Orange gentry who put unfortunate people, who had never done them an injury, to the most cruel death. Yet those who stigmatise this rude son of Neptune as a monster, &c., pass over lightly enough the diabolical atrocities perpetrated by the infamous Hunter Gowan and his compeers. So great is the influence that the accident of birth or of social position exercises over some minds.

The 14th of the same month witnessed the death of another individual of the same detested class. The people resolved to extend no mercy to such vile traitors, regarding them as enemies to humanity, whose existence was a continued danger to the community. At this period the frequent requisitions made for the different camps pressed rather heavily on the resources of the townspeople, but the majority of them were not unwilling to suffer some loss of property in providing for the wants of the brave men who perilled life and liberty for the common cause. To force compliance from the more selfish and griping the threat of burning their houses was made use of by the insurgents, and always with the desired effect. Things went on quietly in Wexford, and were it not for the occasional arrival of parties of the warlike peasantry, the town would have enjoyed the most undisturbed tranquillity, and no one could suppose from the peaceful aspect it presented that a fierce war was raging outside its walls. It is not, however, to be supposed that crimes and outrages of various kinds were not perpetrated during this disturbed period.

Individuals of vile and base character are to be found in every class and in every country, and in times of civil commotion such persons do not fail to avail themselves of the opportunity then presented of indulging their evil propensities.

The existence of the class referred to in Wexford was but too plainly shown by the numerous robberies and other outrages that became frequent. The insurgent chiefs did their utmost to check these disgraceful proceedings, and such of the depredators as were caught suffered condign punishment. In extenuation of the offence of the marauders in question, it is but fair to say that many of them had been totally ruined by the forays headed by Hunter Gowan, Hawtrey White, Archibald Hamilton Jacob, and other magistrates of the same class. As the latter still pursued their course of crime and outrage, the popular assembly thought it necessary to issue the following proclamation:—

"*Proclamation of the People of the County of Wexford.*

" Whereas, it stands manifestly notorious that James Boyd, Hawtrey White, Hunter Gowan, and Archibald Hamilton Jacob, late magistrates of this county, have committed the most horrid acts of cruelty, violence, and oppression, against our peaceable and well-disposed countrymen. Now, we, the people associated and united for the purpose of procuring our just rights, and *being determined to protect the persons and properties of all religious persuasions, who have not oppressed us, and are willing to join with heart and hand our glorious cause,* as well as to show our marked disapprobation and horror of the crimes of the above delinquents, do call on our countrymen at large to use every exertion in their power to apprehend the bodies of the aforesaid James Boyd, Hawtrey White, Hunter Gowan, and Archibald Hamilton Jacob, and to secure and convey them to the gaol of Wexford, to be brought before the tribunal of the people.—Done at Wexford, this 9th day of June, 1798. 'God save the People!'"

To illustrate the good feeling that existed among the Catholic population of Wexford and their desire to conciliate their Protestant fellow-townsmen, we may mention the following event. The crowded state of the gaol having caused the disease known as gaol fever to break out therein, the Protestants suggested that their own church should be used for the accommodation of the sick; but to this proposal the Catholics firmly refused to give their assent, and eventually a sloop was fitted up in the harbour for the purpose.

An incident now unhappily occurred to disturb for a brief space the calm that reigned in Wexford, and throw the populace into a state of violent excitement. It fell among the slumbering passions of the mob like a lighted brand into a powder magazine, and produced a similar explosion. The occasion of this popular ferment was the discovery of a pitch-cap in Wexford barracks, together with a commission for the establishment of an Orange lodge. This double discovery produced a fearful tumult. The horrid instrument of torture was inseparably united in the minds of the people with Lord Kingsborough, who was credited with being its inventor. Breathing vengeance, a furious crowd hurried to his lodgings, with the ugly object that recalled so many revolting scenes elevated on the point of a pike, resolved to make him experience in his own person the torture he had designed for others. But Kingsborough's aristocratic friends stepped between him and the enraged populace.

It shocked the genteelly constituted minds of these persons that the head which was destined to wear a coronet, should be crowned with such an ungraceful head-dress as a pitch-cap. So persuasively did the gentlemen in question plead in favour of the prisoner, that the people, whose anger rarely proved unappeasable, at length relented in their purpose of putting him to the torture. They, however, insisted that he should be conveyed without delay to the sloop, and kept prisoner there. This demand being complied with, they dispersed. Next day Kingsborough's friends had the sloop condemned as unfit for the purpose to which it had been designed, and the prisoner was brought back to his former lodging. There is little doubt that Lord Kingsborough would have been put to death by the people could they have procured evidence of the cruelties he had practised elsewhere; but, luckily for him, his crimes had been committed at a distance from Wexford, and in the absence of witnesses, the justice of the people refused to inflict upon him the death he undoubtedly deserved.

Meantime, affairs in the county were hastening towards a crisis. On the 5th of June a messenger arrived in town from the camp at Gorey Hill, for the purpose of obtaining from the townspeople a supply of ammunition for their intended attack on Arklow. The latter gave, though not without great reluctance, one barrel out of the three they had captured shortly before.

Soon after this event a despatch came from Vinegar Hill, urgently demanding a reinforcement of men from the town as an attack of the royalists was apprehended on that camp. In compliance with this request a force of one hundred and twenty gunsmen, under Captain Murphy, marched out of town on the 10th of June, and arrived the same night at the 'Hill,' where they remained till the 20th.

These men were distinguished for their good conduct, and their interposition put a stop to the executions that had been but too frequent before their arrival; for latterly the insurgents had adopted severe measures of retaliation, and for every one of their party put to death by the Orangemen, sacrificed one of their prisoners. It was, indeed, verging towards a war of extermination on both sides; on the Orange side it had, in truth, been such from the very outset; they had been but too faithful to their wicked oath. The rumours of excesses committed by the partisans of Government reached Wexford, and excited no slight apprehension amongst the loyalist prisoners. They considered themselves in imminent danger of falling victims to the vengeful feeling such reports aroused among the people in whose power they were at present placed.

Popular hatred still burned against Lord Kingsborough as the representative of Orangeism (a system that in the minds of the people embodied everything that is hateful and detestable in principle and practice), and manifested itself in such a way as to put that young nobleman in terror of his life. To arrest the evil that he feared from some sudden outburst of popular anger, Kingsborough wrote a letter to the Lord Lieutenant, in the name of his fellow-prisoners, in which he besought him to endeavour to procure better treatment for such insurgents as might be captured by the king's troops, as otherwise he and his fellow-captives had good reason to fear certain destruction.

However, this epistle did not reach its destination, for Captain Dixon, aware of its being despatched, rode on before the bearer, Lieutenant Burke, and induced the Enniscorthy insurgents to seize the messenger and intercept the letter. The captain put no trust in the faith of Kingsborough, and suspected his messenger of being the bearer of more than the contents of the letter, viz., important information of the plans of his fellow-insurgents. Were it not for the *emeutes* evoked by the captain, the town would have enjoyed almost complete tranquillity. This rough sailor seems to have sworn undying enmity to the Orangemen, since magistrates of that faction unjustly (upon the evidence of a perjured informer) sentenced his relative, the Rev. Mr. Dixon, to transportation. From that time forth he allowed no opportunity to pass of exciting against them the angry feelings of his followers. During his brief reign as king of the mob the captain was wont almost daily to sally forth from the town at the head of an armed band, and pay domiciliary visits to the habitations of the neighbouring Orange gentry, with a view, as he alleged, of seeing that they were plotting nothing against the people—in fact, using against them their own tactics. In one of these excursions he entered the house of a certain Colonel Le Hunt, near the village of Castlebridge, where he alighted upon an object of whose use he was ignorant, or at least feigned to be so, and to which his excited imagination attributed a terrible significance. This object was nothing more or less than a fire screen, bordered with orange-coloured fringe, and painted with a grotesque representation of the heathen gods. The captain hastened back to town, which he entered on horseback, accompanied by his wife Madge, likewise mounted, bearing aloft the yet mysterious prize, whose nature and purpose he began to descant upon to the mob, that, as usual, thronged around him. He declared that the aforesaid grotesque figures signified nothing less than the tortures to be inflicted by Le Hunt and his fellow-Orangemen on the Catholics. This, and other appeals of the worthy captain, roused the multitude to a desire for instant vengeance on foes whose crimes were black enough to dispense with the addition of imaginary horrors.

The populace, inflamed by Dixon's address, rushed to the house where the unlucky owner of the fire-screen lodged, seized and marched him down to jail, preparatory to holding a trial on him and other obnoxious persons. The tumult was, however, at length appeased by some gifted speaker of the committee, who explained to the excited crowd the harmless nature of the object that had aroused their anger.

But the insurgents at Vinegar Hill were of fiercer and less relenting temper than those who abode in Wexford, and many unfortunates were there put to death as enemies to the popular cause. Nor did their vengeance confine itself within the limits of their own camp; for, on the 16th, they despatched a party of pikemen to the town, who, having seized upon four of the prisoners confined in jail, led them off with them to the "Hill," where they soon after suffered death.*

Leaving the town of Wexford for a time, we now proceed to visit other scenes where events far more important are in progress.

* Concerning the number of loyalists put to death at Vinegar Hill camp, accounts vary: some assert that as many as four hundred were executed—fifty would be nearer the truth.

CHAPTER XIII.

The Insurgents leave Gorey and march upon Arklow.—Their number and equipment.—The battle of Arklow.—Death of Fr. Michael Murphy.—Absence of Father John.—Contest between Esmond Kyan and Colonel Skerret.—Return to Gorey.—Massacre of the wounded insurgents by the English soldiery.—Cannibalism of the "Ancient Britons."—Loss on both sides.—The falsehood of General Needham's despatch demonstrated by various authorities.—State of the country.—Merciful spirit displayed by the insurgents.—Their respect for the fair sex contrasted with the brutality of the loyalist officers and men.

THE leaders of the insurgent army on Gorey Hill having decided to march forthwith to attack the royal troops, who had possessed themselves of Arklow, and having made every possible arrangement to carry their enterprise to a successful termination, issued orders to those who followed their standard to be ready to set out on the expedition.* At about ten o'clock on the 7th of June they were in readiness to march. Of the twenty thousand men who composed the insurgent force on Gorey Hill, not more than two thousand were armed with firearms, many of which

---

* Of the attack on this town the Rev. Mr. Gordon says:—"Had Arklow been attacked immediately after the defeat of Walpole, it would have been taken, but during the delay many troops arrived, till the force consisted of 1600 men." Sir Jonah Barrington states that "the rebels boldly but indiscreetly declared their intention of storming the town. The alarm of the metropolis at this intelligence may easily be conceived, and immediate reinforcement of the garrison of Arklow could alone prevent an attack on Dublin, and an insurrection of the populace. The Cavan militia, commanded by the present Lord Farnham, was instantly despatched to succour General Needham." "The first attack on Arklow was made by a column which advanced by the sea shore, and assailed what was called the Fishery. The main attack was made on the regiment of Durham Fencibles under Colonel Skerret, whose line extended across the fields in front of the barracks."—Gordon.

were out of order and of little use, gunsmiths not being at hand to repair them. Three thousand of their number, at the utmost, had pikes; the rest were forced to be content with scythes, pitchforks, and whatever other rustic implements they could use as weapons of offence. However, the spirit that animated these men seemed to counterbalance their lack of the ordinary weapons used in waging war. They directed their march through the village of Coolgreney, where they halted for a short time to take some slight refreshment, and, after a march of about fourteen English miles, arrived in front of the enemy's position, whom they found well entrenched in preparation to receive them. The insurgents perceived a number of field-officers riding in front of their enemy's line of battle,* but a volley from their sharp-shooters soon compelled these gentlemen to retire behind their line. One of them, having fallen under the fire, was carried off the field either killed or severely wounded. The insurgent artillery, under Esmond Kyan, commenced the battle, and, by the first well-directed volley, dismounted one of the enemy's cannon. While Kyan kept up an effective fire from his few pieces of artillery, one division of the insurgent army corps filed to the right, and commenced a vigorous attack on the Fishery, where the royal troops were in great force, and, having to cross an open field in front of the hostile entrenchment, suffered considerable loss from the enemy's fire. Being reinforced, however, by another corps, they made a determined assault on

* " The conflict took place in a level field at the extremity of the town; the royal infantry being on a line on open ground, with two pieces of cannon at each wing. . . The fire began as regularly as between disciplined armies; the pikemen formed a crescent on a range of hills just over the royalists, and waited for any disorder to rush down and exterminate them."—Sir Jonah Barrington's " Rise and Fall of the Irish Nation," p. 448.

the position of their foes. The main body of the insurgents had by this time arrived, and the battle became general, and after an obstinate defence, during which the insurgents were repeatedly charged by the regular troops and yeomanry, who, on this occasion, manifested unusual spirit, the latter were finally driven with great loss from their position. Nothing could withstand the terrible onset of the pikemen, who, regardless of the loss inflicted on them by their trained adversaries, continued the combat with the utmost bravery. Their chiefs proved themselves worthy to command such gallant men, and charged with dauntless courage at their head. Numbers of the insurgents fell, but the rest still pushed forward with dauntless determination, heroically resolved to conquer or perish.

General Needham, seeing his troops beginning to quail before the repeated and fierce onsets of their undisciplined foes, deemed it prudent to retreat before the mass of the pikemen came to aid their comrades, whose determined onslaught had already made such havoc in his ranks. He feared lest his troops might become utterly panic-stricken and imitate the disgraceful flight of Walpole's, the remnants of which corps, cowed by their recent defeat, now began to waver.

In vain the various corps of yeoman cavalry, who, as we have intimated, showed more spirit on this day than heretofore, charged furiously down upon the firm ranks of the pikemen. They were scattered like chaff before the wind, and finally retired utterly broken and discomfited. The first of the yeoman corps to charge the insurgent ranks was that called the Castletown; at their head rode Captain Thomas Knox Grogan, of Johnstown. This corps was also routed and its captain slain. Nor did the cavalry regiment of Ancient Britons, so infamously notorious for their cruelty, fare better— they also being forced to retire with severe loss. It was in repelling one of the cavalry charges that the insurgents lost one of their leaders, the Rev. Michael Murphy, who fell by a mortal wound in the fury of the strife.*

While the battle continued to rage with such fierceness between the insurgent pikemen and the cavalry of the royalists, to the increasing disadvantage of the latter, Esmond Kyan maintained an artillery fight with his few pieces of ordnance with Skerret, the Colonel of the Durham Fencibles, a cautious officer, who kept his men behind their entrenchments, and was content to return the rather feeble fire directed against his position by Kyan.

At last Kyan succeeded in driving the colonel from his position, and was proceeding to complete his success by a further effort, when, unfortunately, he was wounded severely by a cannon ball, which carried off a cork arm he wore, together with a piece of the stump to which it was attached. This most untimely accident to poor Kyan gave his opponent time to choose a new and better position, and strengthen himself therein. Thus poor Kyan lost his arm, and Skerret gained a reputation to which in truth he had little claim.

This position might have been easily taken by a vigorous charge of pikemen, but the simple, though valiant peasants had formed altogether too high an estimate of the value of their artillery, and many of

* Father Michael fell while leading on a large body of pikemen to the charge. His death at this critical juncture was a terrible blow to the insurgents. It was the common opinion that had he lived he would have led his victorious troops to Dublin. In this action he was the recognized leader; for I have been assured on reliable authority that "Father John" was not present at this battle, though Miles Byrne asserts that he was. It was well known among the old insurgents, a few of whom survived to our own time, that Father John strongly disapproved of the attack on Arklow, and remained behind at Castletown.

them were satisfied to stand idly by, absorbed in admiration of its thundering discharges. This battle, in which such gallantry had been displayed by both sides, had now lasted for four hours with great slaughter, till, at length, the royalists began to give ground, and victory crowned the unparalleled bravery and determination of the insurgents. Their opponents gave way on all sides—completely beaten and borne down by the successive and resistless onsets of the pikemen.

It is true the Durham Fencibles* still defended the second position, behind which they had securely ensconced themselves, and in comparative security beheld their routed comrades scattered far and wide over the field so long and so fiercely contested.

This victory, so glorious for the insurgents, was, however, dearly bought, for many of their most valued and trusted chiefs, and hundreds of their gallant brethren, lay stretched on the field, dead or severely wounded. Amongst those brave chiefs who were slain in the conflict was, as we have already mentioned, the Rev. Michael Murphy—a sad loss to the insurgent cause, for, in addition to the qualities that form a gallant chief, his priestly character made the people follow him with more courage into danger.

Michael Redmond, the leader of the men of Little Limerick (a Wexford village), also received a mortal wound whilst leading his men into the town after driving the royalists out of the Fishery.

Now that victory had rewarded the efforts of the insurgents, and their routed enemy were in full retreat, it seems almost incredible that the victors should have

* "General Needham and most of the officers were disposed to retire as a matter of necessity; but Colonel Skerret, of the Dumbarton Fencibles, resolutely declared that his regiment would never retreat."—Sir Jonah Barrington's "Rise and Fall of the Irish Nation," p. 418.

neglected to secure for themselves the fruits of their dearly bought success, and retired without pursuing the enemy, whom they might easily have made prisoners and obtained possession of their arms and ammunition, of which they stood in such great need. Yet such was unhappily the fact. The insurgent army received orders to march back to Gorey Hill, leaving their routed foe to pursue his flight unmolested. Had the English soldiers been pursued as they retreated in panic and disorder, their total rout would have been inevitable; but the occasion was lost, and with it the fruits of a victory that cost the lives of so many brave men. The insurgents on their march back to Gorey carried some hundreds of their wounded comrades with them, leaving, unfortunately, many others on the field, who were slaughtered without mercy by the enemy on their return. Not only did these wretches murder the unhappy and defenceless wounded, but they mangled the senseless remains of those whom death might have protected from all but the vengeance of fiends. Imagination sickens at the contemplation of the horrible deeds perpetrated by the Ancient Britons, who, having fearfully mangled the remains of the Rev. Michael Murphy, tore out his heart, roasted it, and ate it.*

Does history record another so fiendish deed of the soldiers of any country? Thus ended the battle of Arklow, glorious for the bravery displayed therein, but unfortunate for the unaccountable neglect by which its fruits were lost.

The King's troops engaged in this action amounted

---

* This horrid fact is recorded by a Protestant clergyman, the Rev. Mr. Gordon, who, as an avowed loyalist would not lightly cast an imputation on the king's troops. Tradition states that all who partook of this cannibal banquet died raving mad.

to about 1600 men, together with about a dozen corps of mounted yeomanry. Of this number they are supposed to have lost about 200 in killed and wounded. The insurgent loss was greater, as they were the assailants, and including those wounded, who were butchered after the action by the military, amounted to about 500 men.

The following is the shamelessly mendacious account given of this action in the "Official Bulletin," Dublin, June 10th, 1798 :—

"Accounts were received early this morning by Lieutenant-General Lake, from Major-General Needham at Arklow, stating that the rebels had in great force attacked his position in Arklow, at six o'clock yesterday evening. They advanced in an irregular manner, and extending themselves for the purpose of turning his left flank, his rear and right flanks being strongly defended by the town and barrack of Arklow. Upon their endeavouring to enter the lower end of the town, they were attacked by Fourth Dragoon Guards, Fifth Dragoons, and Ancient Britons, and completely defeated. All round the other points of the position they were defeated with much slaughter. The loss of his majesty's troops was trifling, and their behaviour highly gallant."

The substance of this despatch was furnished by General Needham to his military superior, Lake. Needham knew the art of forging despatches better than he did that of fighting insurgents; his brother officers esteemed him little better than a coward, and his retreat at Arklow would have been converted into a flight but for the firmness with which Skerret stood his ground. To refute the false assertions contained in the above-given despatch, we need only cite the authors who have made mention of the affair in question. Sir Jonah Barrington says :—"The insurgents, dispirited by the fall of Father Murphy, advanced no further; . . . they began to retreat, but without precipitation; the royal army did not think it prudent to pursue." "The rebels ceased from combat as soon as darkness came, and retired unpursued towards Gorey."— Rev. Mr. Gordon. "The insurgents retreated when their ammunition was expended."*—Hay.

The insurgent army, on their return from Arklow, once more encamped on Gorey Hill, where they remained till the 10th, when they returned to Limbrick Hill. Meantime the country where the various battles we have attempted to describe were fought, continued to be the theatre where innumerable scenes of cruelty and bloodshed were exhibited. The yeomanry and military yet infested the country in small bands, taking care to avoid any place where the dreaded pikemen were in force, and wherever they went the shrieks of the tortured victims or the death-cry of some hapless wretch too surely announced their presence. Old men were slain, whose nerveless arms could not defend them, and whose white hairs might have moved the pity of less ruthless foes; and the wives, sisters, and daughters of a people far-famed for their purity, fell victims to the brutal lust of England's vile soldiery and foreign mercenaries.

---

* Mr. Hay seems inclined to think that the military had actually begun to retreat. He says, " variously did the fortune of the day seem to incline ; it is necessary, however, to mention that rumours of a retreat of the troops were circulated, and that orders were given, and seeming preparations made for that purpose, and, as the proverb has it, 'all's well that ends well.' The insurgents, after having displayed singular bravery, courage, and intrepidity as long as their ammunition lasted, retreated when it was expended to their former position at Gorey; and thus ended the battle, at the very moment that it is alleged the army had determined to retreat, and *most undoubtedly my information warrants me to mention that some of the military had already retreated.*"

The sons, brothers, and fathers of those unhappy victims stood on the hill-side, or slept in the rude camp under the free air of heaven; but the patriot's sleep was haunted by the woeful vision of a desolated home, and the suffering of those who were dear to his heart; and can we wonder that, with a sense of these wrongs ever present to his mind, he swore the direst revenge on those who had wrought them.

Had the insurgents borne calmly such injuries and forborne all retaliation, they had been more or less than human. They did in some instances retaliate; but we venture to affirm that never did a people so foully wronged, so ruthlessly trampled under the iron heel of military despotism, exhibit so many instances of merciful forgiveness to those they knew to be their mortal foes. Of this gentle spirit of the people we give two instances. Owens, a Protestant minister, an Orangeman, and a magistrate, had long exercised his power in a most cruel way. This man fell into the power of the people, and though it was proved that he had put many innocent men to death, his life was spared, and his captors decided that as he had inflicted the torture of the pitch-cap on so many, it was but just that he should have an opportunity of proving it himself—to this punishment he accordingly was subjected. The chivalrous spirit of the insurgent peasantry manifested itself by giving women an entire immunity from even the slightest injury. As an instance of this we may relate what occurred to the daughters of Hunter Gowan. These young ladies, who were so numerous as fifteen, being encountered on the road by a band of armed insurgents, were stopped and questioned as to who they were and whither they were going. They told both, and were dismissed unharmed, to appreciate, if they could, the chivalrous generosity of the brave peasants. It is, moreover, admitted even by the bitterest enemies of the gallant insurgents, that during all the time they were masters of the county no insult or injury was offered by them to any female, even the relatives of their most merciless foes—a fact that forms an admirable contrast to the brutal war waged against female honour by those who fought under standards of a nation which boasts itself preeminently civilised and Christian.

Concerning this admirable trait in the character of the insurgent peasantry as contrasted with the infamous conduct of the soldiery, Sir Jonah Barrington remarks:—" It is a singular fact that in all the ferocity of the conflict, the storming of towns and of villages, *women were uniformly respected by the insurgents.* Though numerous ladies fell into their power, they never experienced any incivility or misconduct. But the foreign troops in our service (Hompesch's) not only brutally ill-treated, but occasionally shot gentlewomen. A very respectable married woman in Enniscorthy (Mrs. Stringer, the wife of an attorney) was wantonly shot at her window by a yeoman, in cold blood. The rebels (though her husband was a loyalist) a short time after took some of those foreign soldiers prisoners, and piked them all, as they told them, 'just to teach them how to shoot ladies.' "

Nor were the officers, English or Irish in the royal army, a single pace behind these vile foreign mercenaries in the pursuit of beast-like brutality. We cannot here more than allude to such infamy, of which abundant historical proof already exists. But it would scarce be credited that so fearfully had the minds of people been perverted by the frenzy of religious hatred, that a *lady of fashion,* on being told of the respect shown by the insurgents to the fair sex, merely remarked with an air of disgust, that *it was owing to a want of gallantry in the " croppies,"*

CHAPTER XIV.

Movements of the insurgents and royalists.—Position of the contending forces.—Encampment on Mount Pleasant.—Vaunts of the royalist general.—Retreat of the royal troops.—Insurgent challenge refused.—Insurgents proceed to Vinegar Hill.—Attack on Borris-house.—Battle of Longsaig or Fooke's Mill.

EARLY on the morning of Saturday, the 16th, news was brought to the insurgent camp on Limbrick Hill, that Generals Loftus and Dundas had quitted their camps at Tullow and Hacketstown, and were on their march from these places with the intention of making a combined attack on their position. On the receipt of this welcome intelligence, the camp on Limbrick Hill was broken up, and the insurgents were once more on the march to meet their foes. They reached Carnew without encountering an enemy; and thence they continued their march to Tinahely, where their advanced guard came in view of a like body from the hostile army, whom they put to flight, making many prisoners. They also captured a great number of cattle which were in possession of their enemy. The insurgents reached Mount Pleasant that night, where they encamped.

At an early hour next morning the united forces of Dundas and Loftus came in sight of the insurgents, drawn up in formidable array on Mount Pleasant. The good position occupied by the insurgents, and the appearance of military discipline they exhibited, considerably cooled the ardour the royalist officers had the day before manifested to encounter the "rebels." They had openly boasted that the "bloody croppy rebels" would fly on the appearance of such a formidable force as they commanded. But no sign of fear or inclination to fly was shown by the fierce array of warlike peasants. On the other hand, these pot-valiant generals, so ready to put rebels to flight over their cups, now that they had them present, did not seem over-anxious to come to close quarters with them.

The English force came to a halt at a safe distance; and no doubt they then deemed it would be much safer to have been out of sight altogether. The insurgents, burning to meet those now despised foes, received with warlike ardour the command to advance, and charged at a quick pace down the hill in the direction of their foes.

The latter did not choose to withstand their onset, but retired with great precipitation, leaving a large herd of cattle and a considerable quantity of provisions to be seized by their courageous foes. The cavalry of the royal army attempted to cover the rear of the retreating forces, but were unable to prevent the insurgents from making a considerable number of prisoners. The royalist army continued to retreat before the insurgents till they reached a hill at a considerable distance, where they halted. While the main body of the royal troops were thus retreating from their dangerous proximity to their enemy's line, detached bodies from the insurgent army hung upon their rear, and gave occupation to the numerous corps of cavalry engaged in covering the retreat. Among these skirmishing parties from the insurgent forces, a force of two hundred Arklow men, under the command of Denis Doyle, made a great figure; for, in addition to their possession of that brave spirit that animated the entire insurgent army, they had, by constant training, acquired a great promptitude in the execution of military manoeuvres, and bore themselves as steady as veteran soldiers. Night at length fell over both armies, and put an end to the pursuit. The tumult of the fight was succeeded by silence, and the triumphant insurgents retired to their camp on Mount Pleasant, to seek the repose they so much needed. During the ensuing day the insurgents remained on Mount Pleasant, where intelligence reached them of the utter failure of the insurrection in Dublin and Kildare, and of the supposed immediate invasion of the country by Bonaparte. On the same day, the chiefs held a council, in which the next steps to be taken were debated. It was finally decided to endeavour to force the enemy to give battle. This they sought to do, as it was then known that the various English forces in the county were about to be concentrated for a combined and irresistible attack on the great rendezvous and rallying place of the insurgents on Vinegar Hill. Accordingly, the insurgent army quitted their camp on Mount Pleasant, and took up a position on Kilcavin Hill, thus drawing near to the headquarters of Lieutenant-General Lake, at Gorey. But the English generals, with a large body of regular troops and yeomanry, remained stationary behind their barricades in Gorey, and refused to accept the challenge of the gallant band of Wexford and Wicklow peasants, who, seeing the evident reluctance of their enemy to engage them, advanced boldly to the very walls of Gorey, where they found the king's troops drawn up in preparation for an attack. The few pieces of artillery the insurgents possessed were now brought to the front, and commenced to play on the enemy's line.

The royal artillery replied with spirit to the insurgent fire, and many men fell on both sides. The pikemen, who had hitherto been kept in reserve, now received orders to advance. This command they obeyed with their usual alacrity, and pushed rapidly forward to encounter the red coats. The latter retreated slowly before the impetuous advance of the insurgents, who continued to pursue them till night put an end to the conflict. This engagement took place between the advanced guards of both armies, for the main body of the insurgents yet remained on the hill, while that of the royalists kept behind their entrenchments at Gorey. While a part of the insurgent army were thus engaged, their comrades on the hill were busy discussing the contents of despatches which in the interim had arrived from the general-in-chief, which were to this effect—that, being unable to maintain his position before Ross, he was forced to fall back with his division to cover Wexford; and that he considered it expedient that the forces now on Kilcavan Hill should forthwith set out for Vinegar Hill, in order to act in concert with his army. The wisdom of the proposed step being discussed among the chiefs, it was decided by the majority to abandon their present position on the very evening that had witnessed the glorious success of a portion of their army, in combat with a far more numerous force of the king's troops. That night the insurgents set out for Vinegar Hill, halting to repose at Ferns, well nigh exhausted from excessive fatigue and want of food. On the next morning they resumed their march, proceeding slowly, in order to give time to some who had gone in quest of food to rejoin their corps. Great was the rejoicing in the English camp at Gorey when it was known that their dreaded foe had quitted their encampment, and were retreating towards Vinegar Hill. Soon those English troops, whose cautious generals had hitherto kept them cooped behind entrenchments, which they had hardly hoped would protect them, issued from their shelter; and forthwith commenced a vigorous pursuit. It would be vain to attempt a description of the enormities perpetrated by these worse than savage troops, as they hung on the rear of the wearied pikemen. Suffice it to say that in their progress through the country everything of value they could lay hands on they plundered, every woman that fell into their hands they brutally violated, and every man they put to instant death. The insurgents, meantime, continued their retreat in good order, a rear-guard keeping the enemy at a distance. Their movements were, however, considerably impeded by the vast multitude of helpless women and children who, flying in terror before the advance of the royal army, sought protection from their armed countrymen. Weary and exhausted, the latter at length arrived at the foot of Vinegar Hill just at nightfall, and encamped around it. A hundred fires, lighting up the dark night, made visible the great numbers who had sought protection in the vicinity of the army of the people.

The division of insurgents, under the command of Father Philip Roche, were now encamped on Lacken Hill, an eminence situate between Ross and Enniscorthy, with the intention of making another attack on the former town. But to carry this intention into effect, the insurgents were sadly in need of arms and ammunition.

To obtain a supply of these they resolved to attack Borris House, the residence of Mr. Kavanagh,* which was known to contain a large quantity of the material of war. In this attack they failed, as they did in most others in which they had to fight enemies sheltered behind stone walls. The house in question was so strongly built, that the fire of the howitzer the insurgents brought with them had no effect on its walls. This fortress-like mansion was defended by a party of the Donegal Militia. The attacking party carried on the assault with great determination till evening, when they desisted from it on perceiving the approach of Sir Charles Asgill, at the head of an over-

* Mr. Kavanagh was the grandfather of the late representative of Carlow in the Imperial Parliament.

powering force. The baffled insurgents then returned to their encampments on Lacken Hill. There on the morning of the 19th, one of the chiefs descried, by the aid of a glass, a considerable force of horse, foot, and artillery marching towards them. When their general, the Rev. Philip Roche, was apprised of this, he gave orders to the small force under his command (then diminished to some four hundred men) to prepare for battle.

This command was, however, prevented from being carried into effect by Captain T. Clooney, who considered it would be decidedly rash to hazard a battle with such inferior force as the insurgents possessed. "Acting on this opinion, he desired the men to draw up two-deep on the hillside, fronting their enemy, and, at the same time, placing their hats on the ends of their pikes, to raise them above their heads, so as to deceive the enemy, by making their small force seem more numerous than it in reality was."* They were, at the same moment, to raise a shout, as if about to charge the advancing enemy. These orders were obeyed, and the stratagem succeeded. The advancing royalists halted, seemed to be thrown into confusion, extending their line, as if to prevent themselves from being outflanked by the insurgents, whom they supposed about to attack them in great force. While this confusion prevailed amongst the king's troops, the insurgents made a hasty retreat in the direction of Wexford, and, before the enemy were in readiness to pursue them, were at a safe distance.

Mr. Clooney admits that the number of the royal troops did not exceed that of the insurgents, but considered that, as the latter had but a few rounds of ammunition for their muskets, and no cannon, an engage-

* Clooney's "History of the Insurrection of 1798," p. 73.

ment could only end in their defeat. He affirms that Father Roche, on being told of the enemy's approach, immediately issued orders for battle, *without even inquiring what force he had to encounter.**

At a late hour that night the insurgents arrived at the encampment on the Three Rocks, considerably augmented in numbers on their way thither. They heard on their arrival that Sir John Moore, at the head of a large force, was encamped at Longraig, a village midway between Ross and Wexford. In consequence of this intelligence a council of war was held to deliberate concerning the next steps to be taken. Some officers suggested a night attack, but this was opposed by the majority, and it was finally resolved to set out at an early hour on the following morning. Accordingly, at daybreak next morning, the insurgents, being reinforced by a body of gunsmen, who had been summoned by express during the night from Vinegar Hill, set out to give battle to fifteen hundred chosen troops under the command of one of the bravest and most skilful generals in the English service. When the insurgents arrived at Goff's

---

* The Rev. Mr. Gordon and other authors ascribe the success of this retreat solely to Father Roche. "They (the insurgents) might have been pursued with slaughter if Roche had not practised stratagems. He distributed a number of horsemen with banners displayed, as it were in defiance, which gave the appearance of a force prepared for battle, and intimidated the royal troops from sudden onset, while his infantry were retreating at full speed. Himself was the hindmost in flight from the hill. He overtook his infantry and marched to the post of Three Rocks, without loss of a man."—Gordon. "History of Ireland," vol. 2, p. 421.

Sir John Moore in his despatch concerning this action acknowledges the gallant conduct of the insurgents, speaking of it as a "sharp, brisk action." *His statement of the loss he sustained was suppressed* by a Government which required its generals to assert what was false and suppress what was true, when the honour of the British army was concerned.

Bridge, within sight of the enemy, they halted, and the gunsmen, who had been mingled with the pikemen during their hurried march, were now arrayed into a separate body—forming a line four deep, and amounting to about six hundred and fifty men. At this critical juncture, when the insurgents were about to engage their enemy, the chief, who has been already mentioned as having betrayed the cause at Ross, left the field at the head of his detachment, under pretence of taking up such a position as would enable him to cut off the enemy's retreat in case of their being defeated. While Captain Cloonoy was engaged in remonstrating with this recreant, General Roche, with his usual promptitude, issued orders to his men to advance towards the enemy, who were drawn up in line of battle at Fooke's Mill.*

* The following account of this action is given by the Rev. Mr. Gordon, who, though a staunch loyalist, is acknowledged by all his contemporaries to be perfectly truthful and honest: "On the same day as Enniscorthy, was possession also of Wexford obtained by the royal troops. *General Moore at the head of about twelve hundred men* had, on the evening of the twentieth, in his march towards the former, been intercepted by an army of five or six thousand, led from Three Rocks by Philip Roche, at Goff's Bridge, near the church of Horetown. The forces of Moore, in loose array, or disposed in small parties over a wide extent of ground, and the gunsmen of the *rebels, only five hundred and sixty in number*, maintained a contest with considerable slaughter during four hours. From the nature of the ground, the manœuvres of the soldiery, and their own inattention to the commands of their leaders, the pikemen came not into action; and as their store of powder was at length exhausted, the whole body of insurgents retreated in good order to Three Rocks. *Except at Arklow the royal troops fought better here than in any other engagement in this rebellion; yet such military skill and resolution had an undisciplined and unorganized mob acquired in the short space of three weeks that the combat was long doubtful.*"—History of Ireland, vol. 2, p. 428.

The extraordinary fact that less than 600 insurgent gunsmen

During the battle which ensued the pikemen were forced to remain inactive, the nature of the ground chosen by the English general rendering their advance impossible, and consequently the combat had to be maintained by the gunsmen. The latter continued to pour their fire upon the English line till their ammunition was exhausted; then, perceiving two cavalry regiments, under Lord Dalhousie, approaching to reinforce the enemy, the insurgent general unwillingly ordered a retreat.

No attempt was made to molest the insurgents, who retired from the contest slowly and in good order, bringing with them five out of the six small pieces of cannon they had conveyed with them. There is little doubt that the failure of the insurgents' ammunition saved the English force from destruction, as in case of a retreat they would have been charged by the resistless pikemen. The great loss, amounting to about five hundred men in killed and wounded on the side of the English, sufficiently accounts for the unmolested retreat of their enemy. In this action the loss of the insurgents did not amount to half that sustained by the royalists. The main body of the insurgents encamped on the Three Rocks, while a party belonging to the town took up their quarters there for the night.

maintained a conflict for four hours with double the number of royal troops under an able general, affords an idea of the progress the insurgents had made in the art of war.

CHAPTER XV.

Alarm of the English Government at the long-continued resistance of the Wexford men.—Combined movements of the English generals.—The entrance of Wexford harbour blocked up by men-of-war.—How the insurgents at Vinegar Hill prepared to encounter their enemy.—Commencement of the battle.—Gen. Needham accused of cowardice.—Scarcity of ammunition among the insurgents.—Number engaged on both sides.—Sir Jonah Barrington's description of the fight.—Women take part in the conflict.—Operations of the insurgents under Father Kearns and Mr. Barker.—Death of Father Clinch.—Retreat of the insurgents towards Wexford.—Wounded insurgents slaughtered by the soldiery.—Fate of Barker.—Slaughter of the defenceless people who followed the insurgent retreat.—Small number of the *fighting* men slain at Vinegar Hill.—The insurgents from Vinegar Hill and those from New-Ross meet at Wexford.—General Edward Roche covers the insurgent retreat.

THE English Government, to render effectual whose vile design upon the legislative independence of Ireland the people had been goaded into this insurrection, now beginning to fear lest the continued and stubborn resistance of the Wexford men might arouse the rest of the country from their unaccountable apathy, resolved to crush the rebellion at once by pouring into the country such a force as would render resistance impossible. It seemed, in truth, from the vastness of England's military preparation, as if she were waging war against the united forces of some powerful and rival nation, not merely against the half-armed peasantry of but one, and that not the largest, of the thirty-two counties of Ireland.*

"When we consider," says Mr. Teeling, "the number of troops engaged, the rank and distinction of the commanders, and the immense preparations for reducing a single county, we may form some idea of the importance that Government attached to the Wexford campaign. After so many severe conflicts between the

* The armies of England employed in continental warfare rarely exceeded 20,000 men.

British and the united troops, it was now evident that Wexford could only be reduced by an overwhelming force ; and we find with others the following British officers employed in this service :—Lieutenants-General Lake and Dundas ; Majors-General Needham, Duff, Hunter, Loftus, Eustace, Johnston, Gascoyne; and Brigadiers-General Moore, Grose, &c. The opposition which this force encountered was evident proof that Government had not overrated the courage of the foe."

From all quarters regiments were on the march to take part in a combined attack on the insurgent encampment.

In obedience to orders from the commander-in-chief, General Lake, the following generals put the troops under their command in motion, and hastened to occupy the positions assigned to them. General Dundas marched from Baltinglass to Hacketstown, there to form a junction with Major-General Loftus, who was to proceed thither from Tallow ; both generals were then to advance with their combined forces to attack the insurgents posted on Mount Pleasant. By orders from the general-in-chief they halted at Hacketstown to wait the signal for attack. While the above-mentioned commanders halted at Hacketstown, Major-General Needham moved, on the 19th of June, from Arklow to Gorey, and on the ensuing day encamped on Oulart Hill. On the 19th, Major-General Johnson and General Eustace, having driven the insurgents from Lacken Hill, proceeded to Bloomfield, where they encamped on the evening of the 20th. On the same evening Brigadier-General Moore took up position at Fooke's Mill, and Major-General Sir James Duff had marched from Newtownbarry, and joined General Loftus at Scarawalsh.

It would be utterly impossible to describe the devastation caused by these various divisions of the English army as they marched to take up their different positions. Corps of auxiliary yeomen followed each of these divisions to render the ruin of the county more complete. On the 20th all the above-named generals had arrived at their appointed stations, where they remained to await further orders from Lieutenant-General Lake, who, with General Dundas, was posted at Solsborough. To aid the concentration of troops on land several men-of-war appeared off the coast, while gun-boats blocked up the entrance of Wexford Harbour. As these troops, strong in numbers and discipline, and amply provided with every munition of war, pursued their way of blood and fire through the devastated county, the unfortunate inhabitants, old men, women, and children, who had hitherto sought an anxious and trembling refuge amidst their native fields, now driven even from this shelter, were forced to seek protection at the encampments where the national flag still waved in defiance to the foe. Many of these helpless and terrified fugitives directed their steps to the town of Wexford of which their countrymen still held possession. Amongst the English generals at the time in Wexford, one alone is recorded to have shown that gracious quality of mercy, without which the soldier becomes a mere mercenary butcher; he endeavoured to put a stop to the executions and half hangings, and the various tortures that had caused such unparalleled misery in Wexford.

The deep slumbers of the brave men who lay around Vinegar Hill* were early broken by the ran-

* "Vinegar Hill is a beautiful verdant, low mountain; the River Slaney rolls smoothly at its foot on the one side, and the large town of Enniscorthy lies immediately under its base upon another; at one point the ascent is rather steep, on the other gradual; the top is crowned by a dilapidated stone building."—Sir Jonah Barrington.

dom shots that announced the approach of the royal army.

The men who were aroused by such a stern call from their much needed rest and reminded of the perilous struggle before them, had proved themselves in many a hard-fought combat the bravest of the brave, and now in this crisis of their career there was no sign of dismay amongst them. They answered promptly to the call of their leaders, and each man betook himself without delay to the place assigned for the assemblage of the particular corps to which he belonged. The cheerful and inspiriting summons of the drum or fife was in the insurgent army supplied by the human voice, and on hearing the name of his native parish shouted aloud, the rustic soldier quickly proceeded to join his comrades. The armies about to engage were nearly equal in numbers, but here all parity ceases. Twenty thousand brave peasants* shouldered pike or musket around Vinegar Hill, while as many trained English soldiery were drawn up in a circle that nearly enclosed their line, prepared to give them battle.

Twenty thousand English troops, led by six chosen generals, and practised in every military manœuvre, furnished with that great arm of war, a formidable artillery, and aided by many corps of yeoman cavalry, might promise themselves an easy victory over enemies so unskilfully led and so poorly armed as the insurgents. Moreover, the royal troops were fresh from the repose of the camp, and vigorous as men should be who never suffered from the want of fitting food or drink.

* Sir Jonah Barrington estimates the number of the royal troops at 20,000. Mr. Hay agrees with him in this statement. The insurgent force could not possibly have been greater than that of their enemies, the entire population of Wexford in 1798 being no more than 150,000.

At early dawn the English troops began to approach the insurgent position, and gradually to form a kind of circle around their forces encamped on the hill and its immediate vicinity. This circle was not, however, complete, for on the Wexford side of the hill it was open, and General Needham, whose division it was afterwards affirmed should have occupied the vacant space, was stationed in the rear to cover a possible retreat, for former defeats had made this at least possible to General-in-Chief Lake.* The rattle of musketry that had roused the slumbering peasants to resume their arms became more frequent as the morning advanced, and soon the cannon was heard thundering from the various advancing bodies of the British army. When the powerful English artillery came within range its concentrated fire was directed against the summit of the hill, whereon the greater part of the insurgent force was massed, amongst whom it did considerable execution. To this destructive fire from so many large pieces of artillery the few small guns, but two, in possession of the insurgents made a feeble response of defiance—it lacked the skill of Esmond Kyan to direct its fire, which soon ceased altogether on the ammunition becoming exhausted.

"Even on Vinegar Hill," remarks Mr. Hay, "there were but two charges for cannon, one of which was fired against the army approaching from Solsborough, and the other dismounted cannon posted at the Duffrey Gate at Enniscorthy."

The ammunition for the smaller firearms failed soon after, and the pike was now the only hope. All this while the insurgents had sustained a murderous fire from the English riflemen, who, finding a con-

* General Needham was accused of cowardice on this occasion and obtained the *soubriquet* of the *late* General Needham among his fellow-officers.—Plowden, p. 754.

venient shelter behind the various ditches and hedges in the vicinity of the hill, poured thence a terrible fire on their exposed enemies. Though their ammunition was all expended, the brave insurgents still continued the fight, and endeavoured to drive their foes from behind their natural entrenchments. It was a fearful sight to behold the gallant pikemen charging up to the very mouths of the cannon with a desperate bravery that has never been surpassed, while their ranks were being terribly thinned by successive discharges of every species of deadly firearm.

Concerning the position occupied, and the bravery displayed by the insurgents during this action, Sir Jonah Barrington makes the following observations:—

"The peasantry had dug a slight ditch around the extent of the base (of Vinegar Hill); they had a very few pieces of small half-disabled cannon, some swivels, and not above two thousand firearms of all descriptions. But their situation was desperate, and General Lake considered that two thousand firearms in the hands of infuriated and courageous men, supported by a multitude of pikemen, might be equal to ten times the number under other circumstances.

"A great many women mingled with their relatives, and fought with fury; several were found dead amongst the men, who had fallen in crowds by the bursting of shells. . . . . It was astonishing with what fortitude the peasantry, uncovered, stood the tremendous fire opened upon the four sides of their position; a stream of shells and grape were poured on the multitude; the leaders encouraged them by exhortations, the women by their cries, and every shell that broke amongst the crowd was followed by shouts of defiance. General Lake's horse was shot, many officers wounded, some killed, and a few gentlemen became invisible during the heat of the battle. The troops advanced gradually but steadily up the hill; the peasantry kept up their fire, and maintained their ground; their cannon were nearly useless, their powder deficient, but they died fighting at their post."

It was a slaughter not a fight, for to the ceaseless beating of the iron storm the hapless insurgents could not reply with even one defiant shot. While the body of insurgents on the hill carried on the contest with such heroic perseverance against such fearful odds, the division that obeyed the joint command of Mr. Barker and Father Kearns had likewise been hotly engaged with the enemy. Their position was at some distance beyond the Duffrey Gate, and this they had successfully defended against the English, under General Johnson, on the preceding day. The attack on this position was renewed in the morning, and continued till the retreat of their comrades from Vinegar Hill. Barker, whose experience in the French service we have already mentioned, showed in this action that he had profited by his past lessons in military art. He first posted a body of reserve on the bridge, where he also placed the only cannon he possessed, which was of small size, and mounted on a car.

He then formed the main body of his brave pikemen, stationing the gunsmen on either flank. Having made this disposition of his force, he charged desperately down on the enemy's line, and continued to hold them in check until they were too strongly reinforced, when he retreated to the bridge, which he held with dauntless determination till the loss of his arm compelled him to quit the field. Father Kearns took his place, but was soon after severely wounded and carried from the fight.

Another priest named Clinch was slain in this action. He was engaged in an encounter with Lord Roden, whom he had wounded, when a trooper, coming up to the assistance of his officer, shot down his opponent.

This unequal struggle, which the insurgents maintained during so many hours against such terrible odds, at length came to an end. Orders were issued by the insurgent leaders for a retreat in the direction of Wexford, the road to which town, as we have seen, was left open to them by the cautious policy of the English generals, who feared to drive their stubborn foes to desperation. The barbarous cruelties perpetrated by the command of General Lake sufficiently evinced that prudence, and not mercy or any nobler motive, prompted him thus to leave retreat open to his hard-fighting foes. To the eternal disgrace of the army to which such a miscreant belonged, he caused the hospital that sheltered the sick and wounded of the insurgent army to be set on fire, and, horrible to relate, all the unfortunate inmates were burned to death in the flames that consumed the building. Moreover, he issued orders that all the wounded on the field of battle, as well as those discovered in the houses, should be put to immediate death.* Indelibly branded is the nation whose flag is upheld by such merciless butchers as this disgrace to the noble profession of a soldier!

Barker, the wounded leader, was saved from the fate of the others in the same case, through the interference of some staff-officers who quartered themselves at his house; however, he was arrested by order of the general-in-chief, and conveyed to Wexford jail, there to await his trial. He was soon after released from prison on account of ill health, at the intercession of his brother, and, pending his trial, managed to escape to France. The insurgent army, thus forced to retreat, were enabled to continue their march towards Wexford

* See Hay, Gordon, and Clooney for proof of this.

almost unmolested. The cavalry, as usual, being upon
their rear, occasionally showed an inclination to assail
their retreating enemy, but the rear-guard kept them in
effectual check. But it fared far otherwise with the defenceless multitude, who had gathered round the insurgent camp on the fatal hill. To these no mercy was
shown: they were inhumanly butchered by the pursuing
yeomanry. These wretches displayed, on this occasion,
their usual thirst for blood, and their swords, so seldom
reddened in fight, were now deeply dyed in the blood
of unarmed fugitives. The number slain in battle on
that day *was small in comparison with the* multitude of
unarmed who fell by the swords of the victors.[*]

With respect to the number who were slain on the
insurgent side *during the battle*, Sir Jonah Barrington
says:—" Cavalry and mortars were brought to force
their line, and even against such an attack they made
a long and desperate resistance, and *retreated from that
large and disciplined army with very little comparative
loss.*" Surely, such a retreat was more glorious than
many a victory.

When the insurgents arrived at Wexord they found
it already occupied by the division of their army which
had retreated from Ross; and thus, after three weeks
of almost incessant fighting, wherein thousands of brave
men had fallen, the remnants of both divisions again

---

[*] Mr. Plowden says: "Nearly all the *real rebels* escaped."
"Historical Review," p. 753. The Rev. Mr. Gordon makes a similar statement, "few of the real fighting men were killed."—"History of Ireland."

"It is asserted that eighty-seven wounded peasants whom the
king's army had found on taking the town in the market-place,
used as an hospital, had been burned alive; and that in retaliation
the insurgents burned above a hundred royalists in a barn at
Scullabogue."—Sir Jonah Barrington, "Rise and Fall of the Irish
Nation," p. 455.

met, less sanguine, indeed, than when first they parted, but still not hopeless of the future.

We must add, the insurgents were greatly aided in their retreat by a large force under General Edward Roche, who arrived too late to join in the combat at the hill, but in time to render his defeated comrades this important service. It was his force that covered the retreat. While the battle was yet raging at Vinegar Hill, the reports of the distant artillery were borne ominously to the ears of the inhabitants of the town of Wexford. At length they ceased, and soon after the news was brought that the royal forces had won the day, and were already on their march towards the town.

Insurrection of 1798.   193

CHAPTER XVI.

On the rumours of a French invasion the Government redouble their efforts to quell the insurrection.—Great increase of the English forces.—Insurgents resolve to maintain the contest to the last extremity.—They concentrate their forces at Vinegar Hill.—Anxiety felt by the townspeople.—Reinforcements despatched thence to the chief rendezvous.—Captain Dixon plots the destruction of the Orange prisoners.—Steps taken by Mr. Hay to foil the Captain.—Mr. Hay on his return from the Three Rocks finds the town occupied by a fresh force of insurgents under General Edward Roche.—The latter unable to persuade his men to accompany him to the hill.—Frenzied state of the multitude.—Resolve to put the Orange prisoners to death.—Efforts made by Mr. Hay to save them.—Dixon prevails by the aid of two Orange informers.—Execution of prisoners on the bridge of Wexford.—Father Currin comes to the rescue.—His appeal to the people.—Its effect.—Esmond Kyan's intercession.—Noise of the engagement at Vinegar Hill heard in Wexford.—Lord Kingsborough sends for Mr. Hay.—Inhabitants of the town assemble to concert measures for their safety.—Captain Keough delivers up his sword.—Dixon and his friends oppose the capitulation.—Despatch sent to General Lake and his answer thereto.—Route taken by the defeated insurgents.—Desire the same terms as the townspeople.—Kingsborough's promises.—Timothy Whelan attempts to put an end to the negotiation for the surrender of the town.—Surrender to General Moore.—His humanity on this occasion.—Wounded insurgents in hospital put to death by the yeomen.—Disappointment of General Lake.—His character.

THE rumours now rife of a French invasion increased the anxiety of the British Government in no small degree, for could the Wexford men prolong the contest till the arrival of a Gallic force to their aid, the result of their combined efforts might prove fatal to British dominion in Ireland.

To quell the insurrection before the arrival of such formidable auxiliaries was now the object towards the accomplishment of which all the vast resources of England were employed. Regiment after regiment came pouring into Wexford till the insurgents found themselves confronted with an overwhelming power.*

* That the apprehensions of the Government were not unreasonable is admitted by most authors. Mr. Teeling in his personal narrative, referring to the Wexford men, says: "The rapidity of their movements, the boldness of their designs, their courage,

It is computed that previous to the action at Vinegar Hill there was a force of fully 90,000 men collected in the county of Wexford, so that there were at the least two soldiers to every insurgent. These were fearful odds against the patriots, who, though entertaining but small hopes of ultimate success, determined, nevertheless, to maintain the struggle to the last extremity. Around Vinegar Hill they decided to assemble their dispersed forces, and accordingly from that post messengers were despatched in all directions to summon thither the insurgents who were still in arms. In this emergency the dismayed and perplexed inhabitants of Wexford assembled together to consult concerning what measures they should adopt, but while they were yet engaged in deliberation an imperious summons arrived from Vinegar Hill, commanding all the fighting men to be there at day-break. Many of the townsmen set off that evening to join the chief rendezvous, while, to appease the insurgents in their vicinity, a party of sailors employed themselves in conveying to the Three Rocks the six small cannon taken from the Guinea cutter. On the evening of the 19th a band of Wexford gunsmen returned to town from Vinegar Hill with imperative orders to bring out reinforcements to that camp. At day-break on the ensuing day the drums beat, and all the armed inhabitants marched out, leaving none behind save those who formed the guard.

On the night preceding the departure of these men a band of some seventy pikemen, from the northern parts of the county, had arrived in town, and were lodged in the barracks by Captain Dixon. Mr. Hay, who seemed the good angel of the Orangemen, while the Captain

perseverance, and astonishing success, had given such powerful ascendancy to their arms, as baffled every effort of their enemies, and seemed to threaten the very extinction of the power to which they were opposed."—p. 161.

might be termed their evil genius, suspecting that the
latter entertained sinister designs with regard to his
protégés, resolved, if possible, to thwart him in their
accomplishment.

With seventy pikemen at his back Dixon might act
the dictator in the town, and sacrifice those he deemed
the enemies of his country. To prevent him from putting into execution such a sanguinary scheme, Mr. Hay
mounted his horse, and rode off on the spur to the camp
at the Three Rocks, to represent the matter to the chiefs
of the insurgent army.

He succeeded, though not without great difficulty,
in obtaining the aid he sought, in the shape of a party
of 120 of his fellow-townsmen, who had a few days
before joined the camp. However, four days elapsed
before Mr. Hay could gain what he sought, and on his
return found, to his dismay, the town thronged with
armed insurgents.

This force had been collected in the county and
brought in by General Edward Roche, preparatory to
their proceeding to reinforce the camp at Vinegar Hill.

On the morning of the 20th, when General Roche
desired to lead this body to the hill, he found, to his
great mortification, that they were unwilling to accompany him thither. They were led to adopt this
course by the advice of Captain Dixon, who, having
first aroused the spirit of vengeance in their breasts by
a recital of their wrongs, represented to them that a
fortunate chance having placed in their power the chief
inflictors of these evils, it would be folly to permit
them to escape unpunished. Dixon urged this point
with such artful eloquence that they determined to aid
him in the execution of the sanguinary schemes he
had long meditated. Mr. Hay thus describes the
excitement of the multitude:—"When the people were
assembled, and that General Roche thought to lead

them towards Enniscorthy, they peremptorily refused to proceed, representing Wexford, from the suggestions of Captain Dixon, as more vulnerable: wherefore, the general himself thought it more advisable to continue with this body of the people, now consisting chiefly of the fugitives from the northern parts of the county.

"These were continually relating their misfortunes, the cruelties they suffered, and the hardships they endured, to those with whom they took refuge; which roused and irritated the populace to such a pitch of fury as admits not of description, and of which none but an eye-witness can have an adequate idea.

"All entreaties and remonstrances to soothe or calm the exasperated multitude were in vain. However, continuing still on horseback, I endeavoured to address, explain, excuse, and expostulate, and in the course of these attempts, many pikes were raised against me, and several guns and pistols cocked and pointed at me, and vengeance vowed against me as an Orangeman; for they vociferated that I had distinguished myself by no other feat but activity in protecting their enemies, the Orangemen; that I had never attended their camps, or I would be a judge of their miseries, by the view of general desolation. One man would roar out that I had not been flogged as he had been; another pathetically related that his house had been burned, and that he had been driven to beggary with his whole family, and that he would have the death of the person that injured him; a third lamented the death of his father, another that of a brother, others of their children; and the appeal was made to me to decide on all their varied sufferings and misfortunes, while they perseveringly declared they only wanted to be avenged of those who had actually done them wrong, and I was asked, if similarly circumstanced, would I not take revenge for such injuries as theirs?"

Mr. Hay then implored them to grant the Orangemen at least a trial, but was answered by the universal cry, "What trial did we or our friends and relations obtain when some were hanged or shot, and others whipped or otherwise tortured, our houses and properties burned and destroyed, and ourselves hunted like mad dogs."

At length the people yielded to the entreaties of Mr. Hay and others, and consented to grant the prisoners a trial. A tribunal of seven men was constituted to determine their sentence. Of this number four proved favourable to mercy, and could not be brought to alter their decision by the arguments or threats of Captain Dixon. The latter, in despair of gaining their acquiescence, was on the point of yielding, when aid came to him from an unexpected quarter.

Two Orangemen, named Jackson and O'Connor, came forward and proffered their testimony as informers against the prisoners.

Dixon was now triumphant. The news of an event which favoured their views was soon spread abroad among the angry multitude, and a demand was heard for the instant execution of such as should be found guilty on the strength of the lately found testimony.

Mr. Hay and his fellow-intercessors retired from the scene, and the bloody tragedy began. The first who suffered was a man named Matthewson, who was shot outside the prison door. A batch of eighteen unfortunates was then conducted to the bridge at the request of Dixon, he himself, flanked on either side by an informer, heading the horrid procession. The manner of their trial was as follows:—Placed on their knees on the bridge, they were confronted with the two informers, who gave their evidence against them, if the alleged crime was considered deserving of death. Before the sentence was pronounced by Dixon, it was asked of the people who thronged around did they know of any good action that might be thought sufficient to counterbalance their crimes and entitled them to mercy.

Several of the prisoners found an intercessor among the spectators, and were thus snatched from death. But in case no such intercessor came forward, the death-signal was given by the judge, and the condemned was instantly piked.

The bodies were then thrown over the railing of the bridge into the river, nothing being taken off the person, for the object of the insurgents was vengeance, not robbery. This terrible tragedy went on for some time uninterrupted, till a Mr. Kellet, on being brought before the summary tribunal, bethought him in his extremity of summoning to his aid the parish priest of the town, the Rev. Mr. Currin. This was the first intimation the reverend gentleman had of what was going on. He came running to the bridge in time to interpose between the person who had summoned him and a bloody death. The pikes of the executioners were uplifted to be again reddened with the blood of another victim, when the minister of peace came upon the scene where angry and revengeful passions had full sway, and Christian men had forgotten, in the remembrance of their dreadful wrongs, the most sublime of the Redeemer's precepts—forgiveness of injuries. The good priest threw himself upon his knees beside the intended victim, and implored the people who stood around to join him in prayer. Many of them yielded to his entreaty, and knelt down. Then in solemn and fervent tones he prayed the Almighty Judge to show hereafter the same mercy to the people as they would show to the prisoners. This produced a deep impression upon many of them. Mr. Kellet's life was spared, but the trials were resumed, and others whose guilt was more evident were put to death. A new intercessor soon after appeared. This was Mr. Esmond Kyan, who, though suffering from a severe wound received at the battle of New-Ross, had arisen from his sick-bed, and caused himself to be borne on a litter to the spot. He added his entreaties to those of Father Currin, and at length the slaughter ceased. In all 36 persons fell victims to popular vengeance. Referring to the humane exertions of Father Currin and Mr. Kyan on this occasion, a Protestant gentleman afterwards remarked: "I have heard of hundreds of Catholics who risked their lives to save those of Protestants, but not of one Protestant who encountered any danger to save the lives of Catholics."

On the same evening at about eight o'clock General Roche marched off with his men towards Vinegar Hill, but too late to form a junction with the insurgents assembled there, for the hill was already surrounded by the English troops. On the 21st the engagement at Vinegar Hill took place, and the thunder of the English artillery was distinctly heard in Wexford, warning the inhabitants to provide for their safety, for little hope was entertained by them that the scale of victory would incline in favour of the insurgents. At an early hour on the same day Lord Kingsborough sent for Mr. Hay, to concert measures for the safety of the town.

The drums were beaten to assemble the inhabitants. They met at the house of Captain Keough, and there decided to send a deputation to each of the three royal generals, who with their divisions were now approaching Wexford.

One of these had arrived at Oulart, another was posted at Enniscorthy, while a third had arrived at the Three Rocks. It was also decided at the meeting in question to appoint Lord Kingsborough military governor of the town, and to reinstate Dr. Jacob as mayor.

Lord Kingsborough having received the sword which Captain Keough reluctantly resigned, proceeded to write off despatches to the different British commanders. These despatches ran as follows: "That the town of Wexford had surrendered to him, and in consequence of the behaviour of those in the town during the rebellion, they should all be protected in person and property, murderers excepted, and those who had instigated others to commit murder; hoping that these terms might be ratified, as he had pledged his honour in the most solemn manner to have these terms fulfilled on the town being surrendered to him, the Wexford men not being concerned in the massacre which was perpetrated by country-people in their absence." With the foregoing document another was forwarded from the people of Wexford; it was as as follows:—
"That Captain McManus shall proceed from Wexford towards Oulart, accompanied by Mr. Edward Hay, appointed by the inhabitants of all religious persuasions, to inform the officer commanding the king's troops that they are ready to deliver up the town of Wexford without opposition, to lay down their arms and return to their allegiance, provided that their persons and properties are guaranteed by the commanding-officer; and that they will use every influence in their power to induce the people of the county at large to return to their allegiance; and these terms it is hoped Captain McManus will be able to procure.

"Signed by order of the inhabitants of Wexford. *Wexford, June* 21, 1798. MATTHEW KEOUGH."

Captain Dixon and his friends were strongly opposed to the capitulation, but their opposition was overruled by the majority of the townspeople.

Mr. Hay and Captain McManus, who bore the despatch sent to Lieutenant-General Lake, were well received by that commander, who, however, declared that he did not consider himself bound by any promises made by Lord Kingsborough. He sent Mr. Hay back to the town with his answer to their request. This reply was couched in the following severe terms:—

"Lieutenant-General Lake cannot attend to any terms by rebels in arms against their sovereign. While they continue so he must use the force entrusted to him with the utmost energy for their destruction. To the deluded multitude he promises pardon, on their delivering into his hands their leaders, surrendering their arms, and returning with sincerity to their allegiance.

"*Enniscorthy, June* 22, 1798. Signed, G. LAKE."

Meantime the insurgents who had been defeated at Enniscorthy, took their route along the eastern bank of the Slaney, crossing the bridge at Ferry-Carrig, and halting near the Three Rocks. The majority of them were unwilling that the town should be surrendered without having first obtained the same terms for themselves as had been conceded to the townspeople.

To obtain such terms they despatched three of their officers to bring Lord Kingsborough to their camp with the purpose of detaining him there as a hostage till what they required was granted, and it was not till the latter had made the most solemn promises of the terms in question being conceded, that the insurgent officers quitted the town and returned to their camp. The solemn promises made by Lord Kingsborough induced many of the insurgent chiefs to remain in Wexford— an ill-judged step as the sequel proved. To prevent the capitulation being effected, and to put an end to all negociations, a man of Dixon's party, named Timothy Whelan, shot Ensign Harman while on his way with a despatch to General Moore. The same person attempted also to shoot Lord Kingsborough, but his pistol missed fire, and Kingsborough had the good fortune to escape on this occasion from the fury of an individual, as he had on a former, the vengeance of an angry multude. Dreading the well-known severity of General Lake, the inhabitants of Wexford, while he was yet on his way thither, surrendered the town to General Moore. It was fortunate they did so, for the latter, like most really brave men, was of a merciful disposition, and averse to shedding blood, save in the field of battle. The gallant and humane officer in question proved himself, at this juncture, not undeserving of his high reputation.

He issued orders that none of the inhabitants should be put to death or in any injured; and fearing lest his troops, in the excitement of their triumphant entry, might proceed to sack the town, which they had threatened to do, he detained them on Windmill Hill till their fury had abated. But he could not restrain the treacherous and sanguinary yeomen, parties of whom stole into the town, and proceeding to the hospital wherein lay one hundred and sixty wounded insurgents, set it on fire—the unfortunate and helpless inmates perishing in the flames.

On the 22nd, General Lake marched out from Enniscorthy for Wexford, but, on arriving near the town, had the mortification of finding that it had been already surrendered to General Moore.

Lake was a second Cromwell in his relentless cruelty towards the vanquished, but without a spark of the military genius which crowned that renowned regicide with unfading though blood-dyed laurels.

CHAPTER XVII.

How the insurgents acted after the disastrous retreat from Vinegar Hill.—March out of the town in two divisions.—The route taken by the division under Father John Murphy and Edward Roche.—Hold a council of war.—Father Philip Roche goes on his fatal embassy.—His character.—Miles Byrne not a leader.—March towards Longraig.—Insurgents penetrate into Carlow and Kilkenny.—Put the yeomanry who oppose them to flight.—Conflict at Kilcdmond.—Force the passage of the River Barrow.—Wexford militia taken prisoners.—Cruel deed committed by the militia.—The Hessians; their brutal character.

WE have hitherto seen the insurgents victorious in almost every encounter, but we must now follow them in their more unpropitious fortunes, and behold how these brave men struggled, amidst ever accumulating difficulties, to prolong the unequal contest. While negociations were being still carried on between the people of Wexford town and the English commanders, the insurgent forces, greatly lessened in number, marched out in two divisions, taking different routes. The Three Rocks were once more the scene of an insurgent encampment. On these heights were assembled some two thousand men, under the command of Father John Murphy, who still, with dauntless courage, upheld the flag he had first unfurled in the name of his oppressed country.

Thus while the timid sued for terms, and even brave men deserted the insurgent standard under which they had so often marched to victory, thousands of true men and trusty leaders still kept the field, resolved never more to place their necks under the yoke of their English taskmasters.

The second division of the insurgent army, under their leaders, Kyan and Garret Byrne, had, on the same day, moved in the direction of Gorey. This division was considerably augmented by five thousand men under Edward Roche, who, having arrived too late to take part in the battle of Vinegar Hill, now bravely resolved to repair, if possible, the loss occasioned by his absence.

To Father J. Murphy and Edward Roche must be given the credit of rallying the insurgents dispersed through the town, and leading them forth once more to renew the contest. The division of the insurgent army that set out from Wexford on the evening of the 21st, halted but a short time at the Three Rocks, and then resumed their march in the direction of Sleedah, a small village in the barony of Bantry. This force numbered in all about 3000 men, who were chiefly from the northern parts of the county of Wexford, together with the brave Wicklow men, who had followed the national flag from the very outset. On the arrival of this small force at Sleedah, the place chosen for the night's bivouac, a council of war was held to deliberate on their future proceedings. At this council were present Father John Murphy, Father P. Roche, Anthony Perry, and Edward Fitzgerald, with other leaders of less note.* Here it was that the Rev. P. Roche declared his intention of proceeding to Wexford, in the hope of obtaining terms from General Lake for himself and his comrades. He further proposed that they (the insurgents) should remain in their present position until they should hear of the terms he confidently hoped to obtain. His brother chiefs, however, did not share in these delusive expectations, and endeavoured to dissuade him from his fatal project. Father John, who, with his usual keen perception, divined the probable result, did his utmost to prevail on his friend to remain, and not thus uselessly to endanger his life in seeking mercy from men who

* Miles Byrne, afterwards General in the French army, accompanied this expedition. It is plain, however, that he was too young at the time to hold any very prominent position. A boy of seventeen years of age was hardly likely to be chosen as a leader by the Wexford pikemen. His narrative of the insurrection, as told in "The Memoirs," is very interesting, but inaccurate in some important statements. Notwithstanding these defects it is still a valuable addition to our national literature.

had never shown it. But the arguments and entreaties of Father John and the rest were of no avail.

Before the day had dawned the unfortunate gentleman rode off alone towards Wexford, hopeful of finding in the breasts of the English generals that generous spirit of mercy to which his own manly heart had never been a stranger. As his friends foretold, he failed to accomplish his purpose, and fell a sacrifice to his fatal error.

On entering Wexford he was seized, dragged from his horse, kicked and buffeted in the most brutal manner, and thrown into prison, which he did not quit till he was led to execution. Of this clergyman, Mr. Gordon says :—" Many Protestants owed their life to his intercession." The same may be said with perfect truth of all the other priests who took an active part in the insurrection.

Father Philip Roche who thus fell a victim to the cruel spirit of the times was a man of commanding stature and fine presence. His manners were bland and courteous, and he evinced during his short career as a military leader considerable talent. He was much lamented, and his death threw additional gloom over the cause in which he had been so conspicuous a leader. Hardly had poor Father Roche set out alone for Wexford than Father John gave orders to break up the bivouac at Sleedah, and prepared to march in the direction of Fooke's Mill and Longraig. At the latter place the insurgents passed over the ground whereon the battle had been recently fought between the force under Sir John Moore and that commanded by Father Roche. The unburied bodies of the slain still strewed the ground and made a ghastly scene for the eyes of the passing insurgents, who, however, did not halt, but pursued their march with unwearied activity. They encoun-

tered but little opposition on their way, the yeomen
cavalry behaving with their usual cowardice, appearing
at a distance, firing at the advancing column, and then
betaking themselves to instant flight.

The insurgents were now marching by a circuitous
route with the intention of penetrating into the neighbouring counties of Carlow and Kilkenny, and thus
drawing the troops from Wexford in pursuit, and
affording to their scattered and disheartened, but, as
yet, unsubdued comrades there, an opportunity of
rallying for another and more successful effort. As
they approached the boundary of the county the opposition offered to their advance increased. The yeomanry
appeared in larger bodies, and seemed more inclined to
come to close quarters. At the village of Killane, the
birthplace of the gallant Kelly, they opposed the further
progress of the insurgents, but were soon put to flight
and pursued till they reached the village of Kiledmond.
At this place, being strongly reinforced, the yeomen
resolved to make a stand, and, with a considerable force
of infantry and cavalry, essayed to oppose the passage
of the insurgents through the town, stationing themselves in the principal street. But they were unable to
withstand the charge of the fierce pikemen, and fled
after a brief resistance, setting fire beforehand to the
village. The insurgents, by command of Father John,
set fire to the barracks they had occupied. Having
thus once more obtained a signal triumph over their
enemies, the small force of insurgents proceeded a
short distance beyond the village, and there bivouacked
for the night. These brave men had been on the march
since early morning, and during that time had traversed
the entire county of Wexford, and crowned the day's
labour by a successful battle.

On the following morning the insurgents were early
astir, and received, with warlike joy, the intelligence

that a regular force of cavalry and infantry was stationed at Goresbridge to oppose their passage of the Barrow. After such a meal as their scanty store could furnish, the men, at the command of their leaders, fell into marching order, and set out in the direction of those new enemies. When they arrived within sight of the town, they were furiously charged by the Fourth Dragoon Guards, but sustained the fierce onset of their assailants without flinching, and forced them to beat a hasty retreat. The defeated dragoons fell back on their infantry, the Wexford Militia, which corps received their insurgent countrymen with a volley of musketry, which, however, did not prove fatal to any. It is probable that the men were unwilling instruments in the hands of their taskmasters, and did not wish to take the lives of their own brethren. The conduct of their officer seems to confirm this view of their inclinations; for, while the force under his command maintained a feeble and apparently harmless fire, he seized the opportunity of mounting behind a dragoon and galloped off in the direction of Kilkenny, without waiting the issue of the contest. Upon this his men ceased to fire, were surrounded, and made prisoners. The result of this affair gives us an idea of the feeling by which a great many of the militia regiments were animated, and how little reliance the British government could place on them to serve as executioners of their fellow-countrymen. The majority, however, of the rank and file of the Wexford Militia were Catholics, whose sympathies were naturally with their fellow-countrymen and co-religionists. The insurgents having achieved this signal success, took possession of Goresbridge, where they obtained a quantity of flour. Thence they proceeded towards the ridge of Leinster, where they pitched their camp for the night. We regret to have to record a cruel deed of revenge perpetrated in the insurgent camp during the night, not, indeed, by the insurgents, but by some of the militia captured in the fight of the preceding day. It seems that amongst the prisoners taken were some Orangemen who had formerly treated with great cruelty their Catholic comrades on the supposition of their being United Irishmen. These injured men, yielding to the fell spirit of revenge engendered by the memory of their wrongs, rose during the night and murdered their former tyrants. It was a cruel deed and a lamentable instance of the sad fruits of the hateful Orange system. Before we further pursue the fortunes of these brave men we will, for a brief while, retrace our steps to consider the condition of the inhabitants of Wexford. The regular troops and yeomanry emulated each other in diabolical cruelty; and, to deepen the horrors of the period, a brutal horde of foreign German mercenaries, called Hessians, were let loose on the people. Tradition has handed down amongst the people the name and deeds of this demon crew, and, for years after, the mere mention of these loathed and accursed Hessians was sufficient to call the indignant blood to the cheek of manhood, and to cast a pallor over that of woman. In fact, so desolate had the country become, that none save the old, the decrepit, or the idiotic, were to be encountered on the roads, in the houses, or fields. But neither the decrepitude of age, nor the deprivation of reason, that even amongst the fiercest and most savage children of nature throws a shield over utter helplessness, afforded any protection from the indiscriminate fury of England's swordsmen. We would fain pass over in silence the wrongs inflicted on helpless women.*

---

* Both officers and men were wont to boast openly of the outrages they had perpetrated on the wives and daughters of the "rebels," so fiendish was the spirit that animated the Orange party, and so bitter the feeling of hatred entertained by them to their Catholic fellow-countrymen.

Better and more merciful had it been to have plunged the swords that had been reddened in the blood of the hoary fathers of the peasantry in the bosoms of those Irish maids and matrons than to have subjected them to the brutal appetites of the vilest mercenaries.

CHAPTER XVIII.

Insurgents arrive at the village of Dunain, where they are joined by the colliers.—Attack on Castlecomer.—Attempt to take possession of Lady Anne Butler's mansion.—Burning of Castlecomer.—Flight of Sir Chas. Asgill.—Strange apathy of the people of Kilkenny and Queen's County.—Insurgents retrace their steps towards Wexford.—Treachery of the colliers.—Insurgents force their way through Scollagh Gap.—Father John captured.—Insurgents again separate into two bodies, taking different routes.

BEFORE dawn the insurgents set out for the village of Dunain, where they arrived about five in the morning. Here they were joined by a large body of colliers (from an extensive coal mine in the vicinity) armed with swords and pistols of an indifferent description. On arriving at Dunain they heard that four hundred men of the Waterford Militia had just quitted the village, and had gone in the direction of Castlecomer. Father John, whose energetic spirit ever urged him on to some new and perilous undertaking, now set out with a part of his force, including the lately-joined colliers, by a short route across the fields, to attack the English force at Castlecomer, leaving the rest, under another leader, to proceed to the same place by the less direct route of the high road. When the leader of the second division arrived within a short distance of the above-named town, he descried a body of about 200 English soldiery drawn up on the road along which his advance was directed. On seeing the approach of the insurgents, who came

P

on at a running pace, these men raised aloft a white flag on the end of a bayonet, and appeared to desire a parley, evidently with the intention of surrendering. The insurgent chief having halted his men, urged his horse on before them to ascertain the intention of the military; and on drawing nearer found that they were a party of the Waterford Militia, cut off, by the unexpected and rapid advance of the insurgents, from their regiment, and desirous, on receiving suitable terms, of surrendering. The terms they sought were willingly granted by the insurgent leader, who returned towards his own men, riding at the head of the militia, one of whom held his horse's bridle.

But this pacific arrangement was unfortunately disconcerted by an untoward occurrence. One of the insurgents, who happened to be absent during the negotiation, suddenly emerged from the fields upon the road, and seeing the strange position of his captain, naturally supposed him to be a prisoner, and without further reflection drove his pike into the body of the soldier who held his rein, whereupon one of the militia officers, supposing this to be part of a preconcerted plan, discharged the contents of his pistol at the insurgent chief, while another ordered his men to fire upon his followers. The leader's horse received the missile intended for his master, and fell. But the body of the insurgents advancing swiftly towards them, the soldiers threw away their arms and accoutrements, and betook themselves to a hasty flight.

Many of them were captured in the pursuit that ensued, and the few that reached Castlecomer, and rejoined their comrades there, found that they had fared but little better than themselves in their contest with the insurgents under Father John. When the second division arrived in Castlecomer, at the heels of the flying soldiery, they found the town already in possession of their comrades,* with the exception of a large house, the mansion of Lady Anne Butler, into which the defeated troops had retreated, and from the numerous windows of which they now poured out a hot and deadly fire on those who were engaged in its siege.

The house, which had proved so fortunate a refuge for the king's troops, was lofty and very strongly built, and admirably adapted for the purpose which it at present served, and, indeed, could hardly be taken without the aid of battering cannon. In vain did the insurgents attempt to approach the house under the imperfect shelter of loads of hay and straw; the vigilant besieged shot the men who impelled the carts, and thus rendered their efforts futile.† Finding their efforts unavailing to force an entrance under such a heavy fire, the insurgents at length resolved to drive the defenders from the house by setting it on fire, placing quantities of dried wood and other combustible matter at its rere. The house was soon on fire, and the insurgent chiefs, desirous to save the lives of the besieged, sent from amongst their prisoners a black servant, bearing terms to be granted in case they surrendered. The messenger in question, carrying a flag of truce, was admitted, and presently returned with the answer of the garrison, that they were willing to surrender, but only on condition of receiving a written protection from the chiefs. This protection was immediately despatched, but the black soon after returned to say that the besieged now refused to surrender, as they had

---

* Mr. Gordon, in his History of Ireland, states that the insurgents took possession of Castlecomer, and plundered it, killing fifty of the loyalist defenders—that during the fight the town took fire (page 437). The same author estimates the loss sustained by the insurgents at about seventy men.

† Not being possessed of artillery, the insurgents were obliged to have recourse to this primitive method of attack.

descried a large force of royal troops hastening to their assistance. This unexpected news received immediate confirmation. Loud volleys of musketry, now heard coming from a hill outside the town, announced the approach of a new enemy. The force from which this firing proceeded being as yet at some distance, the insurgents found time to collect their scattered forces, and take up a favorable position on a rising ground that fronted the advancing enemy. This newly-arrived foe proved to be General Sir Charles Asgill, who had marched with his division from Kilkenny to the aid of the royal troops in Castlecomer. The insurgents proceeded some distance outside the town before coming in sight of the English force.

At length, having passed a large grove that lay on their right flank, they came in full view of Asgill's force drawn up in line of battle at no great distance. Strange to say, the insurgents were allowed to gain the position they desired, marching all the while with their right flank exposed to the enemy. While the insurgents were pushing rapidly onwards to gain their intended position in front of Asgill's force, a soldier was observed running at full speed towards them from the hostile ranks. He was fired on by those he had deserted, but had the good fortune to escape unhurt, and joined the insurgents with the welcome intelligence that many of his comrades but awaited an opportunity to desert the English standard. The insurgents at length attained the desired position, and awaited with their usual ardour the signal for attack. However, no sign of hostility was shown by their red-coated foes, from whom they had expected a very different reception. Great was their astonishment on beholding, a few moments after, the entire division of the English general—horse, foot, and artillery—wheel about and commence a rapid retreat towards Kilkenny, from whence they came on their abortive expedition. The tired insurgents continued their march through the apathetic population of Kilkenny, and encamped for the night in the Queen's County, whose inhabitants seemed equally indifferent with those of Kilkenny, with unaccountable folly neglecting this grand opportunity, afforded the first time during centuries of slavery, of shaking off the yoke of their English masters. Seeing the unwillingness of this miserable people to join their ranks, the gallant Wexford men directed their march towards their native county, with the design of re-uniting their force to that which had left the county town on the 21st of June to proceed in the direction of Wicklow. During all this day they pursued their homeward march without encountering an enemy, and at a late hour in the evening arrived at the hill of Kilcomney, where they pitched their camp for the night. When the insurgents awoke on the ensuing morning from their sorely-needed repose they discovered that an act of unparalleled treachery had been perpetrated by the villanous colliers, upon whose assistance they had so much relied. These treacherous allies foully deceived the brave men who had so confidently trusted them, and, while the latter were buried in sleep, had arisen and deserted them, plundering them of almost all their fire-arms, and leaving them, as far as was in their power, at the mercy of their numerous foes.* Detestable treachery, the thought of which fills the heart with indignation that words fail to express! Surrounded on all sides by their cruel and merciless foes, foully plundered and betrayed by the in-

---

* "In this hope the Wexford men were grossly deceived; when those who had been thus overcome with lassitude and distress had thus lain for a while, they found themselves stripped of their arms and everything that the colliers could carry with them to their pits and dens."—Kelly, p. 182.

famous colliers, wearied and travel-worn, the grand spirit that had animated these heroic men from the outset still upheld them under their accumulating misfortune. But a fresh trial now awaited their courage and endurance. They ascertained from one of their scouts that the king's troops were gathering round them, advancing from different quarters.

This intelligence determined their leaders to lose no time in making a vigorous onset on some one or other of the approaching forces. They resolved to direct their attack against a body of troops stationed to defend the Pass of Scollagh Gap. Accordingly, the insurgents, to the number of about 4,000 men, the pikemen forming the main body, marching in columns, with as many gunsmen as they could muster on either flank, and in the rear, advanced up the Pass. The soldiery stationed in the defile made but slight resistance to the furious onset of the pikemen, while the few insurgent gunsmen, sheltering themselves behind the rocks that project on either side, picked down every officer that was exposed to their deadly aim. Thus did the insurgents once more put to a disgraceful flight the trained mercenaries who marched under the proud flag of England.* General Asgill, though in the vicinity with 4,000 regular troops, prudently shunned an encounter with the insurgents, finding, doubtless, far more congenial occupation in the cold-blooded butchery of the unfortunate and defenceless people of the district around Kilcomney.† In this, as in the other battles

---

* Of this action the Rev. Mr. Gordon says:—"They forced their way (through the gap) with little loss, with the defeat of the opposing troops, and directed their march north-eastward, by the dwarf woods, near Ferns, to the mountains of Wicklow, reduced by desertion to a much less number, and deprived of their leader, Father John, who was taken after the battle, and hanged at Tullow."

† "They glutted, however, to satiety their savage thirst for blood, with the murder of the county people all around."—Kelly, p. 184.

fought by the insurgents of this division, they were possessed of no artillery. Now, alas! to use the words of Miles Byrne, "a dismal cloud overcast all the hopes of the insurgents." Their most beloved and trusted chief was missing. He had planned the successful passage of Scollagh Gap, had been seen in the combat that ensued, but soon after mysteriously disappeared. The loss of Father John was irreparable, for he had been the soul of the enterprise. Wise to plan, and full of energy to execute, he had ever led his brave and devoted men to certain victory. But now, alas! he was to be seen no more at their head. This was the severest blow that adverse fortune had inflicted on these gallant patriots, who had hitherto continued to struggle with invincible courage against the most fearful odds. It was commonly believed amongst those who with such deep sorrow deplored his loss that, having ridden out to reconnoitre, he had been surprised by a party of the enemy, and slain while resisting capture. In whatever way he may have met his death, his loss inflicted a severe blow on the insurgent cause.* Having, as we have seen, effected so gallantly the passage of Scollagh Gap, the insurgents halted to consult together on what

---

* The *Carlow Magazine* gives an account of his death at Tullow, and a curious old ballad, in the author's possession, confirms the statement therein given. According to the *Magazine*, when taken prisoner, he was discovered to be a priest by a stole and pyx found in his pocket. Before his execution he received 500 lashes with a cat-o'-nine-tails, which he endured without a groan. His head was then cut off, and his body thrown into a lighted pitch-barrel, which was placed at the door of a Mr. Callaghan, a respectable Catholic, in order, as the Orangemen said, that he might enjoy the smell of a roasted priest. His head was stuck on a pole at the chapel gate, where it remained for a long time after. The words in the old ballad referred to, relative to Father John, are as follows:—
"It was by their means (the Kilkenny colliers) Father John Murphy was taken in his retreat to Castlemore. He was brought to Tullow and used most basely; with faggots blazing they burned

steps were next to be taken. But the voice of their
wisest and bravest leader was now unheard in their
council. A difference of opinion as to their future route
arose amongst them. Many were of opinion that the
wood of Kilaughrim, some five miles distant, would
be the best position, whilst others were desirous of
proceeding in the direction of Wicklow to join the division from which they had separated at Wexford town.
They finally separated, to form two bodies, one party
taking the direction of the Wicklow mountains, while
the other sought the cover of Kilaughrim wood.

his bones." The above account of his death is confirmed by a
letter written by Dr. Caufield, R. C. Bishop of Ferns, to Dr.
Troy, of Dublin, dated Wexford, September 2, 1798. Dr. Caufield
was an ardent loyalist, and suspended every priest who joined the
United Irishmen —*See letter to Dr. Troy, in " Plowden's Historical Review of the State of Ireland."* It is also related that, when
he was brought before the court-martial, a certain Major Hall had
the meanness to put several insulting questions to him, which the
high-spirited rebel, undaunted by the terrors of the place, answered
by knocking down with a vigorous blow the ruffianly interrogator. (For further particulars see Appendix).

CHAPTER XIX.

The insurgents halt at Monaseed, where they hear of fresh Orange atrocities.—They fall in with the force they are in quest of.—How the division of insurgents under Garret Byrne, on their way to Wicklow, are met by a horrid spectacle at Gorey.—They take vengeance on the murderers of women and children.—The engagement at Hacketstown.—Just retribution that befel the Ancient British cavalry.—Defeat of the Orangemen at Ballyrakeen Hill.—Attack on Captain Chamney's house.—Resolve to destroy all strongly-built mansions.

MONASEED, the birthplace of so many brave insurgents, lay directly on the route of those who moved in the direction of Wicklow; and there they made a brief stay, and heard with joy of the many splendid achievements of the gallant band they were in quest of. There, too, with feelings of anger and indignation too deep for utterance, they heard of the numberless deeds of inhuman cruelty perpetrated by the yeomen and the regular soldiery on the wounded and defenceless who had the misfortune to fall into their power. One authentic instance, selected from hundreds equally so, may suffice to afford some idea of the conduct of the loyalists of the period. "Hunter Gowan," that incarnation of fiendish cruelty, being his Majesty's *Justice of the Peace*, and likewise captain of yeoman cavalry (consequently enjoying complete dominion over the property and lives of the mere Irish of the day), entered the house of a neighbour of his, named Patrick Bruslan—one of the bravest men in the insurgent army, and then lying ill of a wound—and inquired in the kindest terms about his health. The wife of the wounded man, of whom he made these apparently friendly inquiries, conducted him, at his request, to her husband's bedside, that he might, as he said, "enjoy the pleasure of a chat with his old neighbour." Gowan stood at the bedside of the wounded insurgent, and stretched out his hand, as if in friendly greeting; but when the unsuspecting Bruslan grasped it, Gowan drew a pistol from his pocket with the disengaged hand, and shot him through the heart. Then, turning to depart, he said to the unfortunate widow he had just made—"You will now be saved the trouble of nursing your d——d Popish rebel husband." The insurgents soon quitted Monaseed, and, pursuing their march, had the good fortune to encounter at the White Heaps the division of their army with which they desired to effect a union. The chiefs of this division were Garret Byrne, Esmond Kyan, Edward Roche, and Nicholas Murphy.* Many others, however, had fallen in the different combats that had taken place since their departure from Wexford. This united force bivouacked for the night at Ballyfad, where their number was augmented by the arrival of many who had quitted them to visit their families. Having now to narrate the history of that division of the insurgent force which quitted Wexford on the 21st to proceed in the direction of Wicklow, we must go back to the day of their departure. This division, as well as that which left the town about the same time under the command of Father J. Murphy, was considerably thinned by the delusive hopes created by the negotiations for peace at Wexford. However, at setting out on their march they mustered about 7,000 men, armed in the usual way, and, as commonly happened, very much in want of ammunition for the few firearms they possessed. They proceeded on the first day as far as Pippard's Castle, where they rested for the night. On the ensuing morning the chiefs agreed to march towards the Wicklow mountains, and with their usual promptitude set out at once on their way thither. When in the vicinity of Gorey they alighted upon a horrid spectacle.

* Nicholas Murphy was a brother of Father Michael.

The road along which they marched was strewn with the dead and horribly-mangled bodies of women and children. Many of these victims lay with their bowels ripped open, and presented to the eyes of their countrymen a ghastly spectacle, well calculated to fill them with mingled feelings of horror and compassion, and to rouse them to a determination to take the direst vengeance on the cowardly perpetrators of such worse than savage barbarities. This massacre was occasioned by the insurgents' retreat from Vinegar Hill; for the English regular soldiery and their bloodthirsty associates, the Orangemen, or yeomanry—the terms were synonymous—who had taken shelter within their entrenchments from the furious storm of insurgent warfare, on hearing of this unexpected step on the part of the insurgents, sallied out from their lurking-places, and immediately overran the country, flooding it with the blood of its unfortunate inhabitants, and practising every vile and inhuman cruelty that their inventive malice could suggest. Against this horde of murderous villains the vengeful insurgents now directed their arms. Changing for a time their route, they began to search for their scattered foes in the vicinity of Gorey. Many of the marauders were surprised in the houses of the peasantry in the very act of perpetrating their unspeakable villanies. Being caught red-handed, they were slain on the spot. The alarm being spread through their dispersed forces, they rallied together in considerable numbers. They were routed after a brief resistance, and pursued to Gorey, where, attempting to make a stand, they were again signally defeated, and pursued with severe loss towards Arklow. Such of the insurgents as were mounted pursued the flying foe as far as Coolgreny, where many of them fell by the hands of the victorious avengers. While this pursuit was maintained by some detached parties of the insurgents, their main body halted at Gorey, awaiting the return of their absent comrades. On the return of these the entire column set out for Croghan Hill, at the foot of which they encamped for the night. The day on which the gallant insurgents so well avenged the terrible wrongs inflicted on their wives, mothers, and children has been called the "bloody Friday," on account of the blood that was shed so abundantly thereon.

The forces engaged in this massacre of the defenceless and unresisting were the Ancient Britons—a Welsh regiment—in conjunction with many of the yeomanry corps of the county, whose chiefs were Hunter Gowan, Beaumont of Hyde Park, Ram of Gorey, the Earl of Courtown, White of Midleton, and the Earl of Mountnorres—names to be met with in the different narratives of those fearful times, when the demons of cruelty and bloodshed reigned supreme. Notwithstanding all these dreadful deeds of cruelty, of which their friends and relatives were the victims, be it here recorded to the honour of the valiant peasantry, so foully aspersed by Orange historians, that though they had taken numbers of prisoners, none suffered death at their hands, for which humanity they got little credit. The insurgent army remained encamped on Croghan Mountain during this day, and employed themselves in gathering provisions and collecting ammunition, in both of which employments their success was but limited.

On the morning of the 25th of June, the insurgents marched to Hacketstown, encountering on their way some corps of yeoman cavalry, whom they put to immediate flight. On drawing near the town they found the English infantry drawn up in a field outside it, prepared to dispute their entrance. Upon this force, numbering about 200 men, the pikemen fell furiously, soon routing them, and leaving their captain (Hardy) dead upon the field, together with thirty of his men. The insurgents now entered the town, and proceeded to attack the barracks, in which their discomfited foe had found refuge. Adjoining this building, but projecting farther into the street, stood a large malthouse, in which a party of armed loyalists had taken post for the purpose of aiding the royal troops. The front of the barracks and one side of the malthouse met and formed an angle, so that from one building a direct, and from the other a flanking fire could be poured upon the attacking party.

Both the buildings in question were of great strength, and in fact well-nigh impregnable to assailants unprovided with artillery. The roof of the barracks was surrounded by a parapet, from behind which the besieged could take aim with almost perfect security. To obtain possession of these buildings was the object to which the insurgents now bent all their energies. A low wall, running parallel to the front wall of the barracks, afforded a partial and insufficient shelter to the insurgent gunsmen, from behind which they could take aim at such of the loyalists as showed themselves at the windows of the malthouse, or over the parapet of the barracks. The insurgents, indeed, fought at great disadvantage, and under the galling fire of their well-sheltered foes numbers of them fell. But nothing could exceed the heroic resolution and rare intrepidity they displayed in the course of this unwise attempt to take a fortified house without the aid of even a single piece of artillery. Their leaders in this affair were Garret Byrne, Edward Fitzgerald, Anthony Perry, and Michael Reynolds.[*] The latter gentleman signally distinguished himself during the action. The Wexfordians, accustomed as they were to see men bear themselves bravely in bat-

---

[*] It was Michael Reynolds who led the attack on Naas, described in a former chapter.

tle were struck with admiration at the extraordinary coolness displayed by Reynolds, who exposed his person fearlessly on all occasions when it was necessary to direct the efforts of the assailants, not seeming to regard in the least the bullets that showered around him thick as hail. While the unequal contest was maintained by the gunsmen on both sides, a party of the insurgents endeavoured to drive the enemy from their retreat by setting it on fire. This daring attempt they persevered in for several hours, one party after another advancing to the assault under such cover as featherbeds and loads of straw fastened upon cars afforded. Many gallant men lost their lives in these useless efforts, for the bullets of the defenders reached them through and under their insufficient cover. But undeterred by their heavy losses, they still carried on the desperate conflict, reckless of life, and resolved to prevail or perish.

And, in truth, could the most persevering and dauntless resolution have effected the object they aimed at, it would have been accomplished. It was in advancing to one of the assaults referred to that young James Murphy, a nephew of Father Michael, lost his life. He was shot by one of the soldiers posted in the barracks, an excellent marksman, who had already slain several of the insurgents. But the death of this brave young man was soon after avenged by his friend Myles Doran, of Cloughmore, who brought down the sharpshooting red coat with a well-directed bullet.*

---

* A still greater loss was that of the brave leader Reynolds, who was mortally wounded as he mounted a ladder carrying a lighted brand, and covered (*but ineffectually*) with a feather bed; his companions carried him into a neighbouring cabin where he soon after expired—exhorting them with his dying breath to persevere in the cause in which they were embarked.

Towards evening a partial success seemed to reward the persevering intrepidity of the insurgents. The malt-house was abandoned by its loyalist defenders; but the fire from that building had scarce ceased when a fresh one was opened upon them from the house of the Rev. Mr. M'Gee, a Protestant clergyman, within which he, with several of his friends had barricaded themselves, resolved to assist, with all their powers, the besieged soldiery, and inflict a crushing defeat upon a common enemy.*

But still the latter maintained the conflict with unabated fierceness, although the bodies of their dead and wounded comrades strewed the ground even more thickly as the hours passed on; nor did they desist from an enterprise they should never have attempted till darkness began to gather round the scene of desperate strife, and rendered its continuance impossible. During the night the insurgents withdrew from the place where so many precious lives had been unavail-

---

* The above account of the engagement at Hacketstown was communicated to the author by several of the insurgents who took part therein. Amongst those were his maternal grandfather and grand-uncle. The latter was standing by James Murphy's side when he received his death-wound. All these witnesses spoke in enthusiastic terms of Reynolds' gallantry.

An old lady, a relative of Father Michael, informed the author that she was present when he entered his brother's house to bring his young nephew with him to the camp. The boy was sitting in company with his mother and the younger members of the family when his uncle came into the room where they were all assembled. Father Michael having announced his purpose of bringing James with him, his mother expressed her unwillingness that he should leave her to take part in so perilous an enterprise, reminding the priest that he was but a "child." The patriot priest, in reply to the remonstrances which her maternal tenderness suggested, said, "Sister, it is true that he is very young, but not too young to fight, and, if needs be, to die, for his country."

ingly sacrificed, carrying with them their numerous
wounded, but leaving upon the field of conflict the dead
bodies of upwards of two hundred men.* The total loss,
in killed and wounded on the side of the loyalists did
not amount to more than fifty of their entire number.

Next day the Irish army marched towards Croghan
Hill—one of the Wicklow mountains. Here they remained unmolested by the enemy during the 27th and
28th of June. On the morning of the 29th, having
resolved to attack the town of Carnew, they set out at
an early hour on their march thither, halting for a
short space at Monaseed, to obtain whatever refresh-
ments the little village afforded. The insurgents had
quitted the village but a short time when it was
entered by the celebrated cavalry regiment of Ancient
Britons, followed by several corps of mounted yeomen—the latter desiring to act as executioners on the
insurgents, whom they hoped to see soon defeated
by their more warlike comrades. Amongst these infamous villains were the Earls of C—— and M——,
who were not ashamed to be the leaders of such a
vile crew of cowardly cutthroats. These royalist
forces having learned at Monaseed that the insurgents
complained of being extremely fatigued by their almost
incessant marching, and, moreover, that their ammunition was quite exhausted, considered them a sure
prey; and, elated by the hope of a complete victory,
and supplied with such an amount of Dutch courage as
their abundant potations at Monaseed could inspire,
they rode on in pursuit of an enemy they had al-

---

* "Every effort to set the barracks or M'Ghee's house on fire
having failed, the insurgents relinquished the attack, which had
already deprived them of so many brave companions; after nine
hours' fighting, they withdrew their force, marched to Blessington,
and encamped there for the night."—Kelly, p. 183.

ready, in imagination, vanquished. The regular cavalry led the advance, while their numerous yeoman allies followed, as was their wont, in the rere. They were now about a mile from Carnew, and were come to a place where the road was bounded by an old deerpark wall on the right, and on the left by a huge ditch, which ran in the midst of swampy ground. While riding at a hand gallop along the part of the road thus enclosed, they found that their further advance was arrested by a barricade formed of cars thrown across the road. This unexpected obstacle of course brought them to a dead halt. Before they had time to advance or retreat, their hitherto concealed foes rose suddenly from behind the ditch and wall we have described, and while the gunsmen poured a deliberate fire, every shot of which told, into their surprised and dismayed ranks, the more dreaded pikemen sprang forth from the same ambush, and were in an instant in their midst. We might pity these unfortunate dragoons had not the ferocious character of their crimes closed our hearts to all softer feelings. After a fight that lasted about half an hour, every man of the regiment that rode from Monaseed in all the pride of anticipated conquest, lay on the road either dead or dying. Thus perished the infamous cavalry regiment called the Ancient Britons, receiving the retribution that falls upon such red-handed sons of Cain sooner or later. But where were the burly yeomen who rode so gladly in their train to aid in an enterprise that promised such an abundant harvest of blood? These heroes remained on a rising ground at some distance on the right, while their accomplices in crime underwent their bloody ordeal, without offering them the slightest aid, and when they saw that all was over gave spurs to their horses, and rode off in the greatest terror and dismay. The intelligence of the defeat and total destruction of the Ancient Britons at Ballyellis was carried rapidly over the entire country, causing great joy to the defenders of liberty, and striking terror into the hearts of tyrants and their instruments. It reached the English infantry on their way from Carnew to the scene of action, and caused them to retreat. They took refuge in a large malt-house, where they fortified themselves as best they could, and awaited the attack of their rapidly advancing foes. Here the scene that occurred at Hacketstown was re-enacted—insurgent bravery wasting itself vainly on stone walls, and many brave men losing their lives in a fruitless essay to take a strongly-built, well-garrisoned house without artillery. The insurgent leaders, deeming it a useless sacrifice of life to continue the attack on the malt-house, drew their men off, and marched to Kilcavin Hill, where they remained for the night, greatly elated by the victory they had achieved. On this morning the insurgents shook off slumber at an early hour, and, before the sun had risen, were on their way to Shillelah, and, passing by that village, took post on Ballyrakeen Hill, where they remained for the night.

July 1st.—This day being a great anniversary with the Orangemen, these miserable traitors, whose dastardly triumphs are all founded on the humiliation of their country, whose curse and ruin they have ever been, resolved to signalise it by a furious and decisive onslaught on the few brave men who held aloft the national flag on Ballyraheen Hill. Towards the hill in question came troops of the various corps of yeoman cavalry, while their infantry showed an unusual determination to come to close quarters with their ancient enemies. With equal ardour the Irish troops—for though the Orangemen were born in Ireland their constant and unnatural hatred of her cause deprives them of all right to be called Irishmen—rushed to meet their treacherous foes, charging down the slope of the hill in a firm phalanx of pikemen, intermingled and flanked by gunsmen, on their enemy's lines. In vain the hostile cavalry essayed to check by their furious charge that unyielding cohort of brothers who fought in the sacred cause of country; in vain their infantry poured the leaden hail into their ranks. Every man in the insurgent ranks was a hero resolved to conquer or perish in a sacred cause. The insurgent force was now assailed on all sides by the cavalry, who, confiding in their numbers, and, perhaps anxious to retrieve their characters from the too well-merited stigma of cowardice, continued the attack with unwonted spirit. But this could make no impression on the ranks of their opponents, and they retired from each unsuccessful charge with diminished numbers. The gunsmen attached to the insurgent force remained to protect the flanks, answering with well-directed volleys the fire of the enemy's infantry. At length, after nearly an hour's fighting, victory again favoured the brave insurgents. Hundreds of their foemen lay stretched upon the ground dead or severely wounded, while their comrades, cavalry and infantry, unable to maintain any longer the combat against such determined foes, took to flight in different directions—the cavalry galloping away at fox-hunting speed, leaving their infantry to make the best retreat they could.* The latter, being closely pursued by the pikemen, took refuge within the mansion of Captain Chamney, which stood at the foot of the hill, and from its safe shelter defied their victorious foes. Here again bravery that had proved invincible in the field in fair fight was foiled when opposed by stone walls that sheltered a beaten foe. Seeing the uselessness of prolonging such an at-

* In this affair Captains Chamney and Nixon were slain.

tack, the men at the command of their leaders desisted from it, and marched off in the direction of Wicklow Gap, having obtained by the day's victory a fair supply of firearms and ammunition. The fruits of many hard-fought engagements having been lost to the insurgents by reason of their enemies taking refuge in large isolated, strongly-built mansions, it became evident to the leaders that to pursue their enterprise with any chance of success all such buildings must of necessity be destroyed. They came to this resolution with regret, but it was with them a question of life and death, and half-measures in such a position are simply madness. The insurgents pursued their route towards Wicklow Gap, marching all night, and, having arrived there on the following morning, pitched their camps, remaining during that day and the ensuing night.

CHAPTER XX.

Insurgents proceed to the Wicklow Gold Mines, where they burn the English camp.—Receive a reinforcement from Killaughrim Wood.—"The babes in the wood."—They attack General Sir James Duff, and force him to retreat.—Mr. Plowden's narrative of the battle of Cranford or Ballygullen.—Insurgents divide their force.—Wexford men return to Carrigrew.—Wicklow men retreat to Glenmalure.—Wexford insurgents quit Carrickburn and proceed to Kildare to join Aylmer.—March towards Athlone.—Attack a fortified house occupied by Lieutenant Tyrrell.—The Wexford men separate from the Kildare insurgents and penetrate into Meath.—Encountered by the Limerick militia and forced to retreat.—Capture and execution of Father Kearns and Anthony Perry.—The Wexford insurgents cross the Boyne and enter Louth.—Attacked by a large force of cavalry near Ardee.—Approach within seven miles of the metropolis, where they are routed by a squadron of the Dumfries dragoons.—The Rev. Mr. Gordon's account of the last stand made by the Wexford insurgents.

ON this day, July 2, at their usual early hour, the insurgents set out for the Wicklow Gold Mines, with the design of burning the English camp, which was there erected in '95. Having accomplished the desired feat, they returned by way of the Whiteheaps, and took up a position at Ballyfad. The insurgents, notwithstanding their great losses, both in men and leaders, were still a numerous force, and fairly armed with the spoils of their many victories. At the time, also, they were augmented by the force under Father Kearns, who had marched from Killaughrim Wood to join them.* While the insurgent camp was pitched at Ballyfad, small parties were despatched in several directions to reconnoitre, and bring back whatever intelli-

* Different military detachments were sent out from Ross and Enniscorthy, and these endeavoured to surround the extensive woods of Killaughrim, supposed to contain them (the insurgents), but their efforts proved fruitless, as they never could come up with the *babes in the wood*, who generally had a rendezvous in the night and dispersed towards morning, into such a variety of lurking places, that but few of them were apprehended; and though several plans for their annihilation were contrived they all proved ineffectual."—Hay, page 298.

gence they could obtain of the motions of the enemy. Towards dawn of day some of the men who had been despatched on the preceding evening on this important commission returned to report the advance of a formidable English force on their position. On the receipt of this intelligence orders were at once issued to quit their present position and take up a better one on one of the hills in their vicinity. While the chiefs of the Irish army were choosing this position the near approach of the English force was announced by a volley from their advanced guard, which passed over the heads of a similar detachment of insurgents. A dense fog, which since dawn had covered all the country around, occasioned some confusion amongst them, preventing them from ascertaining the position of the enemy they knew to be near, and even causing some detachments to stray from the main body. The rising sun at length dispersed the fog, and shining forth in unobscured splendour on the insurgent army revealed to them, as they marched from the hill in the direction of Gorey, a large English force of horse, foot, and artillery following in their rear at about the distance of a mile. This force was commanded by Sir James Duff, who followed in the track of his enemy, but was unwilling to begin the contest till he had received reinforcements he expected from General Needham. The insurgents, however, seeing that Sir James evinced no inclination to attack, rightly concluded that he waited reinforcements, and in consequence, judged it better to give him battle before they arrived. With this resolve, they advanced some two miles along the Gorey road, their cautious enemy all the while hanging on their rear. The insurgents now left the high road, along which they had hitherto directed their march, and proceeded by a narrow cross road that opened on their right and stretched towards the townland of Ballygullen.

When they had proceeded some short distance along this
new route, their gunsmen, in obedience to their leaders'
orders, left the ranks and stationed themselves in ambush behind the fences that bounded the narrow road,
while the main body fell into fighting order, and moved
steadily onward towards Ballygullen, as if they intended
to pursue their march. It was designed by this movement to draw the enemy's cavalry, who had not seen
the execution of the stratagem, and were unaware of
the position of the ambushed gunsmen, under the fire
of the latter. This skilful plan succeeded. The English cavalry, seeing the main body of the pikemen pursuing their march, continued to follow them until they
came to where the concealed gunsmen lay. Then the
latter poured a close and destructive fire amongst them,
killing a considerable number and causing the survivors
to seek safety in instant flight. Had not the impatience
of the insurgents caused them to deliver their fire rather
prematurely, this great body of cavalry might have
been utterly destroyed; as it was, their loss was so
heavy that they made no appearance in the engagement
that ensued. General Duff, on beholding the surprise
and defeat of his cavalry, ordered his infantry to deploy
into line and advance to meet their foes. A most sanguinary and fiercely fought battle now ensued, in which
both sides displayed the greatest bravery. The insurgent gunsmen maintained a deadly fire on the English ranks till their small supply of ammunition was
entirely exhausted. It then only remained for the
insurgent leaders to bring their redoubted pikemen into
action. This they did with their usual gallant promptitude, directing their attack on the right flank of the
opposing force. General Duff, seeing this manœuvre,
and believing that his men had got quite enough
from the gunsmen without encountering those fearful
pikemen, gave orders to retreat in the direction of

Gorey.* The insurgents, though victorious in this hard-fought engagement, which lasted two hours, lost great numbers of their men, and the regret caused by the loss of so many brave comrades was hardly counterbalanced by the knowledge that they had inflicted a far greater loss on their routed enemies. As soon as Duff's shattered force had disappeared, they set out about collecting their wounded, and then quitted the scene of action, and marched off towards a hill some half mile distant therefrom. A council of war was now held, to deliberate on their future course of action. At this council it was decided to divide their force rather than await united the combined and overpowering attack of the large English army at that time assembled in the county of Wexford from all parts of the three kingdoms.

Of this action, Mr. Plowden says:—"Upon the arrival of the insurgents at a place called Cranford, by others Ballygullen, they resolved to make resistance and await the approach of the troops, however numerous they might be, although their own force was then very considerably reduced. They resolutely maintained the conflict for an hour and a half, with the utmost intrepidity; having repulsed the cavalry, and driven the artillerymen three times from their cannon, all performed by the gunsmen; for the pikemen, as on former occasions, never came into action; but fresh reinforcements of the army pouring in on all sides, they were obliged to give way, *quitting the field of battle with little loss to themselves,* and notwithstanding all their fatigue, retreating with their usual agility and swiftness in different directions."

Mr. Plowden here admits that they defeated the force under General Duff, and only retreated on the approach of overwhelming reinforcements, which coincides with the accounts given by other authors.

* Eighty of General Duff's troopers were slain in this action.—Kelly.

The Wicklow men resolved to seek the shelter of their native mountains; some of them, however, choosing to remain with the Wexford men, who marched that same night for their former camping ground on the hill of Carrigrew. Though the battle of Ballygullen, or Cranford, may be said to have concluded the famous insurrection of 1798, as after that engagement none of much importance took place between the hostile forces, we think it right to follow to the end of their career those who took part in the heroic but unsuccessful struggle we have essayed to describe in the foregoing pages.

The Wicklow men, after a brief repose, proceeded towards their proposed destination, passing Ferns and Carnew on their march.

When at length night set in it found them still pushing steadily onward; nor did they halt till they had left Kilpipe and Aughrim far behind, and gained the security they sought among their native mountains.

In this retreat they long kept alive the scanty embers of a fire that had once burned with such bright and cheerful flames. Yet as they never could muster afterwards a sufficient force wherewith to encounter their foes in any considerable conflict, their adventurous and most daring exploits furnish matter suited rather for the romancist than the historian.

In Emmet's Memoirs we find a highly interesting narrative of the adventures of the small but heroic band, who so long maintained those strongholds of nature, their own "native hills," against the numerous forces of military despatched against them, thus rendering their name one of terror to the English garrison of the lowlands.

Hackett, Dwyer, Holt, and Garret Byrne were chiefs of this small band, who never numbered more than two or three hundred men, but whose marvellous courage and activity rendered them formidable to their enemies.

The lone Glenmalure afforded them for a long while a comparatively safe retreat, from which, however, they were finally driven by the king's troops. Their most effective and inveterate enemies were the kilted Highlanders, whose former habits peculiarly fitted them for the effectual hunting down of the brave but unfortunate Wicklow mountaineers.

The Wexford men, with their few Wicklow adherents once more, and for the last time, assembled on the Hill of Carrigrew, having as leaders Father Kearns, Anthony Perry of Inch, and Garret Byrne of Ballymanus. These brave chiefs determined to march forthwith into the county of Kildare and join their forces to those which were assembled there under the leadership of William Aylmer. The desired junction effected, the entire force, numbering in all some five hundred men, set out towards Meath with a view of surprising Athlone.

On their march thither they arrived at the village of Clonard, where their progress was impeded by a galling fire of musketry, directed against them from a fortified house occupied by Lieutenant Tyrrell and a corps of yeomanry under his command.

The insurgents might have passed on, but, irritated by the loss they sustained, they halted to besiege the house. While engaged in this unwise attempt they were warned of the near approach of large royalist reinforcements from Kinnegad and Mullingar. On receiving this intelligence they desisted from the siege, and pursued their uninterrupted march towards the village of Castlecarberry, where they remained for the night.*

* This repulse the Wexford-men attributed to the cowardice of their Kildare associates, who neither aided them in the attack on

Insurrection of 1798.

This daring incursion of the Wexford insurgents into Kildare alarmed, while it enraged, the numerous loyalists of that and the adjoining counties. Corps of yeomanry, mounted and on foot, and detachments of regular troops, were soon mustering to hunt down the daring band. On the ensuing day the latter resumed

Tyrrell's house, nor joined them in resisting the troops. Deeming such allies worthless, they soon after parted company with them, and pursued their career alone. "After this repulse the fierce Wexfordians pursued unaided their plan of desperate adventure; finally separating from their less enterprising associates, against whom before, in consequence of some disputes, they had with difficulty been prevented from turning their arms."—Gordon, Hist. Ireland, page 411.

Of the attack on Tyrrell's house Mr. Kelly in his History makes the following mention, p. 193:—"The insurgents persisting in their hope of raising succours, determined to penetrate into Meath, Westmeath, and to reach Athlone, making their route through Clonard. As the bridge over the Boyne was to be crossed for the object they had in view, the corps of yeomanry commanded by Lieutenant Tyrrell, being apprised of the approach of the insurgents, occupied a large house belonging to the Captain of that corps, who was then in England. In the spring of '98 Captain Tyrrell took strong precautions to protect himself against the Defenders, who were said to be numerous in Meath. For that purpose he converted his house into a kind of garrison, by securing with mason-work the windows and doors of the under-story. Of Captain Tyrrell's mansion, thus fortified, the corps of yeomen were in possession, when the approach of a great body of insurgents was announced to them. The attack commenced against a high turret in the garden, and the house, at the same time. The fire kept up from both places was very destructive to many of the insurgents. In the meantime expresses were forwarded to Kinnegad, Mullingar, and Edenderry for reinforcements. The body of insurgents, having no cannon, were unable to make an impression upon either points, but unfortunately for themselves, were so improvident as to persist in their attempts. While thus engaged, a numerous corps of yeoman cavalry arrived from Kinnegad, and made terrible slaughter among the stragglers and such as were discovered concealing themselves among the hedges."

their march, and passed into the county of Meath, without receiving all the while any aid from the peasantry, while hotly pursued by a host of foes. The first body of pursuers to come up with them was the Limerick Militia, under Colonel Gough. The militia poured a destructive fire upon them, which, as their ammunition was spent, they were unable to return, and were consequently obliged to retreat with the loss of a few killed and many wounded.

It was soon after this contest, if such it can be called, that Father Kearns and Anthony Perry were made prisoners.* Three days after, the Catholic priest and the Protestant gentleman, being tried (and, of course, found guilty) by court-martial, were hanged on the same gallows at Edenderry. They died as cheerfully, as they fought heroically, for the good old cause of fatherland. Though unsuccessful in this affair, the insurgents still kept together, and, crossing the River Boyne, entered the county Louth. But their pursuers pressed so closely upon them that the hunted Wexford-men were at last forced to turn to bay. The place where they made their final stand was on the historic ground that lies between the Boyne and the town of Ardee. It was there that a large force of cavalry, under the command of Major-General Wemys and Brigadier-General Meyrick, charged down upon the diminished ranks of the outwearied and half-famished pikemen.

However, though wearied and outnumbered, they fought with desperate bravery, keeping their array, and repelling the furious and frequent charges of the

* Their brave leader, Colonel Perry, and the Rev. Mr. Kearns, had got as far as Clonbollogue, through tracts of bog, when two yeomanry officers named Ridgeway, and Robinson, from Edenderry, came upon them, and made them prisoners."—Kelly.

English cavalry, whom they often forced to retire in confusion.

But the appearance at this juncture of a large body of infantry, accompanied by artillery, showed them the uselessness of further contest.

Seeing their already thinned ranks still further diminished by the discharges of musketry and artillery, they began slowly to retreat, with their faces towards the foe (whom respect for their prowess kept at a distance), towards a large bog that lay on their right.

Here they remained unpursued during the ensuing night; but, deeming it hopeless to protract the contest, unaided as they were, they resolved to disperse, and thus render their escape more easy. Before the morning dawned the greater number of the now hopeless insurgents began, with heavy hearts, their homeward journey—proceeding singly or by twos or threes; but a small body keeping together, crossed the Boyne, and pushed on towards Dublin. However, they did not succeed in reaching the metropolis, for, arriving at Ballyboghill, near Swords, the disheartened fugitives were encountered and dispersed by a squadron of the Dumfries Dragoons.

The Rev. Mr. Gordon thus narrates the last desperate struggles that closed the military career of the Wexford insurgents:—"Totally disappointed of their expected reinforcements in the county of Meath, which had been lately disturbed, they passed the Boyne, near Duleek, by a rapid motion, into the county of Louth. Assailed on the fourteenth by two divisions of troops between this river and Ardee, they made a desperate stand; but overpowered on the arrival of more force with artillery, they broke and fled into a bog. Hence a part of them took the road to Ardee, and dispersed; but the main body repassed the Boyne, and were advancing directly towards Dublin with their usual swiftness, when they were overtaken in a hot pursuit by Captain Gordon, of the Dumfries Light Dragoons, at Ballyboghill, within seven miles of the capital. As they would have been surrounded by detachments from different quarters, they fled, and finally dispersed, severally endeavouring by devious ways to reach their homes or places of concealment."

CHAPTER XXI.

Great numbers thrown into prison on the entry of the military into Wexford.—Cruel treatment of prisoners.—Heroism of the boy Lett.—Gen. Needham's troops and the Hempesch dragoons.—Executions in Wexford.—Kelly of Killane.—General Hunter's clemency.—Lord Lieutenant's proclamation.—Orange ferocity.—Esmond Kyan's death.—Hunter Gowan.—"Mr. Massacre."—False alarms raised by the Orangemen.—Major Fitzgerald's courage and prudence.—The island discovered by Hawtrey White cannot be discovered when sought for.—Landing of the French expedition under General Hardi.—Surrender of the insurgent general Edward Roche.—Execution of Walter Devereux and James Redmond.

MANY persons who were implicated in the insurrection, relying upon the promises of Lord Kingsborough, remained in town after the entrance of the king's troops.* But their hopes of immunity were not destined to be realized, for soon after the above-mentioned event took place they were arrested and lodged in jail. Amongst these prisoners was Mr. Hay, whose services to the loyalist cause deserved better treatment at the hands of the victors. He thus describes the great hardships which he and his fellow-captives endured during their incarceration:—
"Two sloops were prepared as prison-ships during the

* Others less credulous made a timely escape; amongst these was Captain Dixon, who fled to America, where he died many years afterwards.

insurrection. One of them, however, was immediately condemned as unfit for that service; and afterwards, on the occasion of Lord Kingsborough and his officers being put on board for a few hours, she was again, on the inspection of the butchers of Wexford, pronounced unfit for the reception of a *pig*. After this second condemnation the *Lovely Kitty* (for so this infernal vessel was called) was hauled up on one side of the harbour, where, from her leaky state, she sank within a foot of her deck, and so escaped firing when the other, which had been used as a prison-ship, was burned. This was the vessel the Wexford Committee (loyalist) ordered to be their prison-ship; and accordingly, on the 3rd of July, she was hauled into the channel, a little dry straw was shaken over that which had remained in her hold for a month before, and the prisoners then were sent on board. Our walking on the fresh litter soon made it wet as the dung underneath, so that it was impossible to lie or sit without imbibing the moisture; nor indeed could we have the comfort of resting against her sides, as the planks were water-soaked, and the effervescence of putrid malt accumulated between her timbers was so strong as even to turn silver black in our pockets in the course of a few hours. The stench was insupportable, and there was besides such an infestation of rats that some of the prisoners were bitten by them. The weather at the time was mostly warm, and this raised such an exhalation that, small as the vessel was, we could scarcely see each other from either end of the hold. If it rained, the deck was so open that it was impossible in any part of the ship to avoid being wetted; and, contrary to the usual state of leaky vessels (when the bilge-water is not offensive), we were nearly suffocated while she was pumping. In our own defence we were obliged to be continually at the pump, to prevent our being overflowed; and, though our last occupation at night, we were always summoned to the same task early in the morning." Twenty-one persons were confined in this dreadful prison, under a guard of "Ogle's Blues," as the Shelmalier infantry were designated. Mr. Hay was detained in this loathsome place for some months, when he was transferred to the jail, whence he was not liberated till he had completed a term of thirteen months' imprisonment. Amongst his fellow-prisoners was a boy of thirteen years, Master James Lett, who, with a spirit far above his tender age, had taken an active part in the battles of New-Ross and Longraig. This little fellow was detained a prisoner till the January of 1799, when he was brought up for trial before Lord Kilwarden. When his lordship inquired for the prisoner, the boy was held up for his inspection on a man's arm. The sight of the diminutive prisoner was quite enough for the judge, who ordered him to be instantly set at liberty. But to resume our narrative.

While Generals Lake and Moore with their troops held possession of Wexford, large bodies of military under other commanders were stationed in the principal towns and villages within the county. Of these the force under General Needham, at Ballenkeele, earned an unenviable distinction for the ferocious war they waged upon the defenceless people.

Detachments from this force continually traversed the country, burning houses and putting to death all persons they chanced to encounter.

The Hompesch Dragoons also gained a special infamy on account of their brutal and indiscriminate violation of female chastity. To escape falling into the hands of these banditti the unfortunate people abandoned their homes, and sought refuge in the most wild and unfrequented places they could find, and the country soon presented the appearance of a desert. Scarce a living being was to be seen in the houses, on the highways, or in the fields that bordered them.

While the country presented this shocking scene of desolation, the county-town itself was hardly in a less lamentable condition. Almost all the respectable inhabitants were in jail, having been arrested and arraigned for high treason.

Amongst the prisoners were Captain Keough, Mr. Cornelius Grogan, Bagenal Harvey, and Mr. Colclough—the two latter had been brought to town from one of the Saltee Islands, in which they had vainly sought a secure hiding place.

A court-martial was now instituted, by whose sentence the first who suffered were the Rev. Philip Roche and Captain Keough. They were executed at the entrance to the bridge. Father Roche was a man of large and heavy frame, and his great weight broke the first rope employed in his execution; but a stronger one was soon procured, and the horrid work completed. Captain Keough suffered death at the same time. His head was cut off, and, being stuck on the point of a pike, was exhibited over the Court-house. The lifeless bodies were then thrown over the bridge into the river. Several others of less note were executed at the same time, whose names are not recorded. Mr. Cornelius Grogan was brought to trial on the 26th, but his case was postponed on account of the absence of witnesses.

Within the space of a few days Messrs. Harvey, Grogan, and Prendergast were added to the list of sufferers. The two last-mentioned gentlemen were, beyond all doubt, sacrificed to the vengeful spirit of the time, no evidence of any weight being adduced of their participation in the insurrection.

On the day following the last-mentioned execution Mr. Colclough suffered death. Mr. John Kelly, of Killane, so conspicuous for his bravery at the battle of New-Ross, in which he was severely wounded, was dragged from his sick-bed—his wound yet unhealed—

before the military tribunal, where he was condemned
to immediate execution. Mr. Kelly's head was struck
off, and his body, like those of his fellow-sufferers,
thrown over the bridge. The head of this gallant
gentleman, before being placed beside that of Captain
Keough, was kicked foot-ball fashion about the quay
by a brutal Orange mob, who had assembled to feast
their eyes with the bloody spectacle. On the 28th, Gen.
Lake took his departure from Wexford, leaving General
Hunter in command. The latter, being a man of humane character, did his utmost to restrain the brutality
of the yeomen; in which effort he was seconded by
Brigadier-General Grose, who was stationed at Enniscorthy, and by General Gascoigne, who, with the 1st
and 2nd regiments of the Coldstream Guards, was
posted at New-Ross. The clemency displayed by the
officers in question at length induced the people to
come to their quarters in great numbers to obtain the
protections that they freely granted, and thus affairs
throughout the country began to wear a less gloomy
aspect. But the steps taken by the ancient enemies of
the country's weal prevented these wise measures from
obtaining their full effect. General Lake, before his
departure, had appointed a committee of magistrates
to superintend prosecutions, and to grant passes to
such persons as desired to leave the country. However, the thirst of these Orange magistrates for blood
was unappeased, and they did their utmost to thwart
the efforts of the more humane of the English generals,
and to render null the general pardon issued by Lord
Cornwallis, the new Viceroy, and printed in the "Dublin
Gazette" on the 3rd of July. This document ran as
follows: "Whereas it is in the power of his Majesty's
generals, and of the forces under their command, en-
t rely to destroy all those who have risen in rebellion

against their sovereign and his laws; yet it is nevertheless the wish of Government, that those persons who by traitorous machinations have been seduced, or by acts of intimidation have been forced from their allegiance, should be received into his Majesty's peace and pardon : ———, commanding in the county of ———, specially authorized thereto, does hereby invite all persons who may be now assembled in any part of the said county, against his Majesty's peace, to surrender themselves and their arms, and to desert the leaders who have seduced them; and for the acceptance of such surrender and submission the space of fourteen days from the date hereof is allowed, and the towns of ——— are hereby specified, at each of which places one of his Majesty's officers and a justice of the peace will attend; and upon entering their names, acknowledging their guilt, and promising good behaviour for the future, and taking the oath of allegiance, and at the same time abjuring all other engagements contrary thereto, they will receive a certificate which will entitle them to protection so long as they demean themselves as becomes good subjects. And in order to render such acts of submission easy and secure, it is the general's pleasure that persons who are now with any portion of the rebels in arms, and willing to surrender themselves, do send to him, or to ———, any number from each body of rebels, not exceeding ten, with whom the general or ——— will settle the manner in which they may repair to the above towns, so that no alarm may be excited and no injury to their persons be offered. June 29, 1798." On the 17th of July another Act was passed, called the "Amnesty," qualifying the preceding. and making many exceptions thereto.

Amongst those who suffered from the unsated vengeance of the Orangemen, after the issue of the above proclamation, were the Rev. Francis Redmond* and Mr. Esmond Kyan. The former was put to death by order of Lord Mountnorris, whose house and property he had saved from destruction during the insurrection. Poor Kyan's humanity, evinced at the peril of his life on Wexford bridge, did not save him, nor even his having obtained, together with Mr. Fitzgerald, a free pardon from General Dundas. Meanwhile, General Hunter and Major Fitzgerald rendered themselves honourably conspicuous by the efforts they made to check the villainous proceedings of the Orange magistracy, who attempted to override the law, and carry on in its despite their old trade of murder and robbery. They even went so far as to tear up the protections granted to the country-people by the royalist commanders. However, a threat of being whipped at the cart's tail soon caused them for a time to desist from such proceedings.

Hunter Gowan, one of the most infamous of these banditti, was arrested on charge of robbery, and lodged in prison in Wexford; from which, however, he was

* Father Francis Redmond, although a *loyal* man, found that his loyalty could not save his life. Lord Mountnorris and he had been very intimate before the insurrection, and during that period the unfortunate priest had been looked upon as a zealous partisan of the Government. Mountnorris considered that his former intimacy with the "Papist" priest might prove a blot on his escutcheon, and resolved to wash out the possible stain in the blood of his former friend. By his orders Father Redmond was seized, and Mountnorris appearing as his prosecutor, he was condemned, and suffered death. We have little pity for such a *loyal traitor!* Loyalty! how that word has been abused, misapplied, or misunderstood: we may submit to unjust laws because we are too feeble to resist them, but such enforced submission widely differs from loyalty which is a debt of gratitude men pay to that authority which respects and defends their rights. Men are *submissive* to irresistible tyranny, *loyal* to just and rightly exercised authority.

soon after liberated. To keep alive such a spirit of alarm as would favour their views, the Orange party began to spread abroad the old rumours of massacres plotted by the "Papists" for the extermination of Protestants. An Anglican clergyman presented himself before General Hunter, and recounted to him a story of this description. The general having heard to the end, addressed him thus:

"Mr. Massacre, if you do not prove to me the circumstances you have related, I shall get you punished in the most exemplary manner for raising false alarms, which have already proved so destructive to this unfortunate country." This speech of the general, so different from what he expected, not a little terrified the reverend alarmist, and, to quote the words of Mr. Hay, "the curate's alarm now from general became personal, and on allowing that his fears had been excited by vague reports to make this representation, his piteous supplication and apparent hearty contrition procured him forgiveness."

But the Orangemen, determined not to be foiled in carrying out their wicked schemes, addressed numerous letters to the chief authorities in Dublin, warning them of the approaching outbreak which they asserted was to take place in that district known as the "Macamores."* Such representations, being unceasingly made by magistrates and Protestant clergymen, at length brought the Lord Lieutenant to think that there might be some truth in the matter, and in consequence he sent orders to General Hunter to form a cordon round the above-named district, and in case he found the representations in question well-founded, to punish the intended rebels with the utmost severity, and if necessary to drive them into the sea. However, General Hunter

---

* This district is co-extensive with the baronies of Shilmalier.

and his aide-de-camp, Major Fitzgerald, discovered in
time the falsehood and malignity of these reports.

The latter, undeterred by the efforts made by the
leading Orangemen to prevent him from approaching
the district inhabited by the people whom they had so
foully misrepresented, determined to proceed unarmed
and unaccompanied into the Macamores, and, by the
fact of remaining there in safety, to afford the most
efficacious refutation to reports that he accounted nothing better than lies, forged by the enemies of the
people to bring about their total destruction. Accordingly, setting out without delay upon his journey, he
arrived at Donoughmore, in the centre of the maligned
district, passed the night there, and on the ensuing day
invited the people of the country around to meet him.
The people accepted this invitation, and met together
at the place he had appointed. But while the major
was yet engaged in addressing them, a party of men
in military uniform was seen to approach the place of
assembly.

This unexpected sight spread instant alarm among
his hearers. A murmur began to run through the
crowd that a trap had been set for them—that Major
Fitzgerald was privy to it, and had brought them there
to be surrounded and slaughtered by the soldiery. It
was, in truth, a critical juncture. Fitzgerald's life
was for a time in jeopardy, and nothing but his great
coolness and presence of mind could have saved him.
He assured the people that he had come amongst them
thus alone and unarmed with no other design than that
of clearing them of the calumnies heaped upon them
by their enemies, and pledged his honour that there
was no body of soldiery in the vicinity of the meeting.
This assurance calmed the agitated people, and happily
averted the utter ruin that would have fallen upon
them had they, deceived by the cunning Orange plot

(for the men whose appearance had alarmed them were Orangemen dressed up in military garb), in a moment of inconsiderate panic, slain their generous friend.

With such persistency did the yeomen carry on their depredations, that General Hunter was forced to send detachments of troops, stationing them in different districts, to protect the lives and properties of the now unarmed inhabitants. Hunter Gowan and Hawtrey White still continued to be the scourges of the country. These worthies employed the time, not spent in plundering or burning the houses of the people, in writing to the military chiefs assurances of a general rising of the "Papists" against his Majesty's Government, to be accompanied, of course, with a wholesale massacre of all such loyal Protestants as themselves. General Hunter, who by this time thoroughly understood the character of these alarmists, gave orders for the arrest of Hawtrey White, as one of the most prominent among his class. On being conducted before the military tribunal, and desired to state his authority for what he had reported. he affirmed that to his own knowledge the rebels had formed an encampment on a certain island about two miles from land, whither they betook themselves every morning, after harassing the country during the night.

Having communicated this important intelligence, he made the *modest* request that he, Hawtrey White, should be entrusted with the command of a force sufficient to prevent the rebels in question from landing. General Hunter, though he gave no credit to this story, thought it well to appear to believe it, and to act so as to convict White of being what he knew him to be—a liar and slanderer of the very worst type. He accordingly sent this very ingenious discoverer of plots, in a gunboat, to find out the *island* he had described, and at the same time despatched a party of soldiers to the shore to intercept the *rebels*.

It is needless to say that no such island could be discovered, and Mr. White, now clearly proven a liar and slanderer, was brought back to Wexford. The general was much inclined to have him tried by court-martial, but his advanced age, and the number of persons who interceded for him, induced the placable officer to relinquish his design.

Many of the insurgent leaders now surrendered to General Hunter, amongst whom was the brave General Edward Roche. It was at this time that the French under Hardi landed, but the Wexford men, thoroughly disgusted with those whose cowardice or apathy had allowed them to maintain an unaided struggle against the power of England, could not be roused by the insignificant expedition in question to enter upon a new campaign.

Besides, Hunter and Fitzgerald had won their hearts by their long-continued and strenuous efforts to protect them against the malignity of the Orangemen. The storm of civil war had risen to its height, and at length began to abate. As the year neared its close, executions became less frequent, yet they did not wholly cease. Amongst the Wexford men who suffered death outside their own county was Mr. Walter Devereux, who, having obtained a protection, proceeded to Cork, with the intention of embarking for America.

On arriving in the southern capital, he was recognised by some of the returned North Cork, arrested, brought to trial, and condemned to death on their evidence. Almost the last person who underwent capital punishment within the county, for acts alleged to have been committed during the insurrection, was a man named James Redmond. He was found guilty of the murder of the Rev. Robert Burrowes, a Protestant clergyman residing near Oulart, and was executed on the 30th of July, 1801.

After the insurrection the Orange system became universal, and to be enrolled in a lodge was a necessary passport to any post of honour or authority. As for the unfortunate Catholics they remained for many years deprived of all the rights of citizens. It would be impossible to recount a tithe of the hardships and cruelties to which they were subjected. The fact that between the 27th of May, 1798, and the 18th of August, 1801, thirty-three of their chapels were burnt by the Orangemen, and that no punishment was inflicted upon the incendiaries, may afford some idea of what they endured.

Thus did the people of Wexford pay the penalty of their gallant and persevering, but fruitless effort to wrest their country from the iron grasp of a too powerful enemy.

For months they successfully withstood the military might of the British empire, defeating her ablest generals in fair fight, and flaunting their green flag in triumph on fields where the proud standard of England lay trampled in the dust. If the cause of freedom failed, the fault was not theirs.

Had the rest of their countrymen awakened, even at the eleventh hour, Ireland had not been now an uncrowned nation.

CONCLUSION.

IT has been often and truly said that no people in the world have loved freedom or hated oppression more ardently than the Irish. But at the same time none have shown greater reverence for just authority, or have been more willing to yield to such authority a cheerful obedience. No people have been more gratefully devoted to those who protected or acknowledged their rights. They have, indeed, been grateful to those who little deserved their gratitude, and loyal to those who did little to earn their loyalty. They were a justice-loving people, but the only law they had known for centuries was one which contemptuously ignored or cruelly trampled upon their rights.

They were a peace-loving people, but they lived under a Government whose policy it was to rule by exciting strife and discord—by setting class against class, and creed against creed, and thus perpetuating slavery by promoting disunion.

The Irish people, weakened by intestine strife, thus purposely kindled, were powerless to defend their rights, which, one by one, were wrested from them.

The nation, feeble from disunion, blind from enforced ignorance, yet possessing the elements of greatness, became at length, like another Sampson, the sport and scorn of its enemies. The vigour of its existence had departed; but a feeble life still remained, which, in its feebleness, too closely resembled death. The last remaining vestige of the country's former independence was her Parliament. True, it was but the shadow of a parliament. Representing but a small section of the population, corrupt and servile, it served all the purposes of the foreign rulers of the country.

While it remained in this abject condition, it was

suffered to exist. Its servility and subjection were indeed the condition of its existence.

But at length, outside the precincts of this fettered and degraded legislature, a new spirit was born. That spirit grew apace, and in its strength called forth the Volunteers. For the first time during dreary centuries Ireland beheld a native army encamped on her soil. They had taken up arms to protect their country from French invasion, they used them to set her free from English tyranny. Soon in glittering files they gathered round the ancient halls of their native legislature, whence the spirit of freedom had long departed. They called that glorious spirit back, and bade it announce to an enslaved people the glad tidings of recovered independence. And now, as if at the touch of some beneficent magician, Ireland awoke from the troubled sleep of centuries. Freed from the vampire of foreign rule that had drained her life-blood, the exhausted nation soon began to feel in every vein the warm glow of returning health. Every element of the country's prosperity showed the influence of the change. Her commerce, no longer restrained by alien jealousy, sent Irish keels to plough the remotest seas. Her agriculture encouraged, soon made the desert places of the island smile with the promise of a teeming harvest, for the consciousness of freedom nerved the arm of the tiller of the soil, and called into exertion his long dormant energies. But this picture, so pleasant to the eyes of Irish patriots, was hateful to those of English rulers. They conceived that the happiness and glory of their own country could not long exist, save in conjunction with the misery and degradation of Ireland.

Regarding the Irish Parliament as the source of Irish liberty, and as such a standing danger to English domination, the British prime-minister and his colleagues in power lent themselves to plot its destruction. They could no longer suffer it to exist on any terms, not even those of the most abject slavery, for experience had proved that it was a slave which at any moment might regain its freedom.

What followed this determination has been already told. The Volunteers fell victims to the treachery of Lord Charlemont. An Irish aristocrat began what his fellows accomplished: he betrayed the guard, they delivered up the keys of the National Legislature. However, before this final treachery could be accomplished, the English Government deemed it necessary to drive the people of Ireland into insurrection, in quelling which they might so enfeeble them, that to wrest from them the last and most cherished of their institutions would be no difficult task. How successfully they accomplished their evil purpose is written in letters of blood in the history of the nation.

Armed resistance to authority is the last resource of the oppressed. It is a desperate remedy for a desperate disease, and only to be essayed when all milder ones have failed. If power listens to the voice of justice, and reforms the law, it is a guilty hand that draws the sword. When it refuses to do this, it becomes tyranny. It may compel, but cannot claim, obedience; for if the laws which it frames and enforces are unjust, they lack the very principle that renders obedience to them a duty. To submit to just authority is the bounden duty of Christian men, for authority is the corner-stone upon which the whole social fabric rests; but, on the other hand, the doctrine that teaches submission to tyranny however grinding, would reduce, if universally accepted, the world to a vast slave-market. Against such a doctrine reason itself revolts. Man's hatred of oppression is as inextinguishable as his love of liberty: when he ceases to feel these impulses he sinks in the scale of reasoning nature, and approaches to the condition of the brute. It was tyranny of the grossest kind that in 1798 stirred up the Irish people to revolt. The laws then in force in Ireland were unjust in themselves and unjustly administered. Nor was there any hope of these laws being peacefully reformed, for the remonstrances of the oppressed were treated by the governing powers with scorn and contempt: all civil and religious liberty was trampled under foot.

The august form of justice had descended from the tribunal, and in its place was seen a hideous monster in the shape of military despotism, grasping in one hand an ensanguined sword, and in the other the flaming torch of the incendiary. In the state of society consequent upon such a lawless rule the Christian minister may preach submission, and quote his favourite theologian to prove the guilt that attaches to revolt; but the victim of wrong and outrage is too engrossed with the consideration of the unjust oppression under which he groans to give attention to the nice distinctions of theological schools. Proscribed by the law which ought to protect him, he deems that law an enemy. Placed outside the pale of human justice, he falls back upon his natural and inalienable rights, and resolves to defend them with his life. The higher his appreciation of the value of liberty, the stronger will be his resolution to defend it. He may fall in defence of his rights, but such a death is preferable to slavery. It was in such circumstances, and under such impulses, that the Irish people in 1798 rose in arms against the government of England. We have followed them through the struggle, beheld its termination; we will now inquire into the cause of its failure.

The insurrection in the northern counties of Ireland, being a distinct event from that which took place in Wexford, requires to be considered by itself. It was the fruit to the production of which the great organization of the United Irishmen had devoted its labours for several years. Yet it was comparatively a feeble attempt—a poor result of such long and patient effort. Of what it might have been had its leaders been able to elude the pursuit of Government, it is useless to conjecture: we only know that it was feebly conducted and easily quelled. To attribute its failure to the brave men who took part in it would be surely unjust: we must seek the cause elsewhere. That cause, we are of opinion, is to be found in the nature of the secret, oath-bound society by which the revolt was organized. Such a society never did, and never will, of itself, effect a successful revolution. If this is true of any country, it is evidently so of a country such as Ireland, where the vast majority of the population are of the Catholic religion, whose ministers, whatever their political views may be, are bound in conscience to oppose a society existing under conditions the Church has declared unlawful. Besides, while the oath in question arrays the vast power of the Church against such an organization, it affords no protection whatever against treachery. Traitors have no reverence for the sanctity of an oath; they take and violate it with equal facility. But a society into which traitors have obtained entrance cannot long veil its operations from Government, which watches it with argus eyes, learns through its spies who are its leaders, and what its plans—waits patiently till the time comes when the great scheme has attained its full development—and then to arrest its chiefs, pounce upon its stores of arms and ammunition, is a work soon accomplished. Once the Government holds the chiefs in its power, more than half its work is done. The heads of such an organization are to it what the mind is to the body—when one is destroyed the other is powerless. It may possess strength, but such strength is inert and useless, for it is bereft of the spirit to direct and concentrate its efforts. It may be said that though the sudden arrest of the United Irish chiefs was the principal cause of the failure of the enterprise in question, such an arrest was but an unfortunate occurrence which prudence might have averted. But experience has established the fact that a powerful Government, such as that of England, can at any time lay hands upon those who conspire its overthrow. The inability of such a society as the United Irish to effect a successful revolt will be best seen by contrasting the insurrection which took place in the northern counties with that which occurred in Wexford.

In the latter place there existed no previous organization; had there been, in all likelihood the explosion of the insurrection would have been as feeble as it proved in the North. In Wexford the people rose *en masse*, with the desperate determination of men who are driven to extremity. They had no previously-chosen leaders, no organization, and but a scanty supply of arms. Yet three weeks had scarce passed when they had obtained all three. In that brief space of time they had gained more of the qualities of soldiers than their northern brethren during years of midnight drilling and secret meeting. Government knew nothing of their plans, which were formed on the field of battle; it could not seize their chiefs, for none had been previously chosen. So rapidly did they learn the soldier's trade, that we find them maintaining a conflict for four hours with double the number of royal troops, and only retreating when their ammunition was completely exhausted—even then they left the field unpursued. Unaided as they were, left to continue the struggle alone, it was impossible that the inhabitants of a single county could have long resisted the power of a great empire. But

they were not finally subdued till for every fighting-
man they could muster there were two soldiers—till
30,000 men were confronted with 90,000—then, indeed, they yielded, as a regular army might, nay, must
have done in similar circumstances.

There may be nothing to surprise us in the final
defeat, but their long-continued resistance was surely
marvellous. The struggle would have been much more
protracted had they been able to obtain ammunition.
The lack of this essential requisite more than once
snatched victory from their grasp. At Arklow, at
Longraig, at Vinegar Hill it failed them, and they
quitted the scene of contest, clutching their empty
guns, and execrating the mischance that rendered their
valour useless. But even had they been supplied with
sufficient ammunition, they must in the end have been
forced to submit; for death would thin their ranks
every day, and there were none to fill the gaps it made,
while their enemy, possessing exhaustless numerical
resources, might continue the contest till they planted
their victorious flag over the grave of the last insurgent.

They were left to continue the desperate struggle
unaided. The heavy yoke of the Penal Law had so
effectually subdued the once fiery and high-spirited
Celtic population of Ireland, that they could remain
spectators of such a strife—could behold their countrymen engaged in a death-grapple with the might of
their ancient foe—could see them trodden down by the
swarming myriads of England's mercenaries, without
raising an arm to aid them.

Oppression, indeed, had well-nigh crushed all manhood out of their souls: they had been so long helots,
that they seemed to have forgotten they were descended
from freemen. The deep abasement of the national
spirit is clearly, alas, too clearly, reflected in the *loyal*

addresses and humble supplications addressed at this
period to the British sovereign, or to his shadowy representative in the Irish metropolis. Reading over
these effusions nowadays, one is filled with wonder to
see men fallen to such a depth of abasement. Such
lying and fulsome flattery, such ardent professions of
loyalty and gratitude addressed to the representatives
of a power that had ground them into the dust—that
had spurned them, spewed forth the filth of insult and
contempt upon them—flogged them, starved them, and,
perhaps, less cruel than all, put an end to their misery
by depriving them of a wretched existence; for to
allow them to live on such terms might be accounted
rather cruelty than mercy.

If men of birth and education had fallen so low, can
we wonder that those of the lower ranks were no better?—for worse they could hardly be.

Among a people so degraded it was in vain the
temple of Freedom was thrown open, that her sacred
fire burned in their sight; for the grim form of Tyranny
stood before the portal, awing them with its scowl, and
threatening them with its scorpion-scourge, till their
very souls died within them, and they shrank away in
terror, their misery heightened by a brief glimpse of
unattainable happiness. Since the events we have
recorded took place, three generations of men have appeared in Ireland. The last of the men of '98 sleep
peacefully in their graves, their sons are grey-haired
men; but the nation for whose freedom they fought
still wears her ancient chains—her voice has been unheard amongst the nations, save when agony wrung
from her a cry that reminded the world at once of her
existence and of her misery.

APPENDIX.

NOTE TO CHAPTER I.

ORIGINAL DECLARATION OF THE UNITED IRISHMEN.

IN the present great era of reform, when unjust Governments are falling in every quarter of Europe; when religious persecution is compelled to abjure her tyranny over conscience; when the rights of man are ascertained in theory, and that theory substantiated by practice; when antiquity can no longer defend absurd and oppressive forms against the common sense and common interests of mankind; when all Government is acknowledged to originate from the people, and to be so far only obligatory as it protects their rights and promotes their welfare; we think it our duty, as Irishmen, to come forward, and state what we feel to be our heavy grievance, and what we know to be its effectual remedy. *We have no National Government*—we are ruled by Englishmen, and the servants of Englishmen, whose object is the interest of another country, whose instrument is corruption, and whose strength is the weakness of Ireland; and these men have the whole of the power and patronage of the country as means to seduce and to subdue the honesty and spirit of her representatives in the legislature.

Such an extrinsic power, acting with uniform force, in a direction too frequently opposite to the true line of our obvious interests, can be resisted with effect solely by *unanimity, decision, and spirit in the people*—qualities which may be exerted most legally, constitutionally, and efficaciously, by that great measure essential to the prosperity and freedom of Ireland—*an equal representation of all the people in Parliament.* We do not here mention as grievances the rejection of a place-bill, of a pension-bill, of a responsibility-bill, the sale of peerages in one house, the corruption publicly avowed in the other, nor the notorious infamy of borough traffic between both, not that we are insensible to their enormity, but that we consider them as but symptoms of that mortal disease which corrodes the vitals of our constitution, and leaves to the people in their own government but the shadow of a name.

Impressed with these sentiments, we have agreed to form an association to be called "The Society of United Irishmen," and we do pledge ourselves to our country, and mutually to each other, that we will steadily support and endeavour, by all due means, to carry into effect the following resolutions:—

First Resolved—That the weight of English influence on the Government of this country is so great as to require a cordial union among *all the people of Ireland,* to maintain that balance which is essential to the preservation of our liberties, and the extension of our commerce. Second—That the sole constitutional mode by which this influence can be opposed is by a complete and radical reform of the representation of the people in Parliament. Third—That no reform is practicable, efficacious, or just, which shall not include Irishmen of every religious persuasion. Satisfied, as we are, that the intestine divisions among Irishmen have too often given encouragement and impunity to profligate, audacious, and corrupt administrations, in measure, which, but for these divisions, they durst not have attempted, we submit our resolutions to the nation as the basis of our political faith. We have gone to what we conceive to be the root of the evil. We have stated what we conceive to be the remedy. With a parliament thus reformed, everything is easy; without it nothing can be done. And we do call on, and most earnestly exhort our countrymen in general, to follow our example, and to form similar societies in every quarter of the kingdom, for the promotion of constitutional knowledge, the abolition of bigotry in religion and politics, and the equal distribution of the rights of men through all sects and denominations of Irishmen. The people, when thus collected, will feel their own weight, and secure that power which theory has already admitted to be their portion, and to which, if they be not aroused by their present provocations to vindicate it, they deserve to forfeit their pretensions *for ever.*

NOTES TO CHAPTER II.

SIR EDWARD CROSBIE.—CRUELTIES PERPETRATED BY THE CARLOW ORANGEMEN.

Sir Edward Crosbie, "the gentlemanly knight:" from the *Irish Magazine*, 1811:—"His figure was manly, and his countenance dignified and determined; he was tall and well-made, with penetrating eyes. He saw no company, for he could meet with none whose minds were congenial to his own. He was no party man, but from his hatred of oppression he incurred the deep dislike of the aristocracy of the county. On the 29th of May, while walking before his house, accompanied by two of his children, a squadron of the 9th Dragoons rode up, seized rudely upon him and conveyed him to Carlow, where he was thrown into prison. One of his servants, named Flynn, yielding to threats of torture, turned informer against him; but another, named Taafe, more firm and faithful, refused, though cruelly tortured to compel him to do so. His enemies were anxious to get rid of him quickly, for they knew a respite was expected. The respite came, but was detained by the Orange postmaster till Sir Edward was put to death. No wonder under such a *regime* that Protestants feared to be thought *liberal.*"

In the same journal we find the following account of the atrocities perpetrated by the Carlow Orangemen on the prisoners they made during the burning of that town:—

"Not satisfied with having burned to death 500 men by setting fire to the houses in which they had taken refuge, the Carlow Orangemen proceeded to try the numerous prisoners they had made. As a necessary preliminary they resolved to manufacture informers. With this view they seized upon four men (Catholics), dragged them to the triangle, to which they tied them; so tightly were the ropes drawn that confined their wrists that the bones flew from the sockets with great noise. They were then whipped till the bones were laid bare. During this torture one of the sufferers, named O'Connor, was heard to exhort his fellow-victims thus: 'Irishmen, die like heroes; your country will remember you; shed not the blood of the innocent, let not the word informer be written on the foreheads of your children.' Not being able even by such extreme torture to overcome the noble constancy of these men, they took three of them down and hanged them on the spot. O'Connor they reserved for further torment. Martin, a sergeant of the North Cork, was selected as his executioner. He ran round the barrack-yard twice with the man suspended on his back, while the victim's blood smoked at the feet of the officers standing around. The last words of O'Connor were, 'My country and my God.' After this act of butchery was completed, an informer was brought into the town by the Orange gentry. This wretch was called 'Paddy the Pointer.' He used to ride through the town holding a long white rod in his hand, indicating, from time to time, with the point thereof, those he designed to accuse, who were instantly conveyed to prison. One hundred of these unhappy victims were confined in the small jail of the town—sixty in a place called the Gallows Yard, a stable about twenty feet square, paved with large rugged stones. Most of these prisoners *were starved to death.* Every time the jailor entered their cells he either kicked the victims or struck them on the head with his clubbed musket.

"After the wholesale destruction of the peasantry in the burning houses, the triumphant soldiery formed a mock procession in derision of the faith of the slain. The procession was headed by the trumpeter of the 9th Dragoons, holding aloft a crucifix stuck on the point of his sword, and exclaiming, 'Behold the wooden Jesus. Behold the God of the Papists.'"

Appendix. 263

VARIOUS TRANSACTIONS IN KILDARE COUNTY, AS NARRATED BY P. O'KELLY, ESQ., IN THE WORK ENTITLED " GENERAL HISTORY OF THE REBELLION OF 1798," PUBLISHED IN DUBLIN, A.D. 1842.

Attack on the Barracks at Prosperous, and the fate of Dr. Esmond.

"ALL the people around Prosperous were roused into resistance by the tyrannical sway of Captain Swayne, who, with his North Cork, plundered and almost laid waste the entire district over which his authority extended. The pitch cap was frequently applied during the free-quarters, several cabins and farm-houses were burned, and the Catholic chapel, out of which the poor woman in charge of it was scarcely allowed to rescue the vestments from the flames, was likewise consumed. On the night of the 23rd of May, Captain Farrell, the insurgent leader, and one like Mick Reynolds of Johnstown, Naas, remarkable for his intrepidity, collected all the forces he could muster, and, among the rest, called upon Dr. Esmond, who lived near Sallins, to aid the people in their intended attack upon their unrelenting oppressors, Captain Swayne and his men. With the dawning of the morning the men marched to attack the military in their barracks. Here they met a warm and determined resistance from the soldiery within; but nothing was able to deter them from their purpose, and animated by their spirited leader, Captain Farrell, and encouraged by the presence of Dr. Esmond among them, they kept close to the walls, and thus became less exposed to the musketry from within. Fire being now the only means to overcome the garrison inside, the insurgents began, first by setting the doors on fire, and by throwing faggots of furze and straw to strengthen the conflagration. The fire and smoke so deterred the garrison inside, that they cried out for quarter. No entreaties could mollify the enraged assailants; they vowed the destruction of Captain Swayne and his soldiery, and in a few minutes saw them perish in the flames. . . . The people of Prosperous having gained their ends, by the destruction of the military and their barracks, dispersed to their several homes; and Dr. Esmond, after refreshing himself and changing clothes, proceeded to join his corps, which was called the Sallins Yeoman Cavalry, commanded by Captain Griffith. This corps being called into Naas, to assist the garrison of that town the preceding night, he was proceeding thither, in company with Montgomery of Oldtown Mills and his captain. Another yeoman, named Hickey, being likewise in company, took an opportunity of advising Dr. Esmond to shoot one and that he would shoot the other.

"This proposal, however, did not meet the approval of Lieutenant Esmond (he being also an officer in the Sallins corps), and thus they all four proceeded to Naas.

"Immediately on their arrival, Dr. Esmond was ordered by Griffith to dismount, and was put under arrest. His very horse was put inside the walls of the gaol, and himself sent on to Dublin, under a strong guard. Previously to their setting out with the prisoner, he was put under a summary trial by court martial, and found guilty of having sanctioned, by his presence, the attack upon Prosperous." On arriving in Dublin, he was conducted to Carlisle-bridge, where he was hanged. His remains were buried under a heap of dung in the Royal Barracks. "No man," adds Mr. Kelly, "who suffered in '98 was more universally esteemed."

The Battle of Old Kilcullen.

"The battle of Old Kilcullen was one of the most intrepid and obstinately fought engagements which occurred during the whole of '98. Captain Eskrine, who had been quartered, together with his men (the Buff Dragoons), upon Thomas Fitzgerald of Geraldine, as has been already mentioned, was returning from Dublin on the night of the 23rd of May, and passing through Ballymore-Eustace, he found to his surprise, that the people of that town had risen, and defeated a small military force that had been living at free quarters; the few that escaped from the pike of the insurgents made their retreat to Naas, which was garrisoned by a great force of regular troops—the night on which M. Reynolds made his attack on that town. Captain Eskrine, as it was said by those who saw him when he arrived at Geraldine, the place of his free-quarters, cried out ragingly to his dragoons that 'neither *himself nor his men would breakfast until they should breakfast upon the Croppies of Ballymore.'* . . . . Old Kilcullen lies about nine miles east of Geraldine, through which he had to march for Ballymore-Eustace; and as soon as he had reached the fair-green, adjoining to which stood an old church, he saw some men collecting around its walls. The situation of the place being considerably elevated, was unfavourable for the cavalry to act. The insurgents were armed with pikes; and perceiving these troopers in full gallop, apparently with the view to cut them down, they boldly stood by one another, and received the charge with their pikes extended. Advancing after this they met Eskrine in his second charge, and plied the pike so vigorously that (although their number did not exceed their assailants) their victory was complete. Captain Eskrine fell into a lough or pool of water, where he fought upon his back, cutting at the pikeman's weapon fastened in his body until he expired."

The Battle of Rathangan.

"The battle of Rathangan comes next to be recorded. The attack upon this town succeeded with the insurgents. They were commanded by Captain Doorley, a respectable young farmer, whose residence was Lallymore. The garrison of Rathangan was but feeble, consisting only of one corps of yeomen, commanded by Captain James Spencer, and half a company of militia of the North Cork. The victory gained at Prosperous animated the people around Rathangan to such a height that they succeeded in their first attack, and became masters of the town. The garrison retreated to Philipstown, where the Black-horse were quartered, who were then ordered to proceed to Rathangan, and drive out the rebels. The people planted a tree of liberty in the street, and prepared to repel any attacking force. They formed a barricade to impede the entrance of the Black-horse, and Spencer's corps, before driven out. These returned, but the re-taking of Rathangan was not an easy matter. The Black-horse were the first that made their appearance, but such was the bravery of the people that they were forced to retire pecipitately. However, having met on their retreat a party of the South Corks, commanded by Colonel Longfield, who had a piece of cannon, they proceeded with them in a new attempt to dislodge the insurgents, and retake the town. The people, commanded by Doorley, made a stout resistance, and beat off their assailants." "In the meantime the people seized upon an old gentleman named Spenser, agent to the Duke of Leinster, and during the absence of Doorley, who would have restrained them from such cruelty, put him to death. It happened in a few hours after the murder of Mr. S. had occurred that the insurgents gave way, after a few discharges of the cannon by the South Corks; and the town was speedily evacuated by its late masters, the United Irishmen." Doorley escaped for the time, and joined the United army of Aylmer, Luby, and Ware. He was, however, soon after taken prisoner, and hanged at Mullingar.

The Battle of Ovidstown.

"Ovidstown, near Hortland House, was the spot where this battle of Aylmer and his officers was to be fought with the King's troops. If the battle proved propitious to the insurgents, they were resolved to march for Dublin; 5000 insurgents would have set the city in a blaze. The United army, under Aylmer, on the morning of the engagement numbered about 5000 men.

"They were well officered, but discipline was little known amongst them. The arrival of the army to attack them was unexpected. The men were at breakfast when the alarm was received. An immediate 'stand to arms' was sounded, and the officers, Aylmer, Luby, Ware, Kieran, Doorley, Walsh, and others, strove to arrange their men as best they could. The royal force it was said amounted to near 400 men, Highlanders, Dragoon Guards, and yeomen cavalry. When the latter came in sight of their enemy they halted and made preparations to attack. The United men advanced to meet the soldiery, and the orders given by Aylmer were, to rush with their pikes upon where the cannon would be seen to play from. The strict discipline observed by the military was perceivable to the insurgents, and, notwithstanding the intrepidity of the insurgent officers, there was a sudden halt, which afforded their enemy an opportunity of seeing their confusion. The pikemen, instead of making a rapid advance against the troops, wheeled behind a quick-set hedge, and the two pieces of cannon moving at the head of four companies of Highlanders were instantly turned to dislodge them. It was afterwards said by many intelligent men, that if the pikemen had acted according to orders they would have gained the battle. The grape-shot discharged from the cannon cut the quick-set hedge, as if lopped off by a clipping shears. The men, being in the shelter of the ditch, were yet safe; but soon, when a panic arose among them, some began to fly, the grape-shot had effect, and several were slain. Aylmer's guns-men behaved well for a time. They approached and shot the soldiery who served the cannon; but an impetuous charge of cavalry discomfited the few who were in the act of moving one of the pieces to their own party, and this enabled other cannoniers of this force to act against the insurgents. Aylmer's guns-men, who were said to be about 200, stood firmly together till the cannon began to thin their ranks, and a discomfiture of the entire body quickly followed. About 200 of the insurgents fell; of the army there were killed, two officers, two sergeants, and twenty privates. After this battle the united army in Kildare separated and began to seek protections. Colonel Aylmer, Hugh Ware, and George Luby, surrendered themselves to General Dundas as state prisoners. All three were afterwards liberated from prison, on condition of quitting their native country, which accordingly they did—Aylmer proceeding to Germany and entering the Austrian service, Ware to France, in whose army he became colonel, and Luby to America, where he died shortly after his arrival."

NOTES TO CHAPTER V.

SANCTION GIVEN BY GOVERNMENT TO CRUELTIES EXERCISED UPON THE PEOPLE.—ORANGEMEN.

The Government gave its full sanction to cruelties exercised at this period on the people. In proof of this we cite the following :—

Sir Ralph Abercrombie resigned his command rather than sanction, by retaining it, the excesses of a ruffianly soldiery. For this noble conduct the gallant and humane soldier was bitterly reviled in the English Parliament, being called, amongst other offensive names, "a Scotch Brute." It is not difficult to decide who were "the Brutes" in this instance.

The outrages committed by the Orange yeomen and militia were so monstrous that the brave Sir John Moore exclaimed, "If I were an Irishman I would be a rebel."

The following extract from a speech delivered by Lord Moira, in the English house of Peers, in the year '98, must free the author from any suspicion of exaggeration :—

"Before my God and my country I speak of what I myself have seen. I have seen in Ireland the most absurd as well as the most disgusting tyranny that any nation ever groaned under. I have seen troops sent full of this prejudice, that every inhabitant of that kingdom is a rebel to the British Government. The most wanton insults, the most cowardly oppression practised upon men of all ranks and conditions, in a part of the country as free from disturbance as the City of London. Thirty houses are sometimes burned in a single night, but from prudential motives *I wish to draw a veil over more aggravated facts.*"

The following incident, related in the *Carlow Magazine*, is a further illustration of the animus of the Government of the day:—" Near the town of Newry, on the 23rd of June (St. John's eve), a number of people, gathered round a bonfire, were deliberately fired upon by a corps of yeomanry, many of them being killed and many wounded. When some of the more humane magistrates of the county applied to

Government for assistance, they received from Mr. Trail, secretary to the Duke of Richmond, an answer to this effect:—That the Government could not accede to their request, as any steps taken by them would supersede the exertions of the local magistrates. It is needless to say that no steps were ever taken, and these murderers escaped, at least from *human* justice. Thus did the Government evince its determination to rule through the Orange magistrates, to the entire exclusion of the liberal Protestants."

The Irish people, whether Catholics or Protestants, were better than the infamous laws that had been framed with a view to create enmity and kindle strife amongst them, and thereby to perpetuate the slavery of their common country. Liberal Protestants were numerous in Ireland—men who desired to live in peace with their Catholic fellow-countrymen, and would gladly have seen them restored to civil and religious liberty. When the insurrection burst forth many of this class threw themselves boldly into the ranks of the patriots, and ventured life and liberty for their beloved country. Others of the same class remained neutral, while, unhappily for themselves and their native land, a considerable section of the dominant creed allied themselves with her foreign oppressors.

These were the members of the Orange Society. The name of Orangemen was assumed in honour of King William the Third—before his accession to the English throne called Prince of Orange—the most intolerant of men calling themselves, with a strange ignorance of historical truth, after one of the most liberal Protestants of his time—the ally and friend of Catholic princes. Of these men it must be said that, while acting as a body they were guilty of the most shocking atrocities, individuals amongst them did many a kind and generous deed in favour of the professors of the persecuted creed.

But these occasional manifestations of a better feeling were seen amongst the humbler ranks of the society in question, for the Orange *gentry* were, without exception, cruel and merciless in the extreme. The truth is, then as now, the lower grades of the Orange body were but the tools of their selfish aristocratic leaders, who held them like blood-

hounds in the leash ready to be loosed at the beck of their
English masters. For the aid they afforded in the uphold-
ing of alien domination, the aristocrats received pay and
patronage, while their plebeian followers reaped but small advantage from their unpatriotic services, and were at times
treated like unruly hounds that are driven into the kennel
when the chase is over. It may not be amiss, in this place,
to relate a few of the many good deeds performed by individuals of the Orange body in favour of Catholics—good
deeds which appear, in those dark and evil days, like gleams
of cheerful sunshine seen at intervals in a sky overspread
with gloomy and threatening clouds:—

In the Parish of Blackwater there lived, during this
troubled period, a farmer named Thackaberry—a Protestant
and an Orangeman—who was wont, after the fashion of his
class, to boast of his loyalty to the Crown, and to profess his
utter detestation of Popery and Papists. Yet, withal, the
man had a good heart, and was, as the sequel goes to prove,
by no means inclined to use the power English law gave him
over the lives and liberties of his Catholic fellow-countrymen.
Even " Popish " priests, though marked out as especial objects of persecution, did not find in the rough Wexford yeoman an implacable foe.

On the contrary, he often strove to shield them from the
vengeance of his less merciful co-religionists. On the occasion we refer to, he saved from death one of these proscribed
and outlawed men. The affair happened in this wise. A
Catholic priest had been seized upon, and hurried off to the
house of one Gainfort, an Orange magistrate of the worst
type, to be detained prisoner there until brought to trial. A
friend of the priest's went to Thackaberry and told him of
the circumstance, entreating him at the same time to try and
save the man, whom he knew to be innocent of the crime laid
to his charge—that of administering the oath of the United
Irishmen.

Thackaberry promised that all would be right, and set off
without delay for Gorey. Arrived at that town he hastened
to Gainfort's house, and demanded the instant liberation of
the prisoner. On receiving a flat refusal from Gainfort, he
proceeded to the room in which the priest was confined, drew

a pistol from his breast, and discharging it at the lock of the door, shattered it to pieces. He then entered the room and desired the priest to follow him, and having conducted him safely out of the town, conveyed him to his own house, where he kept him till he could appear abroad with safety.

The following letter, written about a month after the suppression of the insurrection, by Dr. Caufield, R. C. Bishop of Ferns, to Dr. Troy, Archbishop of Dublin, establishes his *loyalty* plain enough:—

"*Wexford, July* 31, 1798.
" To the Right Rev. Dr. Troy.

"It is impossible for me to gratify your curiosity, as I cannot collect or recollect the particulars of our conduct, or the individuals we endeavoured to serve or save, during three long weeks of tragical confusion, and if I could, I really feel that modesty and decency would forbid me, because it would appear that we claimed gratitude from the individuals and acknowledgment from the public, which, as it strikes me, would appear ostentatious and indecorous. Certain it is, we could name many, very many, persons who I apprehend would not be pleased at seeing their names and religious professions published by us. I can say, that not a Presbyterian, Protestant, or Quaker in this town or adjoining baronies of Forth, Bargy, Shilmalier, Ballaghkeen, besides many from Enniscorthy and other remote parts, who fled and flocked in here, except such as quitted the country, that did not call on us for protection, and that we were employed from morning till night writing, speaking, and pleading for them, to procure protection from the leaders or chiefs of the insurrection, and in general we succeeded for the first fortnight. After that the evil sanguinary spirit booke loose, and no protection availed. Our houses were constantly thronged, and every part, garrets, back-houses, yards, every place filled with the people, their furniture, goods of all kinds. But it soon became treason to plead for protection, for they were all Orangemen, and would destroy us all. In vain did we urge humanity, charity, religion, mercy. I declared, if any of them had killed my friend, my brother, or father, that I would protect and save him if he threw himself on my mercy; for it was by showing mercy that I could expect mercy myself. This conduct and language graduated me equal to an Orangeman; my house must be pulled down or burnt, and my head knocked off. This last sentence was boldly pronounced to my face, surrounded as I was by four or five thousand pikes, spears, or muskets, *when I was striving to save Lord Kingsborough's life*, which we providentially effected by gaining over a few of those *rebels* who had influence over the rest. The task engaged me from nine o'clock in the morning till eight in the evening, during which time I had not a moment's rest, nor did I expect it in this wicked world; and I was alone, i. e., without any of the clergy with me the latter part of the day, except the Rev. James Roche, who mostly remained within doors with Lord Kingsborough. There were other priests there too from the country, but dared not show themselves or speak for fear of pikes, &c.

"I remained until the King's army began to come in (it was Thursday, the 21st of June), then I was in as perilous a situation as ever, not knowing but an indiscriminate slaughter might be their first act. *However, I sat down with Lord Kingsborough and some others at his place of concealment to a bit of salt beef at the fall of night, and got a Captain Rourke of the North Cork Militia, a worthy fellow, to see me home.*

"Two days before this the demon of murder broke out, and a *banditti, as if despatched from hell*, assailed the jail and barracks, both crammed with prisoners, and called them out by dozens to be executed, and two prison ships in the harbour to be brought out, two others to be executed on the bridge. The Rev. Mr. Corrin dined with me, for my cry to the clergy was, that we should keep together living or dying; and at the close of dinner a call for him came from Mr. Kellet, who was brought from the ship to the bridge for execution. He ran with all speed, and found Kellet and several others waiting the awful moment.

"He addressed the *wretches* in the best manner he could: warned them that the blood they were spilling and were to spill must shortly appear against them at the awful tribunal of God, and conjured them to stop, &c., &c. They did so, and Kellet and the rest were allowed to live, and after that there was no massacre. Some days before there was a similar attack on the jail, when the Rev. Messrs. Corrin and Broe happened to be there and prevented its intended effect. On the above-mentioned day Mr. Corrin went home with Mr. Kellet, and all I could do could not bring him to town for near a week, although I sent him General Lake's protection. *He had really pined away to a skeleton. My condition was, providentially for me, the reverse; for I never felt myself more vigorous, and the more pressing the difficulty and the more imminent the danger, the firmer and the more steady was I.*

"I had made up my mind to the worst at the set out, and afterwards took every occurrence as preparatory to the fatal moment I apprehended, and thus continued in unimpaired health till the week before the last, when I was visited by a painful complaint for four days, but have well got rid of it, thank God. Indeed, *the clergy of this town conducted themselves with zeal and activity through the whole, except while on board the vessel in harbour, to which they occasionally fled to escape the fire, fury, etc., of the pikemen.* When the *rebels* were defeated everywhere, and the King's army was approaching, a gentleman, my close neighbour, came to me and told me he would go out to meet them at the risk of his life, and represent me to the commanders as the protector of the Protestants, &c. I thanked him, and said that *Government well knew my loyalty*, and I was satisfied that I had nothing to fear from the King's forces, &c."

NOTES TO CHAPTER VI.

AUTHENTIC ACCOUNT OF THE BURNING OF BOOLEVOGUE CHAPEL.

EARLY on the morning of Whit-Sunday, the 27th of May, a party of yeomen came to Boolevogue Chapel, and not finding the priest whom they designed to put to death, they resolved, as the next best thing, to burn the chapel. The only person they found about the place was a poor woman, the wife of a carpenter in the parish named Jack Murphy. This person had charge of the sacred edifice, and when the Orangemen unexpectedly arrived, they discovered her inside engaged in putting things in order for the expected arrival of the priest. Her husband was about to enter the chapel when he perceived the Orangemen approaching, and had time to conceal himself behind one of the ditches hard by.

Mrs. Murphy being questioned by the Orangemen as to the whereabouts of her husband, and refusing to give them the information they sought, was carried by her captors outside the chapel, and assured that, unless she consented to set fire to the chapel, they would shoot her on the spot. Refusing to comply with this cruel condition, she was forced on her knees by the Orangemen, who prepared to put their threat into execution. In this mortal extremity the poor creature's courage failed, as she cried out, so as to be heard by her husband in his hiding-place—" O Jack, save me; you have been at your duty last week, and are fitter to die than I am." On hearing this appeal from his poor wife Jack quitted the place of his concealment, and presented himself before the Orangemen, who instantly laid hands on him. The same alternative they had before offered his wife they now proposed to him. But the brave fellow resolutely refused to commit, even to save his life, what he believed to be a crime, declaring that he would endure a thousand deaths rather than be guilty of such a wicked deed. Having expressed himself to this effect, he drew forth his beads, and, putting them around his neck, awaited with the courage of a martyr the death he believed was about to be inflicted upon him. However, before his enemies had time to carry their cruel purpose into effect, it was frustrated by an unexpected arrival on the scene. The person who came so opportunely to Jack's aid, in this extremity, was an Orangeman named Valentine, or, as he was commonly called, Val Mowles. Val recognised in Jack an old friend, and resolved to save him from the fate that threatened him. He struck up the levelled muskets of his fellow-Orangemen, swearing at the same time that he would shoot the first man that aimed a gun at his friend. This threat proved effectual, and Jack was liberated, with liberty to go where he would. On his friend's departure, Val declared that he would set the chapel on fire himself. This he speedily accomplished by discharging the contents of his musket into the thatched roof of the building, which presently took fire, to the great joy of the spectators. Val is said to have exclaimed as he watched the progress of the flames: "Now let the Virgin put out the fire if she can."

On being liberated, Jack Murphy set out to join his neighbours on Oulart Hill, where he acted a manful part. He lived for many years after these events, and was buried, at his own desire, under the spot upon which he knelt on that memorable Whit-Sunday, awaiting death at the hands of the Orangemen. The people of the vicinity can point out the place of his interment to the present day, and from them the author obtained the account of the occurrence above detailed—of its truth there cannot be the slightest doubt: the father of one of my informants and the uncle of another was present during the transaction.

NOTES TO CHAPTER XVIII.
CHARACTER OF FATHER JOHN MURPHY—HIS DEATH.

THIS celebrated chief was of rather small stature, but of uncommon strength and activity; of such a perfect constitution of body that though he exposed himself to every hardship, he was never known to suffer from the least illness. He excelled in all manly exercises, in which he took great delight, and was reputed the best ball player in the parish. His mind was like his body, vigorous and powerful; and that it was not uncultivated appears from the fact that he won the degree of Doctor of Divinity in the famous College of Seville, in Spain. The gentleness and amiability of his disposition, together with his other excellent qualities of mind and body, endeared him exceedingly to his parishioners. Such was the character of the man stigmatised by Orange historians as a "ferocious bigot;" yet to confirm this calumnious assertion they could not cite a single act of ferocity committed by him during his brief but *glorious* career as an insurgent leader.

Thirteen years after his death (1811) the following account of that tragic event was published in the "Irish Magazine," and may be received as perfectly accurate.

Accident threw in the way of the author an old man (a first cousin and name-sake of the Gallagher mentioned below, Father John's fellow-sufferer), whose narrative of the affair agreed in every respect with that given in the "Magazine," which is as follows:—

"Towards the close of the year 1797, and during that part of 1798 which preceded the insurrection, the murders, rapine, free-quarters, and burning, were carried to such an alarming extent, that the Catholics of the counties of Wicklow, Wexford, and Carlow were compelled to take the field, and abandon their habitations to their persecutors. Father John Murphy, as well to avoid the common enemy, as to advise his fugitive flock, joined them in their encampment, and was obliged to take the direction of their operations, which, as yet, were only defensive. It was at Rockspring he unsheathed his sword. After the dispersion of the rebel force under his command, he took refuge in the village of Tullow, Co. Carlow, but so disguised as not to be known even by his most intimate acquaintances; he was accompanied by a brave and faithful companion of the name of Gallagher, a native of Ferns. As they were strangers they were not long in the town before they became objects of suspicion, and were taken into custody on the information of John M'Nabb; but not knowing who they were several interrogations were put to them respecting their occupation, names, and former residences. The answers not being satisfactory, Gallagher was tied naked to a post, and there flogged and questioned alternately, without obtaining from him any knowledge of who his master was, meaning Father John. After torturing poor Gallagher, by inflicting on him six hundred lashes, he was taken down, and erecting a temporary gallows, they hung him up; but at short intervals would let him down, still demanding him to inform on his friend. His great soul continued to resist all the malice of his tormentors, who were so impatient at his firmness that they at last suffered him to hang till he was dead. They then commenced their operations on the silent and meek minister of the gospel, who was compelled to witness the sufferings of his faithful friend, and proceeded to search his clothes for any documents that might lead to a discovery of his name or former condition. In his pockets they found part of his sacerdotal robes, and a small vial. At the sight of these articles the whole body cried out with one voice, 'Burn him alive, for he is a priest.' *They first whipped him, each ruffian taking his turn at the cat-o-nine-tails, which he bore with astonishing firmness without uttering a groan.* They then procured a pitch barrel, and placed it at the door of a Mr. Callaghan, a respectable Catholic, saying at the same time, in the hearing of Mr. Callaghan and his trembling family, that they should be entertained with a holy *fricassee*, as there could be no objection to the incense of a fried priest. They then made him fast to the gallows on which poor Gallagher suffered, and with many insults desired him, as he was a priest, to save himself. They then cut off his head, stripped his body naked, and some of the wretches disputed about his clothes. They then flung his body into the burning cask, and while it was consuming, compelled Callaghan to open his windows to admit the smoke which they humorously said would redeem him of sin. After the body and barrel were consumed, they gathered the bones and buried them at the threshold of Callaghan's door. The head was fixed on a pole, about fourteen feet high, at the chapel gate, and whenever these executioners met a Catholic they advised him to apply for forgiveness of his sins from his priest (pointing to the head of Father Murphy)."—The "Irish Magazine and Monthly Asylum for Neglected Biography," for June, 1811.

INDEX.

ADDRESS, loyal, of the Catholic aristocracy, 30.
Alarm of the English Government at the long-continued resistance of the Wexfordians, 183.
Ambuscade, Colonel Stapleton falls into an, 47.
Ancient British Cavalry, destruction of the, 225.
Antrim, attack on, 43.
Apathy, strange, of the people of Kilkenny and Queen's County, 213.
Aristocracy, the Irish, 1, 30.
Arklow, battle of, 165.
Arrest of Lord Edward, 17.
Atrocities committed by the yeomen during the flight from Oulart, 92.
Authorities did not apprehend any serious disturbance in Wexford, 56.

Ballinabinch, battle of, 53.
Ballyrakeen Hill, conflict at, 226.
Bank-notes esteemed of no value in Wexford, 154.
Boolevogue Chapel, authentic account of the burning of, 78, 273.
Borris House, attack on, 178.
Boyne, Wexford insurgents cross the, and enter Louth, 236.
Burning of houses and R.C. chapels, 86.

Cannibalism of the soldiery, 169.
Carlow, attack on the town of, 33.
Castlecomer, attack on, 209.
Catholics refuse to allow the Protestant church to be used as a hospital, 156.
Caufield, Right Rev. Dr., letter of, 271.
Chamney, Captain, attack on his house, 227.
Clinch, Father, slain at Vinegar Hill, 189.
Clonard, assault on Lieutenant Tyrrell's fortified house at, 235.

Clough, battle of; second defeat of Colonel Walpole, 123.
Colclough, Mr., arrival in Wexford from Vinegar Hill, 108.
Colliers, Kilkenny, their treachery, 203.
Colonel Walpole's death, 123.
Converts, pretended, in Wexford, 155.
Cork, insurrection in the county, 40.
Courage, marvellous, displayed by the insurgents, acknowledged even by their enemies, 133.
Craneford, or Ballygullen, battle of, 230.
Crosbie, fate of Sir Edward, 35, 261.
Currin, Father; his efforts to put a stop to the executions on the bridge of Wexford, 198.

Deputation, arrival of, from Wexford loyalists at Vinegar Hill, 100.
Despatches, forgery of false, by loyalist officers, 170, 144.
Dixon, Captain; his violence, 156; plots the destruction of Orange prisoners, 195; excites the mob by means of the fire-screens to attack the Orangemen, 162; opposes the capitulation of Wexford, 200.

Engagement at Ballyrakeen Hill, 226.
Enniscorthy, capture of, by the insurgents, 94.
Entry of the insurgents into Wexford from Ferrybank, 112.
Entry of the military into Wexford on its recapture, 238.
Esmond, fate of Doctor, 264.
Execution of prisoners on Wexford bridge, 197.
Expeditions, French and Dutch, 11.

Fooke's Mill, or Longraig, battle of, 182.

Government, sanction given by, to Orange cruelties, 268.

Hacketstown, battle of, 220.
Harvey, Bagenal, 153; his cowardly conduct at Ross, 130; his resignation of the chief command, 144.
Hay, Edward; efforts made by him to save the Orangemen, 196.
Heroines, 137, 56.
Heroism, displayed by a boy of thirteen, 137.
Hessians, or Hempesch Dragoons, 208, 240.
Hunter, General, clemency displayed by, 202.
Hunter Gowan, proceedings of, and other persecutors, 74; anecdote of H. G., 217.

Informers, how made, 65; hatred borne towards them, 156.
Insurgents endeavour to acquire the art military, 148; lack of gunpowder a great obstacle to their success; their gunsmen and pikemen, 149, 150; their freedom from bigotry; moderation of the insurgents when victorious, 99.
Insurrection, why it failed, 256.
Insurrection in the North contrasted with that in Wexford, 253; excited by Pitt to promote the Union, 13.

Johnson, General, dispositions made for the defence of New-Ross by, 131.
Junction of the Wexford and Kildare men, 234.

Kelly of Killane, his brave conduct at the battle of Ross, 132; his execution, 242.
Keough, Captain, measures taken by, as military governor of Wexford. 152; delivers up his sword, 200.
Kilcullen, conflict in the vicinity of, 25.
Kilcullen, old, battle of, 264.
Kingsborough, Lord, capture of, 155; in peril of the pitch-cap, 159.
Kyan, Esmond, services of, 125.

Lake, General, character of, 202; sets fire to the insurgent hospital in Enniscorthy, 190.
Loftus, flight of General, 125.
Loss, sustained by the English troops, as stated by Mr. Fox in Parliament, 128.

Massacre at Dunlavin by Orange yeomen, 29; at Carnew, 76; at Kilmacthomas Hill, 88; massacre of the wounded insurgents after the battle of Arklow by the soldiery, 169.
Meath militia, surprise and defeat, 101.
M'Cracken, Henry Joy, his career as insurgent leader, 42
Miles Byrne not a leader, 204.
Militia, surrender of Wexford, to the insurgents, 207.
Moore, General, humanity of, 202.
Mortimer, rector of Comber. death of, 48.
Mountjoy, Lord, death of, 130.
Mount Pleasant, insurgent encampment on, 174.
Munroe chosen to command the Down insurgents, 50; his execution, 57.
Murphy, Father John; his character, first exploits, 77; death of, 275.

Murphy, Father Michael, joins Father John, at Ballyoirel, 94; his death at Arklow, 167
Musgrave's and Maxwell's calumnies refuted, 62.

Naas, attack on the town of, 22.
Newtownbarry, how won and lost, 117.
North Cork, cruelties of, 70.

Oppression, effects of, on the Irish people, 156.
Orangemen, exclusively the objects of popular hatred, 161; Orangemen, attempt made by them to murder the prisoners in Enniscorthy jail frustrated, 98; Orangemen, 269; cruelties perpetrated by the Carlow, 261; good deeds by individuals of the society, 270.
Oulart, battle of, 89.
Outbreak of insurrection in Dublin and Kildare, 21; in Wexford, 82.
Ovidstown, conflict at, 266.

Persecutors, Orange, 62.
Pitch-cap introduced in Wexford, 71.
Portaferry, attack on, 48.
Prisoners, cruel treatment of, 238.
Proclamations issued by the authorities on the outbreak of the insurrection, 29.
——— ——— issued by the insurgent chiefs to restrain excesses, 143.
——— ——— issued by the same chiefs against Hawtrey White and his associates, 158.
Prosperity of Ireland under her enfranchised Parliament, 2, 251.
Prosperous, attack on the barracks at, 263.
Protestants, liberal, 269.

Rathangan, conflict at, 265.
Requisitions, 160.
Retaliation, measures of, adopted by the insurgents, 151, 163.
Roche, insurgent general Edward, covers the retreat from Vinegar Hill, 192.
Roche, Rev. Phillip; his character; his fatal embassy, 204.
Ross, New, battle of, 132.
Rumours, horrid, abroad the week preceding the insurrection, 75.

Saintfield, insurgent rendezvous at, 49.
Scollagh Gap, insurgents force their way through, 214.

Scullabogue, burning of, 138.
Separation of Wicklow and Wexford insurgents, 233.
Skirmishes, various, that took place in the counties of Dublin, Wicklow, Kildare, and Carlow (detailed in second chapter and appendix thereto).
Social condition of the people of Wexford, 60.
Stand, last, made by the Wexford-men, 226.
Surrender of Wexford to General Moore, 202.

Tara, engagement at, 86.
Tone, Theobald Wolfe, 11.
Torture, fear of, 68.
Transportation of the people, 75.
Troops, number of, employed by Government to suppress the insurrection in Wexford, 254.
Tubberneering, battle of, 121.

Ulster, insurrection in, 41.
United Irishmen, number in Wexford, 69.
United Irish Society, brief account of, 4; original declaration of, 258.

Vengeance taken by the insurgents on the murderers of women and children, 219.

Watson, death of ex-Colonel, 109.
Wexford, description of the county and its inhabitants, 58; capture by the insurgents, 112; its "fleet," 154; a hotbed of Orangeism, 104.
Women, chivalrous respect shown by the insurgents towards them, 172.

THE END.